MORAL
IMAGINATION IN
KAGURU MODES
OF THOUGHT

Moral Imagination in Kaguru Modes of Thought

T. O. Beidelman

With a new foreword by Ivan Karp

Smithsonian Institution Press
Washington and London

First Smithsonian edition 1993

Library of Congress Cataloging-in-Publication Data
Beidelman, T. O. (Thomas O.), 1931–
    Moral imagination in Kaguru modes of thought / T.O. Beidelman.—
1st Smithsonian ed.
        p. cm.
    Originally published: Bloomington: Indiana University Press,
1986.
    Includes bibliographical references and index.
    ISBN 1-56098-236-5 (paper: alk. paper)
    1. Kaguru (African people)   2. Philosophy, Kaguru.
3. Imagination.   I. Title.
DT443.3.K33B45 1993
306′.089963—dc20   93-2031

British Library Cataloging-in-Publication data available

Manufactured in the United States of America
97 96 95 94 93   5 4 3 2 1

For permission to reproduce any of the illustrations, please correspond directly with
the sources. The Smithsonian Institution Press does not retain reproduction rights for
these illustrations individually or maintain a file of address for photo sources.

To my teachers
And to all the hares, past, present, and future

There are imaginations, not 'the Imagination,'
and they must be studied in detail.

William James, *Psychology*

CONTENTS

Foreword

> . . . negative capability—that is, when a man is capable
> of being in uncertainties, Mysteries, doubts, without
> any irritable reaching after fact and reason.
>
> John Keats

Is it possible to write an ethnography that shows how people's beliefs and values form an internally consistent system and at the same time demonstrate that this system creates the possibility for subversion? Can an ethnography of the imagination begin with an analysis of individuals enmeshed in the give-and-take of everyday life? Is it possible to write about representations and provide an account of the fundamentally political nature of the imaginative life? Can morality be explored primarily through negative examples? These are the questions posed by this powerful and innovative study of social categories, imaginative constructions, and pervasive conflicts in the life of the Kaguru people of Tanzania.

T. O. Beidelman's prize-winning book has been widely acclaimed as a mature work of ethnographic analysis that follows more than three decades of study and reflection on the social life of a Tanzanian people. Its focus is the ethnography of the imagination, defined as a set of mental activities involving fantasy and speculation, including reflections about fate and about life in a society in which there is a massive gap between what people desire and what they experience. Social experience lies at the core of imaginative life, particularly the many ways in which people relate to one another, compete and cooperate, strive to achieve their goals, and continuously adjust their strategic and symbolic interactions to changing circumstances.

Despite its attention to how people strive toward their goals, this is not a book about individuals in the commonsense way we customarily think about them. Named persons do not fill the pages, as they do in so many recent works of anthropology. Neither is this book about depersonalized, abstract categories, disengaged from the life world. This study dwells somewhere in between the known personality and the shared systems that social scientists call culture.

Beidelman's subject is the *moral* imagination, that set of ideas, images, and practices through which people reflect on the nature of life in society and dream about escaping it. Just whose moral imagination—subjects' or author's—forms the subject of this book is appropriately ambiguous. *The Moral Imagination in Kaguru Modes of Thought* begins with a discussion of ideas about the imagination found primarily in works devoted to interpreting literature and philosophy. It ends with a meditation on the sources of Beidelman's own moral imagination as they manifested themselves in his life's history.

Between the theory and the personal reflections, Beidelman tells stories about the Kaguru. He follows customary anthropological practice by setting his account in terms of neighboring peoples, local history, environment, economy, and social organization. Yet this is no conventional ethnography. The cultural forms and complex relations Kaguru devise and through which they interact with one another are the social matrix out of which their moral judgments and imaginative life emerge. What we derive from reading this work, as well as Beidelman's many other books and articles, is a *feel* for the complex and frequently unsatisfactory decisions that the Kaguru make on a daily basis.

This is an ethnography whose themes both revolve around and reflect one another. As such it does not make for an easy work to read. Self-reflection (by Kaguru and the ethnographer) blends into an analysis of symbolic classification: The associations of right and left are related to moral judgments. Folktales about hyena and hare are connected to uncontrolled aggression, domination, and ideas about sociability. Perhaps the complex layerings of theme, imaginative constructions, and life experience are the features that appeal to African scholars who have reviewed this work and been struck by its, dare I say it, authenticity.

Yet this observation creates still another ambiguity. Can a book that is so relentlessly skeptical about all claims of knowledge, including the author's, be termed authentic? These are not questions that have answers, and Beidelman does not provide many easy answers in his book. What we expect from a work of social science is analysis. Kaguru life should be broken down into its constitutive elements, and analysts should show how the elements are connected. They should adduce principles that generate the patterns they describe for us. Even a work of interpretive ethnography, such as this, generally strives for some sort of analysis of patterns. But even though there is much analysis as well as plenty of assertions about pattern in this work, somehow each chapter subverts the preceding one.

Take the central part of the book. In succession Beidelman describes cosmology and dualism; moral space; the house; settlements and body etiquette; legendary time; clans and ethnicity; personhood and time; seasons; names and omens. Each of these chapters covers a conventional ethnographic topic but manages to combine materials that have elsewhere only been treated separately, such as the house and body etiquette or seasons and names. He shows how these are connected through principles that organize Kaguru imaginative constructions, and how vital connections among them are derived not only from their cognitive relationship but through the practice and experiences of the Kaguru themselves.

In the chapter on moral space, Beidelman establishes that houses and settlements are major settings that are organized in terms of fundamental moral ideas about types of persons and how they should relate to one another. This sort of analysis is familiar from the literature on symbolic classification. But Beidelman transcends this type of analysis by looking at moral space as a "stage" on which protagonists enact and debate ideas about what is proper and good for one another. Even here, however, he subverts his own point. The idea of a stage suggests both role playing and improvisation, that somehow a narrative is enacted and a conclusion reached. This further suggests that the negotiation of ideas and practices which Beidelman describes are concluded on stage. But Beidelman reverses his own account in a fascinating materialist way. He argues that the very same stages which serve as moral spaces are also settings in which the most fundamental acts ensuring survival and reproduction are played out:

> Kaguru hold formal beliefs and symbolic terms of expression, but how these are interpreted depends upon the occasions and the protagonists involved. This indeterminacy is essential in that it draws Kaguru into continued negotiations as to which tones and meanings will be stressed at various encounters, and what they will mean. . . . What remains pervasive and unnegotiated is the tenor of everyday activities, Kaguru modes of work, cooking, alimentation, play, grooming and sexuality. These routines are molded not only by etiquette and habit but by the very forms of Kaguru settlements, housing and landscape. (P. 64)

Thus the very settings in which symbolic forms are produced are also settings in which the limits of negotiability are experienced. Material constraints, the limits produced by past actions, the materiality of human actions themselves as they produce a "natural" world shaped by human hands and human history are the limits of the world in which the Kaguru, and not only the Kaguru, act.

For all of its dependence on a language-game concept of culture, Beidelman's book does not conform to Wittgenstein's famous aphorism that "the limits of my language are the limits of my world." Instead Beidelman asserts over and over again that "my language bumps up against the changing limits of the world." This realist position is linked to the contents of this book in a challenging way. The conventional materialist approach is content to show how symbolic activity is limited by social and natural content. Beidelman does something remarkably different. He focuses on the experience of limits themselves and on how attempts at transcending the physical, social, and moral conditions of existence are the stuff out of which the moral imagination is made.

"Imagination is an art by which individuals struggle to transform their social baggage into gear that suits urgent situational needs in terms of meanings and moral judgments" (p. 203). This gear is designed to answer the great questions of culture and philosophy, defined in the broadest sense. Identity, fate, distributive justice are all brought into play in the moral imagination. Play is a significant aspect of the continuous process by which imaginative constructions are made and remade, answers to momentous questions are formulated and rejected, but play is a serious matter for the Kaguru, even when it is physical.

Derived from the experience of limits, conflict, domination, and loss, the moral imagination plays upon what Beidelman calls the quotidian aspects of life. Possibility and potentiality are imaginatively elaborated upon the fabric of daily life while leaving lived experience unchanged. Changing society asks too much of the imagination, but the very play of the imagination so well described in this book does produce the possibility of questioning, maybe even challenging the naturalness of everyday life, of the limits of the material and natural worlds.

Because he deals with both social activities and imaginative constructions, the organization and chapter headings of *Moral Imagination in Kaguru Modes of Thought* cover the standard fare of many other ethnographies. Beidelman describes environment and social organization, symbolic classification, concepts of time and space, storytelling, ideas about pollution and cleanliness, notions of sociability, witchcraft and sorcery beliefs, and more besides. These are the usual materials found in a monograph on modes of thought. Yet in Beidelman's hands these materials take on new and subtle shades of meaning.

Not only limits but ambiguity and subversion are recurrent topics that run through Beidelman's seemingly conventional accounts of symbolic classification, ideas about time and space, attitudes toward the life cycle and human body, and notions about kinship and personhood. All are forms through which society is constructed and media by which people pursue their goals. The emphasis on practice found in so much current anthropological writing also covers these topics in much the same ways.

This work deviates from more conventional ethnographies by focusing on how people subvert expectations, fail to conform, or simply fail in their aims. It is not an ethnography of Kaguru successes and public recognition. I think that all ethnographies implicitly advocate a point of view and identify with some members of a society at the expense of others. Most ethnographic accounts, certainly most Africanist ethnographies, ally themselves with the more successful members of society, such as elders, government chiefs, and women who have achieved senior status. Studies of African societies are replete with marriages completed, households formed, lives honored, and children brought into the world and successfully reared, as well as rituals that achieve their goals.

The Kaguru with whom Beidelman identifies are another sort. This is a book of lives blighted by witchcraft, political plans gone askew, houses sundered, and children ill. Nonetheless, the people who are described herein have a splendid and defiant aspect to them. The gaps between goals and ideals and their experience of disjuncture in the life world is filled by the Kaguru with an extraordinary rich and evocative imaginative life. In the Kaguru world, space and time are organized in terms of complex categories; subtle differences in the life course are the subject of meditation, and pleasure is taken not only in worldly success but also in how people pursue their aims.

Now I do not want to suggest that the Kaguru people in Beidelman's perspective are characters out of a Hemingway novel, playing a game they know is lost simply for the sake of playing it. The Kaguru world is filled with far more uncertainty and indeterminacy than Hemingway's. The Kaguru people are not Italian counts playing billiards but African peasants subject to the vicissitudes of environment, invasion by outsiders, and problems of their own making. "To imagine another kind of world is always a judgment about this one," Beidelman tells us (p. 202). Performed as mock judgment or serious judgment, the moral imagination simultaneously links and releases individuals from their social and material circumstances. This is perhaps the most profound observation made by Beidelman in this book. He continually returns to the theme of imaginative freedom and responsibility. The Kaguru people are perpetually in flight from one another, in his view, as they struggle to hold others to them. This contradictory attitude relates to the ways in which their imaginative constructions reflect on and enlarge their world. The options that Kaguru imagine conform only partially to the options available to them in this world. In a way they free themselves from their limits by imagining how those limits may be transcended, even when that is patently impossible. The judgments they make about the world by imagining alternatives create the possibility of more than the world offers. In the face of conditions that American and European ethnographers such as Beidelman have to endure only on a temporary basis, people such as the Kaguru artfully construct multiple worlds while dwelling within the limits of their world.

What is the responsibility of the ethnographer who participates in the life world of another people, but ultimately does not have to respond to the same constraints? In another context Beidelman once wrote of anthropological fieldworkers:

> The social anthropologist himself becomes an illustration of a fascinating cultural puzzle: that of men standing within and without the objects they must understand. In this respect it may not be unduly dramatic to suggest that the greatest of social anthropologists, those from whom we learn the most, appear as the most alienated and therefore perhaps the freest but most troubled of the social scientists. (1970:526)

Both Beidelman and the Kaguru live in conditions that leave them troubled but enable them to be free. The conditions of each are neither commensurate nor equal. Beidelman and most anthropologists who work with people much poorer them themselves are far freer and less troubled in material ways than the Kaguru, for example. Under those circumstances the *responsibility of anthropologists,* their vocation, is to act as witness to how other people live, how they experience their lives, and what they imagine both the experience and the alternatives to be. *The Moral Imagination in Kaguru Modes of Thought* is a splendid act of witnessing, among the very best I know. It responds to the vocation of anthropologists by combining meticulous collection of data with a fine social analysis and a distanced yet participatory account of how the Kaguru do the same. For Beidelman and the best of the social anthropologists I know, ethnography is more than theory linked to data, it is as much an artifact of the moral imagination as the imaginative constructions of the Kaguru people themselves.

March 1993   Ivan Karp
                                                            Smithsonian Institution

Preface

This study has been long in preparation. Preliminary drafts of some of its chapters
appeared as articles twenty-five years ago. None appears here unrevised. Over the
years various colleagues have complained that I have not provided a proper, extended,
synthesized account of Kaguru society. I hope that this volume will go some way to
remedy this omission. I also hope that it corrects and improves upon some of my
earlier interpretations. It should, since some of my earlier publications were followed
by three subsequent fieldtrips. I have postponed this task so long because of my
conviction that most of us are too precipitate in publishing our views on our ethnographic research. The Kaguru material is complex, but probably no more so than that
for many other preliterate societies. My delay stems not from the material but from
appreciation of a general fact about ethnographic fieldwork. Most anthropologists do
their initial research while still in their twenties, as I did. While they undoubtedly
often collect copious and accurate information, their youth probably impedes both
their ability to appreciate society as a totality and, more serious, their appreciation of
the essential pathos and ambiguity of social life. If youth provides the robustness to
facilitate ethnography, middle age provides seasoning and perspective. This book and
a future monograph on Kaguru rites of passage now constitute my more seasoned
judgments on what my data mean.

The aims of this study are threefold. First and foremost, this is an ethnographic
report of one East African people as I encountered them some decades ago. Theories
may change, but ethnography remains at the heart of anthropology; it is the test and
measure of all theory. Second, this is necessarily a tentative theoretical statement about
some problems that have long concerned social anthropologists, mainly issues related
to how exotic, preliterate peoples view their world and society and what lessons our
understanding of such people may teach us about what it means for us to live with
one another in society. I have tried to keep the theoretical statements limited, not
because I lack interest in theory but because I believe that theory is best presented
embedded within ethnography rather than outside and beyond it. In a sense, Kaguru
ethnography may also teach us something about other peoples in Africa. Kaguru are,
to be sure, a relatively small society; they are not in any way unusually remarkable.
They possess no especially different beliefs and institutions that either challenge our
ideas about East African cultures or suggest any great enigma to anthropological
thinking. Yet perhaps the Kaguru's typicality among Bantu-language-speaking peoples
constitutes a useful trait, for coming to grips with how Kaguru think and live may
provide further understanding of how many of the other societies of East and Central
Africa work. In this volume I make no attempt to fit Kaguru into any wider, comparative
picture (though I did in some of my earlier publications), yet those who have worked

with other peoples in this region of Africa should readily recognize many common features. Kaguru social organization, ancestral propitiation, naming, beliefs about misfortune, and oral literature all echo themes represented in numerous other ethnographies. Third and last, this study aims at pointing out some connections and parallels between the findings of social anthropology and the concerns of writers in other disciplines. This aim accounts for what may seem a somewhat odd cast to the kinds of authorities cited in this work. Anthropology has much of value to contribute beyond the discipline. Its concerns, despite some jargon regarding terms about exotic kinship and social organization, about alien beliefs and customs, are indeed about human experience in general. The seemingly alien nature of the social worlds which anthropologists portray should broaden our understanding of the kinds of questions we ask about ourselves, about our own society, not only as it is and may become but as it once was and how it came to be as it is. For all these reasons, anthropological information should interest many others besides anthropologists; it should interest sociologists, historians, philosophers, and literary critics, among others.

To draw attention to this point, stated by most of us but too often neglected in practice, I present my material with more references to non-anthropologists than to my colleagues. As a rule, where both anthropologists and non-anthropologists have raised questions or gained similar insights, I have tried to cite those outside my field, especially where these have presented such material before anthropologists have done so. Even when anthropologists have been especially distinguished in making certain points, I have tended to cite the earliest writers who influenced me although these may not be the more celebrated. I do this for two reasons: in the first case, I want to underscore the fact that the questions that anthropologists now ask are not essentially different from many of those repeatedly asked by scholars in other fields; in the second, I want to point out that even within anthropology, both our questions and many of the answers have been with us for a long time. Much that currently passes for brilliant innovation is merely the recrudescence of past ideas and arguments. Of course, I do not claim that the authorities I cite are necessarily the first to raise such issues. My reading is limited. Besides, in many of the arguments which I raise one might well have to go back to the ancient Greeks, Augustine, or Vico to spot the first significant probings about the issues involved. This is not because anthropology is getting nowhere, but rather because many of the most important questions that concern us today are perennial. Furthermore, I have often found that many of the earlier writers evince a vigor and keenness in their formulations not found in those who later reiterate the same points. Even though I have eschewed citing most current writings in ethnography, unless these pertain directly to this work either in terms of the study of Bantu-language-speaking peoples or in terms of related imaginative imagery in oral literature and belief, I am deeply aware that much admirable work has been recently published in social anthropology. This is, however, essentially an ethnographic account, and so citation of comparative material would be inappropriate. My other publications and various reviews, including earlier versions of these same essays, indicate my interest in the works of others outside my ethnographic area.

I noted earlier that this study represents many decades of interest in Kaguru and neighboring East African societies. For that reason my debts are long and wide. I first encountered the Kaguru in 1957 and subsequently spent over thirty-six months residing with them and their neighbors, in 1957–58, 1961–63, 1965, and 1966. My fieldwork and related archival and library studies in Oxford and London were supported by a wide number of sponsors: my family foremost, and then the University of Illinois, the Ford Foundation, the National Science Foundation, the National Institute for Mental Health, the Wenner-Gren Foundation for Anthropological Research, Duke University, and the National Endowment for the Humanities. Time and funds for writing and preparing this manuscript were provided through a Guggenheim Foundation Fellowship and New York University. The ethnographic description pertains essentially to Kaguruland during the colonial and immediate postcolonial period when I worked.

Various versions of this manuscript were read by Gillian Feeley-Harnik, Michelle Gilbert, Ivan Karp, Rodney Needham, John Middleton, and Annette Weiner. None is, of course, responsible for my final interpretations.

Finally, my greatest debt is to the Kaguru. Unquestionably my time living with them was the profoundest experience of my life. It taught me my limits but also my strengths and abilities. Kaguru were not always an easy people to study, but they showed me much kindness, hospitality, patience, and, yes, fun. Above all, they gave me a lasting lesson in how people can endure and prevail against meddling and persecution by outsiders, in how people can retain dignity, ironic humor, and integrity against adversity. We shared ideas and quarreled, trusted and deceived one another, got drunk, joked, and danced at ceremonies and beer clubs, shared illness, accidents, grief, misfortune, and boredom. Kaguru are a strong people, an attractive people, and I hope this work portrays them with some truth in the ways they merit.

MORAL IMAGINATION IN KAGURU MODES OF THOUGHT

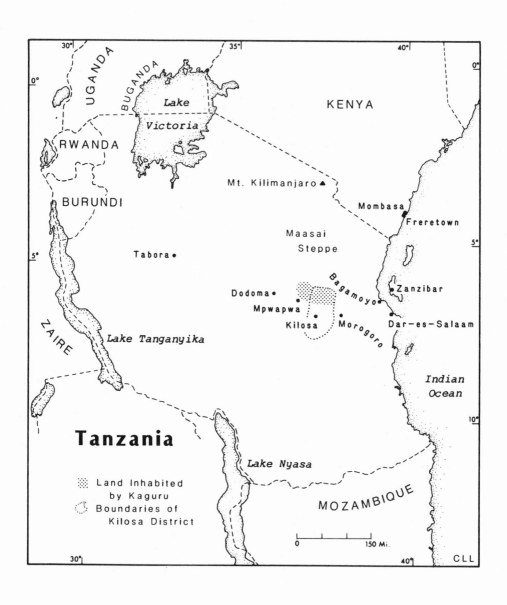

30°

UGANDA

BUGANDA

0°

RWANDA

Lake
Victoria

KENYA

35°

40°

0°

BURUNDI

Mt. Kilimanjaro ▲

Mombasa

Freretown

5°

Maasai
Steppe

Tabora •

5°

ZAIRE

Lake Tanganyika

Dodoma •

Mpwapwa •

Kilosa •

Bagamoyo

Zanzibar

Morogoro

Dar-es-Salaam

Indian
Ocean

10°

Tanzania

Lake Nyasa

Land Inhabited
by Kaguru
Boundaries of
Kilosa District

MOZAMBIQUE

0   150 Mi.

30°

40°

CLL

CHAPTER 1.

Imagining Beliefs and Morality

Imagination, which, in truth,
Is but another name for absolute power
And clearest insight, amplitude of mind,
And Reason in her most exalted mood.
W. Wordsworth, *The Prelude*, Book XIV, 1.190

The rules of the Imagination are themselves
the very powers of growth and production.
S. T. Coleridge, *Biographia Literaria*

This study deals with two abstract concepts, imagination and morality. Neither is easy to define, both concepts being complex and vague in meaning, their use varying greatly with different writers.

I consider the first term, imagination, in three different respects. First, it relates to the ways that people construct images of the world in which they live. In part this reflects the physical and physiological rudiments out of which experience is drawn; more complicatedly it reflects the social and cultural particularities of that world. While it can be argued that each person experiences a unique vision of that world, the incontestable facts of shared social life, of language, suggest that some common picture may be constructed which enables these different persons to interact with one another and to pass on these views from generation to generation, albeit at times in somewhat modified forms. This common, culturally endowed world-picture represents the first such product of the imagination, a cosmology that both shapes people's views of themselves and their surroundings and, in turn, presents a picture in which they measure, assess, and reflect upon the reality of their experiences.

Second, imagination relates to the ways in which people picture a world different from that which they actually experience. It provides a means by which people extend their vision of what may be possible or at least desirable or feared if things are not all that they are claimed to be or seem to be at first. This second meaning of imagination, then, relates not only to ways that society may change but also to ways that its members may stand back to scrutinize, contemplate, and judge their world. In this sense imaginative exercise constitutes means for criticism, for distortion, even subversion, of the social order. It offers the possibility of questioning some aspects of the version of the system in which imagination itself is rooted.

Third, imagination also refers to the very means by which a study of these first two processes could be formulated at all. For a writer to construct an alien culture, whether this be as anthropologist or comparative sociologist, or as social, literary, or art historian, requires imaginative effort. Such a person must somehow draw from within himself or herself experiences, ideas, and feelings that enable a construction of a new and somewhat alien world. If this mode of imaginative thought were not possible, none of these fields of comparative study could exist. Such a task seems formidable, yet few if any of us would entirely reject the possibility, much less the need, for this translation of culture. This final aspect of the concept of imagination leads us outside the Kaguru themselves, suggesting how our imaginative, analytical processes work: my ability to observe and understand the Kaguru depends upon the degree to which I have successfully cultivated this third form of insight. I do not propose to examine this final side of imagination here, yet it remains omnipresent as I play out my version of the first two forms of imagination among the Kaguru.[1] Finally, I assume that it should be clear that some aspects of the imagination, as a means of moral exercise within a society, relate to these more complex interpretive aspects evinced in anthropology, comparative sociology, and history.

The second term in this study, morality, relates both to society and to the individual within it, the person. The word *moral* derives from *mos*,[2] a way of comporting oneself, and, indeed, it is in terms of social interaction that I hope to ground my understanding of how Kaguru apply imaginative thought. Social life is both rewarding and constricting, our benefits secured at the price of accepting, even embracing limitations and some pain and frustration. These rewards and punishments are epitomized by choices, and in our concomitant expectations that others will make similar choices. These choices of action, in turn, derive from others, from judgments about what the world is and should be. Our morality, then, is embedded in a cosmology as well as in our emotions, and both inform and impel our judgments. This is also true of our awareness and expectations of both ourselves and others. To interact with others we must imagine what their own needs and views may be, often working through a process combining projection and introspection. In the pages that follow I first review my concept of imagination and then of morality.

The imagination is central to philosophical inquiry, at least for some (cf. Warnock 1976: especially 194, 202, 207; Sartre n.d). For example, Wittgenstein repeatedly employs the term *imagine* in his efforts to extend philosophical insights, to imagine situations or conditions which lie outside our ordinary ways of thinking and experiencing (1964:40ff). *Imagine* is clearly for him an "odd job word" (ibid.:43), suggesting the complex and diverse meanings it has held for writers as diverse as Hume, Kant, Coleridge, Wordsworth, Brentano, Collingwood, Sartre, and Husserl. "Imagination of reality" could even be termed a form of play by which we comprehend our world (Huizinga 1950:4) and as such is central to all understanding, provided that we consider play to have a very serious side. Likewise, "the *a priori* imagination" is at work in fashioning all history as a form of "perceptual imagination" (Collingwood 1961:242, cf. 247). Nearly all of these writers have recognized, if, in some cases, only by their strenuous denials, that imagination is inextricably linked to the emotions; how could it be otherwise, since imagination is rooted in our deepest convictions, aspirations, and visions of our experiences? Collingwood has put this eloquently:

> Attention or awareness is a kind of activity different from mere feeling and presupposing it. The essence of it is that instead of having our field of view wholly occupied by the sensations and emotions of the moment, we also become aware of ourselves, as the activity is an enlargement of our field of view, which now takes in the act of feeling as well as the thing felt. Practically considered, it is the assertion of ourselves as the owners of our feelings. By this self-assertion we dominate our feelings; they become no longer experiences forcing themselves upon us unaware, but experiences in which we experience our own activity. Their brute power over us is thus replaced by our power over them: we become able on the one hand to stand up to them so that they no longer unconditionally determine our conduct, and, on the other, to prolong and evoke them at will. From being impressions of sense, they have become ideas of imagination. (1958:222).

> Every further development of thought is based upon it, and deals not with feeling in its crude form but with feeling as thus transformed into imagination. (ibid.: 223)

Huizinga's characterization of play comes close to my own notions of what the imagination is and does for society. For him, play represents something yet at the same time contests that same something (Huizinga 1950:13). This is not so different from Wittgenstein's idea of human thought being epitomized by a "word game." The aesthetic yet also agonistic aspects of play figure in imagination. Rituals and myths express many features of a cosmology, while, for Kaguru, other work of the imagination—stories, songs, riddles, and beliefs about sorcery and witchcraft—play with the contradictory, unresolvable aspects of the same system.

One aspect of imagination which all writers seem to recognize is that it spans a range of seemingly otherwise unbridgeable realms. It is in this sense that rituals are "imaginative actualizations" (Huizinga 1950:15; cf. Firth

1973:167) of our visions of what the world could or should be. Yet no ritual
bridges more than a few sides of thought and experience, nor could it do so
any more than one social rule or goal could account for the myriad situations,
impressions, and aims of individuals involved in so many changing roles and
situations. Rituals do allow us to be more conscious of both our ideas and
our emotions; in this they are very highly developed exercises in imagination.
These represent long-evolved, socially accepted forms of what every artist
seeks, a way to focus the imagination upon a certain message through certain
motifs, order, and stress (cf. I. A. Richards n.d.:192–195; Collingwood
1958:222–223). Rituals are both more and less than they portray: more in the
sense that they express a range and elegance of motifs developed and artic-
ulated in ways not possible in everyday experience.

   The sum of all these exercises in imagination constitutes the cosmology of
a society, the ways its members piece together the disparate and myriad shards
of experience. Cosmology is embedded in language yet extends far deeper,
for, after all, a language is merely the currency by which the trade of daily
encounters may be planned, enacted, and judged: "And to imagine a language
means to imagine a form of life" (Wittgenstein 1963:36), and that transcends
words. However fantastic or seemingly odd, imagination remains rooted in
the changing spectra of our total experience. "It is perhaps true to say that
memory is the faculty of poetry, because the imagination itself is an exercise
of memory. There is nothing we imagine which we do not already know.
And our ability to imagine is our ability to remember what we have already
once experienced and to apply to some different situation" (Spender n.d.:121–
122). This enrichment, indeed, this substantiation of ideas and values, secures
a word's or symbol's meaning from a blend of physical as well as social
determinants: "social life is endued with supra-biological forms; in the shape
of play, which enhances its value" (Huizinga 1950:46). This play is sometimes serious stuff indeed, involving the basic lineaments of daily life as well
as the drama of high occasions. As Firth rightly observes, symbols permeate
a vast area, from the mythical and cosmological message evoked at great
ceremonies to everyday and seemingly trivial activities (1973:28–29). This
merger of feeling and thought sustains the existential beliefs of a cosmology:
". . . once Imagination is on the side of Reason it can contribute to Order,
rather than to Disorder, by making reasonable things seem sensible. . ."
(Burke 1970:189). While this is true, we must never forget that a cosmology
is myriad, contradictory, and loaded with conflicting and ambivalently
charged elements. This countervailing character is not, however, a failing but
constitutes the very strength of such a belief system, for real life, even though
conducted through a system of social rules, values, and beliefs, is too diverse
and manifold to be sustained by any entirely consistent system. One of the
main arguments of this study is that it is in the sphere of the imagination that

a people, such as the Kaguru, confront these disparate and conflicting features of their thought and experience.

At the heart of imagination is "the power by which one image or feeling is made to modify many others and by a sort of fusion to force many into one" (Coleridge 1977:414). The force of such modes of thought stems from two interrelated sets of features.

First, we gain imaginative power from metaphors or analogy. "Metaphor is a basic trick of language to cover the unfamiliar with familiar words on account of partial similarity" (Burkert 1979:23). In this way, metaphors extend thought beyond its initial, more literal implications. "A metaphor goes outside the ordinary range, treating it as a source of traditional wisdom" (Empson 1964:332). Metaphor derives from the Greek *meta* (beyond) and *pherein* (carry), to transfer, and it is thus akin to symbol (*sumballein*), to throw together, and even to analogy (*analegein*), to gather up (see Stanford 1972, especially pp. 3–21). In short, these processes relate to a synthetic operation, to what James terms "productive imagination" (1948:302). By this, symbols assume "circularity" (Burke 1957:254–255), "associational clustering" (Burke 1957:18; cf. Hyman 1947:161–196), "compression" (I. A. Richards n.d.:245, 290–291), "condensation" (Sapir 1963:565). Terms link whole domains with one another in order to form overarching systems (cf. Lakoff and Johnson 1980:117), though never a single, entirely pervasive one. Indeed, it is because these modes of thought encompass wide, diverse ranges of activities and references that they so tenaciously hold our allegiance and attention. To be sure, we shall see that some of these domains adhere more steadily to one another than to others. In fact, the force of a metaphor lies in the fact that the primary meaning and its associations are more keenly evoked than are those to which they are compared. Furthermore, we should understand that a powerful belief system repeatedly fuses the processes of metaphor and metonymy so that both are embedded in the same imagery (Barthes 1968:88).

Strength and flexibility are gained by there being some gaps and inconsistencies between some sections of this cosmology, which is never considered in its entirety, except perhaps by anthropologists.[3] Depending upon which of their components are imaginatively conjured up, these different domains may be considered fused or at odds. The systemic nature of Kaguru cosmology is illusory in terms of how Kaguru employ it. The Kaguru social world appears in varied and changing aspects, something whose meaning, sense, and value are constantly negotiated among Kaguru themselves, who imaginatively use the symbols and ideas which stand for their way of living. In this sense, a ritual occasion or a folktale represents a "more perfect" evocation of a facet of cosmology in society because of its selectivity, departing from reality yet suggesting a more intense, sharper experience because of its concision and consistency. Yet all Kaguru social life is informed by changing and contended elements of these beliefs and values.

Above all, imagination involves contemplation and speculation about the ideas or symbols that stand for one's world. For this process to achieve any coherence, the different domains comprising that world need at times to be joined and compared. This sense of inclusion, coherence, and wholeness not only facilitates analysis and appreciation but provides some sense of unity and meaning that is in itself reassuring and pleasing, aesthetically as well as ethically. Yet this cosmology holds profound inconsistencies and these are often skillfully avoided or eluded. At other times, imagination provides vent for profound disquiet and hostility by centering on these very contradictions. It then provides a means to deconstruct a system which may also be viewed as binding and repressive. We shall see that Kaguru beliefs about witchcraft and sorcery may be so understood.

Second, those who discuss both imagination and metaphor recognize that these involve feelings. Collingwood went so far as to argue that the final end of imaginative representation was to re-evocate emotions so as to reinforce and heighten our appreciation and awareness of our conceptualizations (1958:57, 65–66, 274). The synthetic function of metaphor not only connects conceptual domains but, more important, links realms of ideation with those of affect and feeling; ". . . the imagination's close connection with sensory images is thought both to make it highly responsive to the sensory appetite and to make sensory appetites more enticing. . ." (Burke 1970:188). Osgood and other social psychologists have coined the phrase "semantic differential" to refer to the complex yet fundamental means by which affectual and moral tones are attached to seemingly abstract terms through association with sup-posedly more primary perceptions (Osgood 1952; Osgood, Suci, and Tan-nenbaum 1957). Subjecting such abstractions to analytical scrutiny often leads us to find the useful ultimately giving way to the agreeable (Bachelard 1964:33). It is hardly news that "behind every abstract expression lies met-aphor" (Huizinga 1950:4).[4] What must be further remembered is that such metaphorical roots fix these abstractions in a field of affect and appetite. Our sight, touch, taste, and smell, and the appetites and physiological demands of our bodies (sex, nourishment, elimination, shelter) are all recruited both to construct and to patrol the corridors of our thoughts. Such sensations enable us not only to manufacture symbols and ideas but to evoke and contemplate them in the imaginative mind's eye of ourselves and others. These sensations are very powerful, indeed, and they can also rise against and confound the moral assertions to which they are attached.

Some metaphorical associations are what Burke terms "positive" in that they imply no logical opposite. Thus, the embodiment of spirits in birds or snakes or the expression of matriliny in terms of decumbent vegetation implies no logical opposites, however powerfully suggestive such imagery is for Kaguru. Yet other forms of imagery are clearly polar, and these relate to moralistic thinking, suggesting choice and preference (cf. Burke 1970:23, footnote). Since a central feature of symbolic, cosmological systems is the polarity of a wide range of elements (associated with powerful sensory and appetitive motifs), polarity's moral, judgmental force should be apparent. I cannot emphasize too strongly that while symbols assume powerful moral valences, these are neither constant nor consistent. The values and meanings attached to symbols are subject to constant negotiation depending on the social context in which they are evoked. Even where those who employ such terms strive to control and restrict the significance evoked, it appears inevitable that other meanings and associations cannot be entirely expunged and continue to echo through the imagery. The ties between poetic and philosophical vision are deep and are rooted in metaphor (Mackay 1965).

Imagination provides further, even more complex means by which Kaguru and others contemplate and explore the moral possibilities of their conceptions. One of these involves the subversive but liberating power of imaginative fantasy, while the other involves the extensive, solidary possibilities of imaginative sympathy or empathy, with its sometimes dangerous concomitant of resentment.

First, let us consider fantasy. While polar dichotomies and analogical associations focus on moral choices, on isolating qualities and issues, imaginative play may afford something rather different. One should remember that the word *illusion* literally means *in play*. Such fantasy may blur or multiply choices, affording a perspective that transcends ordinary situations and perspectives. Ricoeur observes that "to imagine is to make oneself absent from the whole of things" (1979:152). We free ourselves by transcending our boundaries through imagination (Simmel 1971:355). This fragmentation of reality, in the fantasy of stories and myths, provides a more manageable model or facet of experience, displaying the complexity of experience in reduced, more comprehensible terms. Thus, "the fairy tale only invents what is not the case: it does not talk nonsense" (Wittgenstein 1963:97). "A well-constructed plot should, therefore, be single in its issue. . ." (Aristotle 1961:76), and not encompass all of protean possibilities of experience. "A good tale, over determined and 'crystallized,' may just be too logical to be true" (Burkert 1979:207), but this, in turn, hardly means that it holds no truth at any level. After all, imagination "is part of sense's own recognition of reality that there must be a standard above sense, and one that has the power of veto over it" (Frye 1963:152). As Simmel notes, "individuals [are] only limited realizations of their selves" (1971:xviii); we are all more than our apparent social selves: ". . . the way in which [the individual] is associated is determined by the way in which he is not" (ibid.:12). "Literature should attempt, rather, 'to unexpress the expressible,' to problematize the meanings we automatically confer or assume'' (Culler 1983:57). It is precisely in this sense in reading an innovative philosopher such as Wittgenstein that we encounter the verb *imagine* so frequently in his more challenging and subversive texts.

Thus, the fantastic quality of imagination takes us outside ourselves in two ways, by presenting a version of experience and things that is both less and more than what we ordinarily encounter. It is less in that only one or two facets are considered and explored, often with an oddness determined precisely because other features are ignored. It is more in that this narrowing of scrutiny and development allows an expansion, even a luxuriation of qualities and possibilities not encountered in reality. "This is the vision, not of what is, but of what otherwise might be done with a given situation" (Frye 1963:151). "Yes, but that which I see in those stories is something they acquire, after all, from the evidence, including such evidence as does not seem directly connected with them—from the thought of man and his past, from the strangeness of what I see in myself and in others, what I have seen and I have heard" (Wittgenstein 1971:41). Fantasy is rooted in everyday reality.

It is out of the bewildering complexity of everyday experience that the play of the storyteller can create a kind of strange order in fantastic limitation (cf. Huizinga 1950:10). Imagination evinced in stories and fables allows Kaguru to contemplate their ideas and experience to extremes and degrees beyond the limits of the lives they live, yet this same imaginative experience can inform Kaguru of how they live and consider their working lives.[5]

Second, Kaguru tales represent only an extreme form of what is, in less removed and fantastic form and exercise, part and parcel of everyday experience. For Kaguru, as for others, social action requires a subjective interpretation of the experience and intentions of others (cf. Schutz 1967:8). It also requires imagining how to present a social self, a *persona*, to others, a self that will force or entice them to play one's game. Thus, it involves both demystification and mystification at once. Sartre argues that ambiguity or opacity in our imagination is a source of fear, whereas individuated, resolved imagery is reassuring (n.d.:189). I disagree in one sense, for we shall see that Kaguru gain considerable advantage and even pleasure through their folktales in seizing upon the ambiguities in their social life. They do not seem to find harmony and consistency vital to their peace of mind. These are sources of humor and drama in folktales. Furthermore, by cultivating ambiguities, individuals mask their conflicting obligations, intentions, and feelings, even while at the same time striving to force others, especially those they hope to control, to divulge their explicit allegiances and needs. Much of Kaguru social life is a constant negotiation between self-serving, protective ambiguity and cooperative or exploitative explication of social rights and obligations. Kaguru stories embody such essential processes in condensed forms that Kaguru learn as they are socialized. All Kaguru constantly gauge their acts not only in terms of their own motives and roles but also in terms of how they expect others to react. A shrewd Kaguru is a kind of sociologist reckoning the factors of roles and personality behind each other Kaguru with whom she or he interacts. In part, this is taught through tales, anecdotes, and gossip. In part, it is learned through the experience of trial and error, not only on one's own part but in watching others. Finally, it is understood through imaginative projection. A Kaguru wonders what he or she would do in a similar situation. This, of course, is a kind of empathy or sympathy built up under the assumption that others are of like mind and experience to oneself (Scheler 1954:247). The reverse of this, the view that others may be monstrous, evil, alien, also stems from the imagination. This can lead to a self-poisoning of the mind, which, in its profoundest sense, Scheler terms *ressentiment* (1972:45–46), henceforth termed resentment. For Kaguru this may often be expressed as fear and suspicion of sorcery and witchcraft and represents a central feature of how they judge their relations to their society.

We construct our scenarios of social life from a complex mosaic of experience. This derives from the manifold and often contradictory or competing roles that form our social selves and which define our aims and mold our sentiments. Yet "probably much of what we are forced to represent to ourselves as mixed feelings, as composites of many drives, as the composite of opposite sensations, is entirely self-consistent" (Simmel 1971:77). What Simmel seems to mean here is that these seemingly countervailing tendencies are at one with the wholeness of our full, individual selves, and, indeed, are consistent with what it means to live with others. What these seeming inconsistencies may be at odds with is the nonsituational, unreal construct of a social self which we sometimes fashion when remarking upon conduct and attitudes in the abstract sense as social anthropologists. Much of Kaguru imagination delves into the murky, ambiguous interstices between these different situational definitions of the person, of social roles, values, and beliefs, implicitly contrasting these definitions not only with more public and artificial versions of the self but with the even more complex individual that each of us also is. "A society is, therefore, a structure which consists of beings which stand inside and outside of it at the same time" (Burke 1962:607–608). What these persons are is determined by the never-ending negotiations that constitute social interaction.

The chapters that follow consider various ways that Kaguru imagine, but not merely in the sense that they fantasize or speculate about what might be or cannot happen, or even what should be. As I have noted, to imagine also means to think, to consider the ways one's life and society have led to what one is. Society is a world of myriad relations that require constant work precisely because they are subject to continued change and contradictions; to be one's self within society also requires incessant labor, both to absorb and to use the gifts that society and culture provide, yet also to control, perhaps even to triumph over or fend off, these impingements so as to gain some measure of one's own being. Durkheim and later Simmel long ago brilliantly drew attention to these ceaseless oscillations between society and the individual. Indeed, this interplay forms the very essence of moral struggle. In that sense it remains difficult to separate some forms of sociology from a "higher" form of social psychology. It is around this effort of the individual to imagine what one is and how one functions that this study is centered. These relations are not easily defined or portrayed. It is the quintessential value of ethnographic description that it, more than mere theorizing, may lend some embodiment to such assertions about the meaning of our experiences as human beings.

NOTES

1. I have presented some of my views on these matters elsewhere (1980a, 1981b, 1983). I do not believe that an ethnographic monograph is a proper vehicle for such methodological soul-searching. In part, an ethnography itself should illustrate and vindicate the method. Furthermore, what recent accounts we do have of such methodological moaning and groaning suggest a failure of moral nerve. For another, somewhat narrow view of sociological imagination, see Mills 1961.

2. Throughout this work I refer to the derivations of various words. Although I realize that his work has been criticized at times, I generally depend on Partridge (1961) for such information.

3. I do not intend to embark on an evaluation of other interpretations of symbolic systems. It should be clear that I do not consider any symbols to be axiomatic, to be ends in themselves, much less to epitomize any total reality (cf. Turner 1967:20, 43). At best, they involve only facets of a cultural or social reality which is essentially myriad and contradictory.

4. For excellent discussions of how metaphors and related imaginative processes form key features in the development of Western beliefs and values, see Onions 1951 and Lloyd 1966.

5. To the contrary, Hallpike sees such stories as "atomizing" truth, failing to grasp that these provide insights because of their selectivity. He does recognize that in such societies stories and initiation rather than specific verbal instructions provide moral awareness (1979:109–112). The African use of such stories to undertake moral inquiry has been well illustrated and discussed by Jackson (1982:1–3, 31).

CHAPTER 2.

Kaguru Life

So and no otherwise—
So and no otherwise—
hillmen desire their Hills!
Rudyard Kipling, The Sea and the Hills

The mountains are our sponsors . . .
W. S. Landor, Regeneration

In this chapter I sketch some general features of Kaguru society and culture and the physical environment in which Kaguru live.[1] I do this with two aims. First, it is useful for readers to have some picture of Kaguru life as a whole in order to make sense of the more detailed account I provide in subsequent chapters. Second, some features of the Kaguru's ecological environment and social organization have deeply influenced the ways Kaguru imagine themselves and their world. These contribute a few broad themes that permeate most sectors of Kaguru life.

Kaguru are a people who fled to their hills after having suffered from raids by more warlike neighbors. Consequently, they are justifiably suspicious and devious in their dealings with outsiders. Kaguru are agriculturalists who wish they could sustain more livestock than they do, and who face considerable insecurity over food in some years. Most important of all, they are matrilineal and hold certain values and beliefs resembling those held by many other matrilineal peoples of East and Central Africa. Yet many of their notions, such as those about the dead, God, rainmaking, witchcraft, joking relations, and naming, represent cultural traits shared by other Bantu language speakers regardless of their form of organization. In any case, I believe that the political and economic circumstances of Kaguruland, its subjection to raiding, its thinness of population in relation to the land, and the insecurity of resources, have set severe limits on the development of their political system. These account for the constant coalescence and dissipation of Kaguru settlements and for the lack of any sustained hierarchical political system.

Kaguru are especially aware of contradictions in their aims and needs. They view their world with a keen mixture of power and powerlessness, since some of the very factors that encourage cooperation and submission to others may also work toward division, betrayal, and independence. The precipitous terrain and the meagerness and undependability of resources work against Kaguru establishing any enduring and extensive social framework by which people may be held together. In times of need, Kaguru are likely to posit contradictory courses of behavior. Those in want advocate cooperation and sharing; those in plenty demand subordination for support or even conceal resources in order to survive. In a world of limited goods and precarious fortunes, Kaguru seek to gain their own ends of security and domination, but these are as much ensured through divisive and selfish autonomy as through group cooperation. Yet Kaguruland also has a long history of raiding, not only between neighboring groups but by ethnic outsiders. Without ties to kin and neighbors, each household would stand relatively helpless against the outside. Kaguru society, then, is best seen as a congeries of fragments, perpetually drawing together, dissolving, and regrouping in ever newly negotiated combinations.

The processes recounted above could characterize patrilineal as well as matrilineal peoples. Yet Kaguru matriliny adds further contradiction and tension to the system through its inability to foster the long-term stability of many domestic groups. Kaguru matriliny challenges the stability of certain key relations over time. In the short run, it calls husband-wife relations to risk in competition with ties between siblings. In the longer view, it sets even siblings at odds in terms of the most central bond of the society, mother and children. Since traditionally Kaguruland was short of people rather than arable land, social groups tended to compete and negotiate for the loyalty and control of people rather than access to land as wealth. For Kaguru, people are wealth, yet shortage of resources sets limits to the range of people one may command and hold.

I must emphasize that I do not view these features of Kaguru social structure as failings, though some Kaguru do, in that they sometimes complain that countervailing social rules frustrate their most cherished aims. I do, however, stress that Kaguru society is one on which there is constant negotiation over nearly all social ties, with many deep cleavages becoming not only possible but inevitable. In a sense, however, this indicates that Kaguru, at least the most intelligent and adroit, have considerable avenues available for eluding or manipulating rules so as to maximize their autonomy from others. While I have mentioned Kaguru's repeated advocacy of cooperation and support among kin and neighbors, Kaguru set a very high value on autonomy and experience difficulty in resolving this value with their repeated need to depend on others for security and furtherance of their ambitions.

LAND, CLIMATE, AND ECONOMY

Ukaguru is a highland area in Tanzania about 3,600 square miles in size. Today there are probably about 100,000 Kaguru. Although the population is estimated to have been much less in precolonial times, Ukaguru today is still not an overpopulated country and there is considerable movement within any neighborhood.

Long before the first Arab and European colonists arrived, Ukaguru was a corridor for trade and a refuge for people suffering from drought and warfare. As a result, Kaguru have been subjected to a wide range of cultural influences; yet, conscious to differentiate themselves from those surrounding them, they have managed to absorb some of these influences to form a distinctive society.

Ukaguru comprises three types of terrain. The southeastern fifth is lowland and was only thinly populated in precolonial times because it was frequently flooded, unhealthful, and, most important of all, difficult to defend. The central third of Ukaguru consists of the Itumba Mountains, over 4,500 feet in altitude with many peaks over 6,000 feet. It is a cool, damp area with too much rain for growing much sorghum or millet. Mountaineers favor maize but also grow considerable tobacco, vegetables, and fruits. Some of these areas even sustain cultivation throughout the year. The mountains contain iron deposits that once supported an extensive iron industry. Kaguru say that many of the mountainsides were denuded not for agriculture but to provide wood to feed their smelters. When the first Europeans entered Ukaguru, they found these mountains to be the most populous and prosperous portion of the country, mainly because this area was the easiest to defend against the raids of Maasai, Gogo, Hehe, and Arab slavers and from foraging caravaners. Today the mountains are much more thinly populated, and the plateau area is the most populous. Kaguru say that this is because they dislike the coldness and dampness of the higher areas. They also note that the broader river valleys of the plateau are better for cultivation than are the narrow, steeper valleys of the mountains. They maintain that in the past it was danger from raiding that kept them mainly in the mountains. Still, the many generations of mountain life have left an essentially highland cast to much Kaguru imagery everywhere. At present, however, over two-thirds of all Kaguru live in the plateau (2,000 to 4,500 feet) that surrounds the central Itumba Mountains. This plateau comprises about half of Ukaguru. It is an area of low, rolling hills dotted with occasional mountains and spectacular rocky outcrops. From the Itumba Mountains and these other scattered peaks, streams fan out through the plateau, forming arable valleys displaying a nearly continuous patchwork of cultivation. These river valleys are cultivated every year, while the outlying, less well-watered higher ground is subject to slash-and-burn cultivation. The staple crops in the plateau are maize, millet, and sorghum, the latter two being preferred in the drier, western part of the plateau. Grain is supplemented with a wide range of vegetables, yams, plantains, bananas, manioc, and sugarcane. The main crop for trading is tobacco, which is sought by neighboring Gogo, Maasai, and others in exchange for livestock and handicrafts (today, money).

Most Kaguru keep sheep and goats and some chickens. In the mountains and the western plateau some Kaguru keep herds of cattle as well. Kaguru envy their neighbors, the Gogo, Hehe, and Maasai, who all possess far more cattle than they. Their environment prevents Kaguru from holding as many cattle as they desire. Instead, it dictates an agricultural economy. Yet livestock remain the most valued wealth, and Kaguru persist in speaking about cattle in a way that might lead a stranger to judge animals as more important economically than they really are.

In good years the plateau enjoys about 30 inches of rain while some mountain areas receive several times this. As in most of East Africa, the amount and pattern of rainfall are crucial to survival. It is likely that every third or fourth year may be lean and every seventh or eighth brings severe difficulties, sometimes even famine (Brooke 1967). The annual cycle of rains and dry season dictates the basic rhythm and intensity of all Kaguru work and leisure.

Kaguru view these features of terrain and climate in somewhat contradictory ways. Most Kaguru consider the Itumba Mountains to be the cultural and spiritual heart of their land. This is where customs are said to exist in purest form. This is the region that sheltered Kaguru when they were endangered. Yet the majority of Kaguru, those now living in the plateau and lowlands, sometimes deride mountaineers as poor and backward. Many say the mountains are too hard and uncomfortable for good living. Similarly, all Kaguru anticipate the rains, recognizing that their very survival depends upon when and how they fall. Yet the Kaguru hold mixed feelings about these rains as well. They bring endless toil and discomfort. It is the dry season, when little grows, that is the time for leisure, conviviality, and play. The rains are the key to life, but the time of their absence is when life is enjoyed.

Kaguru imagery emphasizes the contrasts between mountains and valleys, between settlements, with their surrounding fields, and the wild bush, which must be repeatedly cleared for arable land, picturing their very society in such topographical terms. Settlements are characterized as orderly contrasted with the dangerous, encroaching bush; kinship is compared to streams, which represent fertility, continuity, and connectedness.

Securing a livelihood out of this land is the central problem and theme of all Kaguru life. Ukaguru is a beautiful hill and mountain country that, at the height of the rains, appears far more fertile and prosperous than it actually is. It is a constant struggle for Kaguru to secure food for survival. Some years may bring plenty, but everyone knows that real hardship—sometimes drought, perhaps flooding, even rarely locusts, not to mention the depredations of rodents, birds, and other pests—must sooner or later be faced. Granaries may be full at harvest during the early dry season but are usually severely depleted by the onset of the next rains. Many Kaguru worry about making ends meet until the first new crops are harvested. The most important result of these likely shortages is that no Kaguru can afford to reject his or her kin and neighbors, whose help may be essential in hard times. At the same time, most households are wary of the demands of others and are secretive about what resources they really do possess. The single most pervasive theme in Kaguru culture, sustenance, revolves around balancing the demands for sharing with kin and neighbors against commonsensical regard for the survival of one's own household.

MATRILINEALITY AND DOMESTICITY

Kaguru are matrilineal, as are the neighboring peoples to the east and south, the Ngulu, Zigula, Lugulu, Sagala, and Vidunda. Kaguru often contrast themselves with the patrilineal Gogo, Maasai, Baraguyu, and Hehe, who neighbor and raided them. Kaguru, then, are keenly aware that while they are hardly unique, theirs is not the only way a society might be organized. Quite often they ponder why they should be matrilineal rather than organized differently. Indeed, while matriliny is the proclaimed rule, many men at times promote their rights as fathers over those as mother's brothers when they can get away with it. Matriliny is, of course, the chief means by which larger groups may be constructed. Traditionally, settlements were built up around a matrilineal core, and it is through matrilineal ties that major contributions for bridewealth, bloodwealth, access to land, and authority to propitiate ancestors are reckoned. Groups are built up to facilitate defense, to pool labor for cultivating and herding, and to present a solidary face against disputes and claims from other groups. The key strategy for advancement in Kaguru social relations is the accumulation and allocation of people into such groups, rather than any major focus on gaining access to land, ritual knowledge, or livestock. All of these latter advantages are goals, to be sure, but such resources are employed chiefly as means to secure as many followers or dependents as possible and do not constitute ends in themselves. Yet this process is severely checked in that individual Kaguru also value autonomy and repeated shortages of food set limits on sharing.

One tries to retain as many of one's dependents as one can and, if possible, at the same time employ marital strategies as ways for securing even more people. In a man's case, this means wives for himself and his sons and nephews, husbands for his daughters, sisters, and nieces. In a woman's case, it means maintaining residence that gives her and her eventual offspring access to supportive kin who will protect them against affines. Obviously, not everyone can win at such a game. Prosperous and forceful men seek to retain their own children and attract those children's spouses as well. One means toward this end is to provide outsiders with wives for little or no bridewealth. Another is to invite residence in a settlement larger and therefore safer and more prosperous than others. Bridewealth is proportionate to the autonomy that a man can claim. A large payment enables a man to take a wife to reside with him where he wishes and gives him increased rights in his children's labor and the subsequent bridewealth or brideservice which he might receive for his daughters. Small or no payment of bridewealth means that a husband starts out married life living with his wife's people, where he would work out his debt through brideservice; hence the term "affine who cultivates" for a newly married young male. Marriage can therefore represent a wide range of fates. It might mean that a woman must leave her natal settlement and stay with her new husband, either in his newly founded settlement or in her husband's kin's village. In the past, it more often meant that a youth had to stay with his wife's people, who exploited his labor and who were likely to side with his wife against him and other affinal outsiders. Today, the possibility of securing wages outside Ukaguru provides some chance for autonomy to some youths.

A really poor youth might be married to a father's sister's daughter or a mother's brother's daughter, usually with the understanding that he need not provide full or even any bridewealth. No one, however, does something like this for nothing, and in these cases of cross-cousin marriage, the elder has foregone bridewealth because he expects the youth to reside near him. Then the new husband loses considerable independence because of his obligations to his senior kin and also because his wife is as well connected as he within the local kinship network. In anthropological jargon, such matches are sometimes described as preferential marriages. Such an adjective well characterizes how these unions are viewed by some of the elders who exploit them. These unions may even be favored by some women who see this as one way to avoid leaving their natal villages and to continue links between mothers and sisters. Such a marriage is hardly preferred by the new husband himself, who has markedly decreased his autonomy. We can see that a wide range of marital arrangements is possible, depending upon a person's age, wealth, and kin ties. In general, disadvantage lies with that spouse who moves into a new village as an affinal outsider. For women there is the added potential difficulty of sometimes being married to a polygynist whose co-wives compete with her over benefits for themselves and their children.

In general, older men control younger ones in two ways. First, elders monopolize the means by which wives can be acquired. While youths might

dream of securing wealth independently by which they can obtain wives, most
find themselves tied to their senior kin or to affines because of marital debts
in bridewealth or brideservice. Such debts are the price young men pay to
become householders and full adults. Some men, by dint of age, cleverness,
work, and luck, eventually break free from many of these obligations. They
then, in turn, may take additional wives on their own terms and eventually
proceed to exploit their own youthful dependents as well. Second, elders
monopolize access to the dead. They alone consult and propitiate ancestors,
and in so doing determine whose misdeeds have brought about misfortune
from the angered spirits. Before they can lay these disturbed ghosts to rest,
they will attempt to resolve the hard feelings and supposed wrongs at the root
of these troubles. As a result of these duties, elders tend to define proper
conduct in terms likely to maintain their own authority and power, though
most would put this otherwise and maintain that they advocate proper obedience to rules so as to allow the group to cohere. The trouble is that rules
seen from above by elders are often interpreted differently by juniors. Of
course, elders who abuse their advantages by being stingy about enabling
dependents to marry or by interpreting the will of the dead so as to advance
themselves while blatantly harming others risk losing followers. After all,
even in the politically turbulent past, dissidents could often go elsewhere,
since arable land was not scarce, whereas people were in demand. Kaguru
autonomy persists despite efforts at domination and control by elders. In
summary, elders compete for the loyalty of kin and affines, that loyalty ultimately being expressed through common residence and attentiveness to rituals, which elders dominate. Wealth, knowledge, age, and well-connected-
ness all give elders advantages, but these can never be pushed too far. In any
case, for some elders (usually men) to succeed both in retaining their dependents and in recruiting still more inevitably means that some others must
fail. I should add that while some older women appear to exert considerable
influence in local affairs, today this is ultimately expressed openly through
their sons.

There is no question that in the precolonial period Kaguru settlements
resulting from such struggles were far larger than are such settlements today,
and probably more stable. Once raiding was quelled by European rule, all
subsequent historical observers remark upon a slow but steady erosion of the
size of settlements. Yet Kaguru still need each other, though not on the more
day-to-day basis posed by unstable and dangerous political conditions. Now
such mutual support involves sharing resources for costs in law suits, fines,
bridewealth, school fees, ritual, medical care, clothing, and food shortages,
and pooling labor for planting, clearing land, harvesting, herding, and
housebuilding.

So far I have discussed Kaguru matriliny mainly in terms of how elder men employ certain advantages in order to dominate young men who, however, will eventually succeed them. An even more ambiguous and problematical aspect concerns the relations between men and women, especially as these involve the play between women's roles as wives, sisters, and mothers and men's roles as husbands, brothers, and fathers. Certainly all societies constructed around kinship embody conflict between men and women, generally expressed in terms of various forms of complementary attributes and division of labor. It is not only that men and women need one another to produce and rear children; Kaguru men need women to cook, draw water, brew beer for sacrifice and cash, and assist them in cultivation. In the past, women needed men for protection as well as to aid in cultivation, housebuilding, and tending livestock. While men continue to dominate women in their control of ancestral propitiation, divination, and jural proceedings, it is obvious to everyone that men need women more immediately and continually economically than women need men. Even today almost no adult men find it bearable or practical to live without women. Of course, men could cook and fetch water, but it would be considered shameful for them to do so. In contrast, women readily do all these tasks and can cultivate as skillfully as men. As a result, even in the past, and even more so today, many women live comfortably in households alone with their children and without men. A lone woman is quite able to carry out all of the everyday chores that sustain life; if she has children to help her with these tasks and perhaps to tend livestock, she is well off indeed. Women do periodically seek male kin to support and guide them in housebuilding and in various jural and ritual crises, but even then which men they choose to ask for help often reflects a careful playing off of kin competing against one another for their favor. Many Kaguru women are even encouraged by some of their matrilineal kinsmen to reside alone, as widows, divorcees, or even unmarried mothers. This keeps them free of husbands and their kin. These women's matrilineal kinsmen see this as a strategy to increase their own hold on them, since such women cannot play off husbands and affines against their own kin in order to get their own ways. Yet many women view this situation with some favor as a means by which they themselves can partially elude men's steady interference in their affairs, such as controlling how they use the proceeds they gain from selling crops and beer, interfering about the men with whom these women have affairs and from whom they receive gifts, and deciding where and when women visit others. In any case, these maneuvers all point out the continuing uneasiness with which Kaguru men view women's seeming abilities to elude control. In later chapters we shall see that the complex interplay between authority, power, and affection reflects different and ultimately unresolvable aims and strengths of Kaguru men and women. This is not to say that the system is unworkable, but rather that it is propelled along by these countervailing motives.

Kaguru often speak of men as dominating, aggressive, and embodying authority, and of women as passive, conciliatory, and affectual. Obviously these are simplistic stereotypes in that some men are meek and weak and some women strong and assertive. Furthermore, effective authority by men requires affectual support, while strong affect elicited by women brings its own terms of power. Kaguru tell us that men and women may be stereotyped in certain ways, but both their beliefs and their experiences are clearly less cut-and-dried than this. We know that in the past some Kaguru women are said to have held positions as heads of settlements or even larger congeries of people. As this study proceeds, we shall find that for Kaguru men, women present a continual challenge to their aims at controlling junior kin, ironically as much because women are so necessary as allies in this domination as they are potential subverters of it. For Kaguru women, men often serve, unwittingly or otherwise, as the very means by which women elude male authority, or even as the vehicles by which women succeed in influencing other men. Women are key mediating and affectual links in the chains of both domestic and matrilineal authority, but in many cases they do not acquiesce to some men's schemes to have matters end quite as these men would like. Since women, above all else, see their security and fates indissolubly linked to those of their children, they remain especially problematic as the inevitable and staunchest allies of the younger generation against their elders. As juniors, men strive to assert their autonomy against aging males. Women are asked to lend affectual support and council both to the status quo and to those pressing for change. Clever women find ample means to guarantee that their own interests and needs must be considered if their loyalty and affection are to be counted on by such men.

One kind of tension between male and female kin hinges on the fact that though Kaguru are matrilineal, most men generally subscribe to an ideal in which they hope to reside with their wives and children in the belief that they, the husbands, rather than their wives' brothers, will secure allegiance and benefits from these offspring. To achieve this, men rely heavily on the support of their wives. In turn, these same men hope that their own sisters will be raising other men's children (their nieces and nephews) to be their future heirs. Men thus hope for loyal wives yet for sisters disloyal to their own husbands, at least to the extent that these sisters will encourage their children to seek out their mother's brother for some countersupport. At times men even encourage sisters to leave their husbands, especially after they have borne many children so that little or no bridewealth need be refunded.[2] Thus there is considerable tension between women's roles as wives and their roles as sisters, and men's roles as husbands and as brothers. What is never in question is the women's roles as mothers.

Men then are deeply concerned with the fertility of their wives but equally so with that of their sisters, though this has repressive or disturbing aspects for them. This is reflected in Kaguru imagination by way of off-color jokes, songs, and stories where men do retain their sisters and cohabit with them, as well as by way of prohibitions against mentioning sex in front of a sister. Kaguru wryly see an illicit attraction in this, but recognize that the purpose of marriage is more than producing children (after all, unmarried women produce offspring). A sister's marriage converts strangers and enemies into kin, not only as affinal allies but as a broader range of complementary paternal and collateral connections for one's offspring.[3] These kin appear at a disadvantage if one considers them from an unrealistically unadulterated matrilineal purview; but none of these organizational principles makes sense or is workable if considered *in vacuo* or if carried out to its illogical extremity.

Problems arise for a man when his sister so loves her husband that her loyalties to him far surpass those to her brother. The brother would tend to impute this betrayal to her sexual appetite. In such a case, the brother would still hope to win out if their mother were alive, for what decent person would prefer the seductive blandishments of a sensual spouse to the primal affection of one's own mother?[4]

These relations appear quite different, however, when considered from a woman's perspective. While men like to think of all the women and children of a polygynous household as one big family, obviously each household with a different mother and her children has its own competing priorities. Co-wives use the threat of returning to their brothers or parents and the rumors of what these kinsmen have promised to offer as counters against a husband's stinginess or mistreatment. Each wife tends to be set at odds against the others with reference to the interests of her own children. While some matrilineal peoples (such as the Navaho) attempt to alleviate co-wife hostility by advocating polygynous marriage to sisters, Kaguru are appalled at such a prospect. This is consistent with how intensely Kaguru value mother-child relations. They argue that sisters should work to hold a matrilineage together, but are unlikely to transcend the rivalries engendered by sexual cohabitation and even more by competition over the benefits provided for children by that common husband. After all, lineages segment with reference to sisters, but usually sisters whose mothers are dead. In a similar sense, a woman (ego) views her husband's sister with considerable distrust. Such a woman seeks to persuade her brother (ego's husband) to favor her children (his nieces and nephews) rather than his own. One explanation Kaguru give for marrying cross-cousins is that they are already enemies on account of this competition for inheritance, and one should seek to use marriage to convert enemies into friends. A woman and her children also hold similar misgivings about her brother's wife, since that woman seeks to cheat them out of inheritance. Kaguru cite this as one

reason why a woman's son marries her dead brother's widow, because the
widow is a potential enemy. Similarly, different sisters will compete for the
favor and attention of a brother.

What then holds the system together given these constant potential cleavages? In part, of course, these varying competing ties, ever shifting in weight
and locus, lead to a perpetual jockeying between kin and affines courting one
another's shifting allegiances. It is such kaleidoscopic competition that pulls
the system of relations along as much as it may rend it. Equally crucial is
the medial role of women as mothers. The most enduring and powerful of
all Kaguru ties is unquestionably that between a woman and her children.
While this may, in fact, not always be the case, structural logic argues that
the one person who should invariably have a person's best interest at heart
is one's own mother. Her fate and that of her children should be one. For
Kaguru all women other than one's mother prefer their own children's good
to one's own, even one's mother's sister, the person Kaguru say most nearly
resembles a real mother. As for kinsmen, they are all suspect since they are
all caught in the double bind of being husbands as well as mother's brothers
and are thus even more deeply committed authoritatively to two different and
competing modes of inheritance and control. In the final analysis, the bonds
between women and their children are the ties that effectively link together
different segments of a matrilineage. That siblings stick together is mostly
due to the fact that their mother repeatedly evokes claims for affection and
solidarity between them. If lineages split, it is almost always after the mother
linking various members is dead. Kaguru remark, though somewhat illogi-
cally, that it is the very fact that women are, at least formally, excluded from
the male struggle for jural rights over people and goods that explains why
women can be trusted. Regardless of these previously cited contradictions
concerning sisters and collateral female kin, it is indeed true that mothers
should logically always advise what is best for their own children in these
matters, since it is vicariously through their children that women attain real
influence or security. Such views make sense structurally, but they still cannot
account for personal differences of intelligence, sentiment, and even per-
versity. Some women, as some men, just do not do what is in their own best
interests, and, indeed, some men and women are as nasty and spiteful as
others are kind and forgiving.

In view of these overlapping pressures between competing jural rights and
affection, the cleverest woman seeks to play off the various men in her life
against one another, brothers against husband, and husband against father and
mother's brothers. So long as she keeps the primary interests of her own
children firmly in view and does not commit herself entirely to any one camp,
she cannot go too far wrong. Of course, such behavior implies a degree of

calculation, a coldheartedness, and a clever manipulativeness that would be both remarkable and repulsive if carried out persistently. Kaguru women, like people everywhere, only intermittently control the social scenario well. Yet most are pretty much aware of what they would like to do and how they would like to do it and of how the system works. Bringing such things off is another matter, though provocation can prompt spectacular conduct by some women under duress, especially against husbands and fathers.

Gender

It is this undivided locus of ultimate maternal interest that makes women more trustworthy than men yet also more dangerous. In contrast, men are forever torn between their lineal ambitions and duties as mothers' brothers (which means, ironically, also as mothers' sons) and their personal, domestic hopes as husbands and fathers. No one can ever be sure where someone's final priorities actually lie. No one really wants to choose. Given the limited resources available, most men are constantly being pushed first in one direction, then another, by their own and their sisters' children, inevitably annoying one or another competing contingent, however they respond.

Given these motivations in Kaguru kinship, neither men nor women can hope for much success in life without having children. This is both more intensely rewarding yet potentially more difficult for women than for men. Women without children are not full women. They have a dim future and consider themselves failures. Outside the family, they have little scope for activity other than brewing beer, marketing crops, and quasi prostitution. Men, too, need heirs, but they have these in two different ways, through their wives and through their sisters. Furthermore, men have a considerably longer time period as procreators than do women as childbearers. Men can and do wait until they can "get their act together." Women are both forced into and eager for maternity, so as to secure their positions while they are capable of producing young. This does have one unintended structurally significant outcome. Since women tend to marry at an earlier age than men, they have mature and childbearing offspring earlier than their brothers do. Women consequently face different choices regarding their own and their children's allegiances before their brothers do. Men's scope is broader and somewhat more flexible, but the loyalties which women command are less ambivalent, more quickly faced, and therefore more intense.

Barrenness is the worst fate that any Kaguru woman can imagine and is generally associated with supernatural punishment by the dead or the malevolence of kin and neighbors. Who the father of a woman's child may be makes no difference in terms of its lineal affiliation or to the mother's increased value to her kin. The most serious disadvantage faced by unmarried mothers lies in the fact that the child and mother cannot play off a husband-father against matrilineal kin in order to further their own interests. Unless she secures a lover who pays for some rights in the child, both she and the child must depend entirely on her natal kin. For women not to marry is no tragedy; for them not to bear children is. In contrast, to some extent men can surmount the limitations of infertility and even impotence. Men may take more than one wife if they wish to maintain a relationship but suspect that a wife is barren (all men marry), and, on occasion, other men (usually kin) may secretly father children for these men. Obviously women cannot fake parenthood in this way; there is no adoption. It does happen, however, that a woman who suspects her husband of infertility may attempt to conceive through a liaison with some lover. Such children are not usually recognized as belonging to the biological father but to the husband, the one who "bought the womb." Thus, even women's infidelity can serve their husbands while working to women's advantage as well.

As a final word in this thumbnail sketch of Kaguru relations between kin, I must caution the reader on one important point. I have dwelt on the conflict and competition characterizing interactions between men and women occupying different and changing roles in households and lineages. Most of the discussion involved strategies to maximize such protagonists' advantages or to minimize their vulnerabilities. This should not wrongly convey an impression that most Kaguru life is one long series of quarrels, litigation, and intrigues. That is far from the case, and many households move along peacefully for many months at a time. Yet I did witness a good deal of gossip, quarreling, and litigation. This did not, however, strike me as any greater than what I encountered among the two other East African societies where I also did fieldwork. Nor does this seem inconsistent with my readings of ethnography for many other peoples. In any society where so much is reckoned in terms of membership and standing within various kin groups, such disputes reveal how much depends on these ties. Furthermore, if Kaguru do dispute and attempt to manipulate and subvert aspects of their social system and succeed, surely this indicates that Kaguru can find some freedom and fulfillment through the constraints and contradictions within the system. It is precisely these features which seem most to attract and exercise Kaguru moral imaginative thought. Kaguru moral attention is directed to these features not because these are seen as moral scandals (to paraphrase Lévi-Strauss), but because these contradictions allow Kaguru to imagine means by which some persons may employ Kaguru culture in order to succeed. This is possible not only because Kaguru are keenly aware of the quirks and traps within their social world, but because, viewing their system from an occasional imaginative distance, if only intermittently, they no longer allow it to take them over but rather selectively, if not cynically, make it (*viz.*, others) work for themselves. Kaguru beliefs and rites, which Kaguru sometimes speak of as all of a piece, are in fact as ambivalent, contradictory, and open to varying strategies of comment and interpretation as are the matrilineal and domestic interrelations from which they stem.[5]

CONCLUSION

Kaguru have good grounds for wariness, suspicion, and secretiveness; not only have they long suffered from harmful interference by outsiders, but through the shifting and undependable conditions of their environment, they find themselves pulled in opposite directions. At times they seek solidarity of kin and neighbors against outsiders; at others they fear these very ties will sap their meager resources within each separate, contending household. The result is a pervasive view of authority and power in highly ambiguous and ambivalent terms. Guile and manipulative cleverness are both condemned and praised, depending upon the particular contextual perspectives of those caught in any set of interactions. Subversion and trickery, as much as loyalty and honesty, are valued attributes of survival and success.

Kaguru norms repeatedly advocate the rightful dominance of old over young and of men over women (at least in the jural and ritual sense). Yet the two central features of Kaguru organized life, matriliny and domesticity, presided over by males, place men and women in quite different, contending social and temporal frames. Out of this unresolved amalgam, men are drawn in two directions, toward children and wives within their own households, and toward their sisters, whose offspring are their lineal heirs. At the same time women as mothers strategically span both these competing domestic and lineal spheres, accounting for their power and influence not only over their own affairs but over males as well. The strong undercurrent of sexual hostility and male uneasiness over sexual adequacy and female loyalty is a negative side of these same tendencies which ultimately work powerfully for maturing women and their offspring against older males still seeking to control them. Throughout this study, Kaguru are seen as repeatedly striving to resolve these various and contending priorities and needs so as to contain the changes inevitable with the maturation and the corresponding increase in membership of a group. Out of these constant efforts, stemming from domestic developmental cycles, the varying constellations of Kaguru settlements and ritual groups are repeatedly figured. Out of these same efforts, women, at least if they have the good fortune to bear children, increasingly gain in security and influence as they and their children mature, whereas men age only to find that their maturity has heightened the dilemmas which they continue to face and has weakened their personal resources to meet these challenges.

NOTES

1. Space disallows a full picture of Kaguru environment and social organization. The fullest general picture remains Beidelman 1971a. The account I present here emphasizes traditional Kaguru social organization rather than that altered by modern factors. For bibliographical information regarding supplementary reading, see Beidelman 1967a, 1969, 1974b, 1981a.

2. In Kaguru tradition, bridewealth is refunded upon divorce, but a woman's kin deduct a sizable portion for each child she bore her husband. Ironically, this means that the more children women have, the more factors encourage them and their kin to consider their husbands expendable and press for divorce at any domestic crisis.

3. For this reason, while Kaguru recognize the tactical advantages in cross-cousin marriages, they also lament that these waste opportunities to establish ties with new people.

4. Heretofore, I have not paid attention to relations between a woman and her husband's mother, even though these tend to be notoriously difficult in many societies. Oddly, I do not know a single Kaguru story or anecdote dwelling on this relation. Nor did Kaguru repeatedly speak of it in the way, for example, that they harp on brother-sister ties, husband-wife relations, or even those between grandchildren and their grandparents. I inquired repeatedly about such relations and was assured that a daughter-in-law owed great respect to her husband's mother and should go out of her way to maintain even more formal relations toward her father-in-law, that woman's husband. Yet I was also told that relations between such women were likely to be cool, but any real hostility seemed much more likely to be focused on protagonists within one's own generation, such as one's husband's sisters or brothers' wives.

5. Most of the material will strike readers as familiar if they have read Turner (1953, 1959, 1962b, 1967, 1968, 1969), White (1961), Audrey Richards (1956), Stefaniszyn (1964), Grohs (1980), and other writers on rituals and beliefs among matrilineal peoples of Central Africa (cf. Beidelman 1971a:103–111, 1964d, 1965b, 1981d).

CHAPTER 3.

Cosmology and Dualism

The right hand of the Lord hath the pre-eminence.
Psalms 11.16

Man is the hunter; woman is his game.
A. L. Tennyson, *The Princess*, V.i.147

We are symbols, and inhabit symbols.
R. W. Emerson, xiii, The Poet, *Essays*

Kaguru beliefs and values are couched in terms of dualistic categories, countervailing characteristics and forces which both complement and at other times oppose one another.[1] In terms of deeper cultural structure, these are consistent with the social groupings by which various persons are organized and focused around changing goals and needs. These change, of course, through time and place. While these dialectical principles of complementarity and opposition alter in tone and emphasis, broader lineaments of structure and form display some common, enduring features by which human affairs and perceptions are organized. One can reasonably characterize Kaguru as having a coherent and comprehensive cosmology, a way of ordering thoughts, experiences, and social actions, but the affectual and moral tones of these elements undergo constant shifts in emphasis and qualification. These colorings of meaning and values are up for ceaseless negotiation by the Kaguru actors involved.

These dualistic features of Kaguru life so permeate Kaguru beliefs, values, and social groupings that an anthropologist is justified in terming Kaguru belief not only a dualistic cosmology but a dualistic social structure as well. Yet dualism is a deceptive term in that, misunderstood, it might wrongly lead some to believe that this refers to a system that is ever present in one form and always activated in its entirety. Kaguru are, of course, more or less all familiar with dualistic principles and constantly employ some of them in dealing with and formulating particular aims and experiences. Yet different situations, demands, aims, and roles are so varied and contradictory that only some segments of this cosmology are meaningful or usefully activated at any one time. The same holds true for social groups, which only selectively figure in any particular social scenario being staged. Indeed, the value and power of Kaguru thought and society (as in any social system) stem from its ultimately contradictory, richly ambivalent, and ambiguous nature, which demands constant work to be redefined and restated ever anew as different occasions and needs require. The cosmology is myriad, as protean as human experience itself must be in a dynamic society and fluid environment.

Yet there are some central themes and units in this system, and if we commence with these, we can discern some more or less steady principles around which other segments gravitate or rebound. These themes may be approached from two directions, from the social groups they embody or portray or from the metaphors which convey this portrayal. Thus we could commence with men and women and the paternal and maternal groups that lie behind fathers' and mothers' ties to children, or we could commence with the metaphors by which these persons and groups are qualified, such as bodily and spatial orientation, textures, temperature, and colors. That several such approaches are possible is due to the great complexity of this material. Kaguru beliefs and values, their cosmology, may be usefully likened to a great organ console. A vast keyboard makes a wide range of notes available, to be played singly, in chords, or in series; there is also a great number of stops which may be used to color particular notes in certain ways, It is not then simply a question of what symbol or element is evoked, but what aspects of that symbol are used, what are ignored, what repressed, or what merely sympathetically resonated as a result of other associated images and experiences. The difficulty in presenting this system lies in the fact that many of its meanings are contradictory, ambivalent, or ambiguous, and while actors and occasions go far to determine which shades of significance are relevant, often the power of the symbols derives as much from the possibility that more than one implication can be discerned or argued from them. This diversity stems from the fact that the system is constructed, deconstructed, and reconstructed through repeated practices or actions; it is not a static edifice constructed out of discursive endeavor.

Social anthropologists remain divided on how better to approach society: as social groupings using ideas, or as systems of ideas expressed through social groups? To provide an entry into understanding Kaguru cosmology I use both approaches, the social organizational and the more symbolic or metaphorical. I commence with a broad but brief characterization of some of the basic dualistic contrasts between Kaguru social groups or, rather, between different principles by which these groups are conceived. One of the basic contentions of this study is that Kaguru society, and particularly the ways Kaguru imagination is exercised in considering that society revolves about a central core of complementary yet contending sets of groups and loyalties:

matriliny and domesticity (and the related component roles of mothers and fathers, sisters and brothers), and ultimately kinship and alienness. Having sketched out these general features I then develop the material from an opposite, more detailed direction, that of the multifaceted symbolic attributes by which these social groups and roles are endowed with deep physical and affectual meaning and tone through metaphorical association. Each approach flows easily into the other, but it is the existential social order of matrilineal Kaguru society that I take as the heart of the system. It is from this that the most pervasive and persistent tensions and conflicts arise. Once we have these general features firmly in mind, the more complex metaphorical attributes supporting and elaborating these principles may be more easily grasped in all their more contradictory or ambiguous detail.

OPPOSITION AND COMPLEMENTARITY IN GROUPS AND SPACE

Kaguru tend to view groups and space in terms of complementary oppositions. They contrast these aspects of their environment as having different, opposing physical and, more important, moral qualities. Yet this contrast remains both complex and ambivalent, so that the valences assigned these terms shift repeatedly, revealing how these different components not only depend upon one another but even shift at times to assume some of the qualities or tones more often associated with their supposed opposites. I now review these basic sets, starting with the broadest in location, the contrast between Ukaguru and the lands and peoples beyond, and ending with the most specific, the contrast between men and women, as evinced in a married couple. I commence with the broadest because the general features of Kaguru language, society, demography, and environment form the distinctive features of Kaguru thinking and feeling and provide the common terms by which Kaguru associate with one another and define themselves as different from their neighbors. These broad features in turn determine the distinctive contours of Kaguru culture. The more specific or particular features of activities, associations, and experiences, such as settlement, family, homestead, and age and gender, while important, determine less distinctive features of experience and meaning, ones also shared by many of the Kaguru's neighbors and by ourselves. To this extent, the anthropologist must commence with language, society, culture, and environment, not with the individual actors who experience them, even though these actors are ultimately our primary concern.

All of these primary ideational and effectual sets display certain similar characteristics. Central, core-like features are contrasted to lateral or peripheral ones by which groups extend themselves and negotiate with one another. To put it another way, deep and constant effectual loyalties are contrasted with juridical agreements negotiated through exchanges of goods and people that are weak substitutes for more enduring bonds of feeling. Yet there are emotionally repressed and subversive sides even to these contrasts that reverse dominant valences, as we shall see when we consider beliefs about affinity, ritual pollution, joking behavior, and witchcraft (chapters 8 and 9). Such contrasting sets resemble what is often, in current anthropological jargon, termed "deep structure."

At the broadest level, Kaguru contrast their land and themselves with outsiders, with strangers whose language, diet, and customs are different. Kaguru undertake marriage and alliances among their own kind. Outsiders are feared because they are unknown and uncontrollable; they are able to disguise their true thoughts and intents through an alien language, just as Kaguru retreat into themselves through theirs. Yet the greatest dangers of witchcraft and sorcery lie with one's own kin and neighbors, while the most powerful countermagic and sorcery may be secured from strangers. Outsiders and insiders are each dangerous in their own ways, just as they each have uses that are complementary to one another.

Within their concept of their own country, Kaguru contrast the ordered sphere of the settlements with the dangerous sphere of the wilderness or bush. Various modes of culture and order, especially those involving the processing and consumption of food, are contrasted with the raw aspects of wild beasts. Yet the bush is not entirely shunned, for the dangerous forces that characterize it are also associated with periodic quests for power to control the social world through supernatural forces. The dead, rainmakers, and diviners, and, more libidinously, sorcery and witchcraft, may enable individuals to break out against the constraints of social rules.

Kaguru picture a matrilineal kin that forms an armature around which paternal and affinal kin revolve. While matrilineal obligations and loyalties are paramount socially, paternal and affinal relationships are seen as means of extending ties outward from one's own matrilineage to other groups. These lateral extensions are subject to considerable negotiation through exchanges of payments, gifts, and services. Such exchanges are never entirely resolved or completed. In contrast, powerful matrilineal ties are so enduring and deep that they require no shoring up by repeated payments and negotiation. The relative passivity displayed by Kaguru in expressing matrilineal ties actually reflects strength, whereas the frequent, active assertion and reiteration of paternal and affinal connections are necessitated precisely because such bonds are less certain and less reliable. Extension and assertion are male, paternally associated attributes, whereas deeper and more constant central being is female and matrilineal. These structural features are repeatedly expressed through physiologically couched metaphors.

At the most basic level, that of persons, men and women are contrasted

and linked through a series of oppositions and complementarities that are
reflected not only in physiological and affectual metaphors of gender but in
a wide and ever-varying range of metaphors drawn from all of the other
domains mentioned earlier. These metaphors are grounded in contrast between
one's own group and outsiders, between settlement and bush, and between
the various elements which must be combined in order to produce the instruments which bring safety and sustenance to people. The valences attached
to these ever differently combining clusters of metaphors shift and often
contain resonances even opposed to what these metaphors appear to proclaim,
as where disorder also implies power and fertility, or where emphasis upon
rules and authority suggests a dependence upon negotiation and formalism
unnecessary for truly strong and unquestioned affectual bonds. The myriad
field of Kaguru dualistic metaphorical expression not only provides weight
and feeling to Kaguru beliefs but generates countervailing notions and sentiments of subversion and ambiguity in how these elements are judged on
different occasions. The kaleidoscope of metaphors presented in the following
section indicates how rich and diverse Kaguru imagining of their society is.

INDIVIDUAL KAGURU AND THEIR BELIEFS

The abstract notions of continuity, order, disorder, affection, passion, morality, and immorality are imagined through various substances and things to
which they are attributed. There is for Kaguru an interpenetration between
persons and things, between society and the world in which it is set. In a
memorable passage, Durkheim describes this pattern of understanding: "Into
the idea they [human beings] have formed of things, they have undoubtedly
made human elements enter; but into the idea they have formed of themselves,
they have made enter elements coming from things" (1934:235). For Kaguru,
such imagery of social and physical being, of moral and physical realms,
derives greatly from their bodies, from their bilateral orientations in terms of
right and left, up and down, ahead and behind, and from their blood, flesh,
hair, and bones. It is also reflected in Kaguru understanding of the contours
and climate of their environment and its plant and animal life. Most powerfully
of all, it is reflected in everyday practices of household and village life. In
these, imagery of preparing food, eating, the activities of hearth and bed,
evoke the body, forming what Burke terms "associational clusters" (1957:18)
which weld together the social and natural realms where sexual and alimentary
appetites are regulated and enhanced through the home by way of the regulations of marriage and kinship, cuisine and etiquette.

In trying to learn how Kaguru think metaphorically about their world and
values, a researcher is greatly helped by the fact that Kaguru themselves set
considerable store in explaining many such symbols. Kaguru regard the ini-

tiation of adolescents as the central feature of their culture which brings together at one time and place all that is most highly prized as characteristic of their way of life. Such ceremonies are occasions where the wise and informed explicate the imagery of Kaguru beliefs and values, expounding their hidden meanings and associations. Rituals of marriage, burial, and ancestral propitiation repeat many of these same themes. Even before initiation, the hours of nighttime storytelling and gossip provide young people with scattered and suggestive leads to these truths. Both rituals and storytelling constitute rich means by which Kaguru themselves try to imagine what their way of life signifies. In part, these explain how some things have come about; more important, they present and play with the profound contradictions and ambiguities within Kaguru social life. Thus, Kaguru are often adept at formulating deeper meanings to much of their culture, not only for the young but for inquiring anthropologists.

Just as not all Western European Christians are equally aware of the symbols employed in the liturgy and architecture of their churches, not all Kaguru are equally aware of the full implications of their symbolic acts and related concepts. We must not expect all Kaguru, even of one age, to be comparably versed in symbolism, even though they all participate in many rituals and ceremonies. Some symbolic acts and beliefs are held on faith by many. The system described in this chapter is one grasped in varying degrees by the members of Kaguru society but not uniformly meaningful to all. It is certainly doubtful whether any individual Kaguru sees these various clusters of attributes and things forming a single system to be contemplated and discussed at one time; yet Kaguru do see various sets of attributes in interrelation with one another and are keenly aware of the organizing principles of thought behind such methods of categorization. After all, since Kaguru ''live'' their system through their daily acts, they are not in need of any formal exegesis of all its facets in the way that an anthropologist, sociologist, or psychologist would be.

METAPHORS OF BODILY AND SPATIAL ORIENTATION AND SEXUALITY

Kaguru call the right hand or right side *kulume*; the left, *kumoso*.[2] They consider the right hand to be clean (*ela*) and to have physical strength (*ngufu*); the left is considered unclean (*mwafu*) and without strength (*ngufu hechaka*). Masculine qualities are thought to be of the right, feminine of the left. Some Kaguru said that this was because male (*mugosi* or *-ume*) creatures are physically stronger than female (*mwanamuke* or *-ike*) and that likewise the right hand is stronger than the left. Others said this was due to the way persons

were fashioned in the womb, that one was made of two joined sides, the right
deriving from the father, the left from the mother.

Kaguru draw a parallel between the conception and birth of a child and the
legendary origin of the Kaguru people and their matri-clans (see chapter 5).
They tell of a great trek by Kaguru and neighboring matrilineal peoples to
their present homeland, where they divided into their clans at a place called
Chiwepanhuka. Some say that this legend also represents the birth of a child,
whereby a clan is perpetuated through a new member. Kaguru recount this
at the initiation of adolescents with that interpretation in mind. The name
chiwe (small rock) *panhuka* (fall out or away from a larger mass) may have
a triple meaning. It may refer to a rock fallen away from a larger formation;
it may refer allegorically to a clan broken away from the undifferentiated
tribal group, or to an infant broken away from its mother at birth. By *chiwe*
(small rock) people may sometimes even mean "buttocks," or "vagina," or
the female fundament. In the great trek, Kaguru are said to have come from
the west, which is associated with the womb, and traveled eastward, associated
with the outer world. Of course, the west is also associated with the dead,
whence the unborn come. Not only were the marchers' right sides turned
southward and their left sides north, but people marched in double files, men
on the right of a column, women on the left, and the entire group going toward
higher ground. I should add that in some contexts Kaguru also associate high
ground with attributes related to masculinity and valleys with those related
to femininity, though by now I have clearly taken the discussion far beyond
associations of right and left or strong and weak.

Further possible indication of the dualistic classification of east and west
may be seen in certain Kaguru practices associated with sorcery and countersorcery. A man wishing to perform countersorcery cuts the bark of a *mwi-
yegea* tree (sausage tree, *Kigelia pinnata*), first on its west side, then on its
east, whereas a person practicing sorcery cuts first the east side and then the
west. Ordinary or natural processes are associated with a progression from
west to east, whereas unusual or powerful, even dangerous supernatural ones
may be associated with a progression from east to west. Right and left also
are associated with certain other beliefs about the supernatural. In divination
(*maselu* or *imulamuli*) signs must appear on both the right and the left before
prognostication is regarded as completed.[3] In omens (*ndege*, sing. and pl.)
(see chapter 6) the right signifies importance or favorability, the left insig-
nificance or even malevolence.

Opposition of the right (male) and left (female) hands may be seen in many
everyday Kaguru practices where the right is associated with cleanness, physical strength, auspiciousness, and the left with uncleanness, physical weakness, inauspiciousness. Kaguru encourage all children to use the right hand.
A child who grows up favoring the left is not punished, but people sometimes

jokingly comment on this and, if it is a left-handed boy, may sometimes say that he is "like a wife" (*kama muke*) in this respect. Kaguru eat with the right hand, and use it for greeting persons and for shaking hands. None of these acts could be performed politely with the left. Although gifts should be given and received with both hands, the right sometimes may be used alone, but never the left. When both hands are used, the left should be placed behind and beneath the right. The left hand is used to handle unclean material or to perform unpleasant tasks. It is the hand used to clean after defecation. It is also favored in sex play. Kaguru men sometimes speak of lying on the right side during coitus as being advantageous to them because it enables the man to conceal his right hand and keep his left hand free, and forces the woman to lower herself into using her right hand in such performances.[4] When a Kaguru visits a doctor for treatment, he makes the first payment to the doctor with his right hand. When the treatment has been successfully completed and the patient cured, the final payment is made with the left, presumably because a magical or supernatural process is involved. The right hand, however, precedes the left in ordinary sequences, just as it is usually placed above the left. This is consistent with associating right with males, left with females. Kaguru men precede women when walking on paths, when entering rooms, and in being served, and Kaguru paternal kin usually (although not always) precede maternal kin in performing rituals or duties in which both groups take part. Some Kaguru say that when God created the world he created men first and then women, but, of course, this idea may be the result of Christian missionary teaching.

The Kaguru apply the divisions of right (male) and left (female) to their beliefs concerning the physiology of kinship and to the terms and activities associated with the two major kin groups—paternal and maternal—which compose each individual's relatives. Kaguru report two apparently contradictory principles of physiological kinship, which they themselves do not seem to find contradictory, As I noted above, some Kaguru speak of the right side of the body being formed from the father, the left from the mother. Most, however, speak of the father's sperm (*udoko*) combining with the mother's blood (*sakame* or *sakami*)[5] to form a pregnancy. The blood and the sperm feed the pregnancy and for this reason a couple should have frequent sexual intercourse after conception. The sperm is believed to circulate through a woman's body and contribute to her sexual physical development. A nubile girl's breasts and buttocks are thought to develop steadily with her sexual experience with men. A child is believed to have been formed of both paternal and maternal elements: the bone, cartilage, teeth, and hair, the hard solid parts of the body, come from the father; the blood, the fluid parts, come from the mother. Presumably, the flesh, insofar as it, too, is red and not firm like bone, may be considered to fall into the latter, liquid category.

Since a Kaguru child, flesh, blood, and bone, is the product of paternal sperm (bone) and maternal blood (flesh), consideration of the various attributes associated with blood or flesh and bone is a convenient way to approach the complex problem of Kaguru masculine and feminine symbolism. The most contrasting attributes of blood and bone are their colors and physical states, the redness and fluidity of blood and the whiteness and solidity of bone. To a lesser extent, this is also true in contrasting sperm and vaginal blood.

For Kaguru, the fluidity of blood has several important characteristics readily associated with femininity. It conveys the idea of flowing, of continuity, of perpetuity, of vitality, and it is through women that continuity is achieved in Kaguru society. It is perhaps for these reasons that some Kaguru attempt to derive the word *lukolo* (matri-clan) from a similar archaic word meaning "a place where water flows," rather than from the more popularly credited origin, "root." As Kaguru say, men have no proper descendants and it is only through women that a matri-clan continues. Obviously, fluidity is associated with fertility. Kaguru society is based on agriculture and depends upon the annual rains and upon the few semipermanent valley streams for its economic survival. The most important areas of Kaguru cultivation are river valleys, and various Kaguru initiation songs firmly establish their symbolic significances, which are more or less agreed to by both women and men.

One song goes: *Malagili sigemite mwigenge galangilila ng' holongo sikoga*; "those standing on the riverbank look to see those bathing below." The meaning given to this is: the testicles do not enter inside the vagina during intercourse, although the penis does. Here the riverbank (*mwigenge*) and the channel (*ng' holongo*) of the stream are associated with the female (fluid-below). Similar imagery is found in the song: *Kunyika kuya kutonyila fula; yakulilisa fileuwa fowela*; "there in the bush it rained; it washed away the maize stalk." This is said to mean: the blood at childbirth washes out the afterbirth. Here fertilily of women is associated with their blood and with rain (*fula*). The Kaguru euphemism for the blood of childbirth, "rain" (*fula*), is a play on such concepts. This song also hints at the destructive or dangerous power of the rain and thus of women's fertility and the process of birth, for it calls attention to its violence, comparing it to the sudden destructive rain which sometimes erodes valuable valley land and washes away crops. The word *kunyika* (in the bush) is a common euphemism used in songs to refer to the genitals. The analogy is between two wild, dangerous areas which are difficult to control but from which great power may be gained. Finally, Kaguru say: *Mafula gose kutonya fula dya mihili chimola magenge*; "all rains rain, but the rain of January (*mihili*) erodes riverbanks." This is said to mean: the blood of menstruation and the blood of childbirth are similar, but the blood of childbirth is shockingly great. Here, again, the blood of childbirth and menstruation are compared to rain, emphasizing the powerful and dangerous aspects of female sexuality and fertility. Kaguru do not appear to recognize that women are infertile during menstruation. Indeed, Kaguru say only a witch would have sexual relations with a menstruating woman and that menstruating women are not permitted to sleep in bed with their husbands. While one Kaguru expression for blood of childbirth is *fula* (rain), calling attention to the fertile aspect, another term for childbirth is *ng'hondo* (battle), emphasizing the dangerous aspects as well. Successful childbirth, then, is a victory and, as such, proves a woman's bravery and strength, just as battle proves the bravery and strength of a man.

Kaguru also sing: *Muke mutumbe kwilage mwitembe, nokwila ule fula ikutonya*; "mother's brother's wife, climb on top the house; how can I climb there myself when it is raining outside?" Kaguru say that this means: a menstruating woman soils anything which touches her. The singer of the song is here, figuratively, a woman, although youths also learn this. The singer cannot climb on top of her hut, presumably to secure food or tools, or to repair it, because she is menstruating, and she asks her mother's brother's wife to do this.[6] Here the symbol of rain itself is assigned a powerful or dangerous association. This may be suggested in: *Pule dya ng'ombe dili munakano mwaka no ukwija dili munakano*: "the nose of the cow is moist, all through the year it is moist." This is said to mean: a woman's vagina is always moist. Here the reference to moistness (*munakano*) refers positively to her fertility and receptivity but also possibly negatively to her potential for pollution through menstruation.

The dangerous aspect of sexuality is indicated in the expression *chitwi che duma* (head of a wildcat), which sometimes refers to the vagina or penis, as does the euphemism *mumwiko* (that which is forbidden).[7] The term *kunyika* (in the bush), with its dangerous and wild implications, also refers to male genitals: *kunyika huya kusina nhungu setu singi simapinga*; "in the bush, there are our calabashes, some full, some partly full." This is said to mean that depending upon the frequency of intercourse, a man's testicles are full or not full of semen. The Kaguru sing: *Mutama mhato temela mwitumba ya musingisi ng'hameka mhate*; "you cut the stubble in the Itumba Mountains, but in Musingisi Lowlands one never sees that the stubble has been cut." Kaguru give this two meanings: (a) One can always tell whether a boy has been circumcised, but one cannot always tell by looking whether a girl has undergone some kind of labiadectomy. (b) Circumcising boys makes them clean by removing the moisture-producing foreskin (feminine part), but cutting girls really does not remove moisture or periodic pollution, since they continue to menstruate. It is said that girls are cut to facilitate their abilities to bear children, to soften them, but not to transform them in the physical or moral sense that boys are made jurally responsible after being cut. The use of the mountain/lowland motif is clear enough; but there is also a suggestion of

contrasting order and disorder. The stubble seems to stand for hair (see Beidelman 1963h: riddle 10). For Kaguru, hair, especially pubic hair, is associated with uncleanness and perhaps, therefore, with failure to observe the
proper conventions in human relations. I was told that a proper person would
not want to have sexual relations with someone who had neglected to pluck
or shave his or her pubic hair, because such persons are unclean. (In actual
practice, this was not true.) Still, this is hardly the whole story, for pregnant
women who have been treated with medicines to induce delivery where a
safe term is in doubt let their hair grow long and ungroomed, implying a
quest for special, fertile powers.

The Kaguru sometimes refer to the human penis as *mukila* (tail), apparently
with a notion of the wild or animalistic attributes of the genitals. Man's penis
is that extension of himself linking him through copulation with his more
unruly counterpart, woman; it is a source of pollution. This attribute of a tail
is often emphasized by Kaguru in their folklore; for example, in many popular
Kaguru tales baboons don clothing and try to dupe humans into accepting
them into society. Eventually their tails, hairiness, and rough eating habits
(eating raw food and eating in a slovenly manner) betray them and lead humans
to drive them back into the bush.

The Kaguru speak of the dirtiness (*mwafu*) of the foreskin (*usubu*), sometimes also called *amakunja* or *kusika* (lower part) (Swahihli, *ngovi*), which
should be removed. The root *-sika* has associations both of moistness and of
lowness: *kusika* also means downward, lowland, the direction in which
streams flow, low (in both a physical and a moral sense), and genitals—in
contrast to *kuchanya*, upward, highland, direction from which streams flow;
masika is the term for the rainy season (chapter 6). The uncleanness associated
with the foreskin is, in part, also associated with immaturity, with lacking
jural authority, something the immature share with women. Thus a wife
wishing to abuse her husband in a serious manner may tell him publicly that
he is not circumcised, *viz.*, that he does not act like a man.[8] Kaguru themselves
do not speak often of this contrast between the cleanness of male genitals and
the repeated uncleanness of women's, but they explicitly make this distinction
at times of abuse and with reference to the alleged aim of male initiation.[9]
Once the foreskin is removed, men no longer suffer from unavoidable uncleanness in the sense that women do periodically each month until menopause.

Kaguru associate the sexual act itself with uncleanness, sometimes even
calling it bad (*fiha*), although here I think the word "dirty" would be a better
translation. Sex is sometimes associated with shame (*chinyala*).[10] After sexual
intercourse, a person should wash before meeting others, and the act should
most appropriately be done in the dark when the participants cannot see each
other well. Finally, the act itself seems to partake so strongly of the uncon-

trollable and passionate (*moto*, heat) that it should not be performed by persons involved in any difficult or important undertaking.[11] In discussing the songs above, I refer to the dangerous aspect of feminine fertility, an aspect expressed through the themes of the violence of rain and floods. In this sense, fluidity not only signifies continuity and fertility but also uncontrollability. Indeed, the powers and advantages which bearing children confers on women present considerable challenge to some aspects of men's sense of security. Women's strengths through their offspring are invulnerable to the crosscutting claims of men and, if anything, undermine some aspects of male authority.

The dangerous and uncontrollable aspects of blood and of women in general are symbolically represented in still other ways. The color red serves admirably in this respect because of the association between the shedding of menstrual blood and pollution. Blood is also more positively associated with fertility and birth, but negatively with battles and death. Indeed, all spilling of blood is considered immensely polluting and deaths in which blood is shed are the worst kinds. Some fatal illnesses in which unusual quantities of blood are expelled for no obvious reason (perhaps due to cancer, tuberculosis, or dysentery) are so inauspicious that the bodies of persons who die from such illnesses are thrown into the bush and not given proper burial. Such persons cannot become ancestral spirits. Blood (red) then evokes both life and death, warmth and nurturance, yet also polluting disorder and destruction, depending upon the contexts in which it is encountered. Blood's immensely powerful associations are unequivocal.

FIRE, FOOD, AND SEXUALITY

Kaguru also associate red with fire (*moto*), which, like blood, is useful and important but requires careful control if it is not to be dangerous. The expression *kuhegesa* (to make fire by firesticks, to consume with fire) may also mean "to have sexual relations." The active, upper firestick is known as *luhegeso lugosi* (male firestick) or *mulume* (husband) and the lower, passive one as *luhegeso lufele* (female firestick) or *muke* (wife). Furthermore, the color red is associated, through both fire and blood, with heat (*moto*), both literally and figuratively; sexual activity is said to generate heat. The notion of fire is a complex one, fire being what Bachelard terms "a privileged phenomenon" in its power to explain a wide range of disparate things (1964:7). The hearth is the center of a home, and the idea of a fire as a place about which a social group lives is an important one for Kaguru (cf. chapter 4). It is the place where food is cooked and thus made different from that of wild animals. The term *umoto* (at the fire, the hearth) is best translated as "custom" or "social practice." There is also a probable parallel between the Kaguru use of redness as an allusion to sexuality and their association of the redness of baboons' sexual areas with a disorderly, antisocial nature (Busse 1936–7:64). It also echoes the association of baboons with improperly initiated humans (Beidelman 1965a:22–24).

Kaguru women and men believe that a woman's menstrual flow (*kutumika*, to menstruate, to be taken up with something) is associated with the height of her sexual power, when her blood overflows in its plenitude, whereas at pregnancy her blood is directed toward building a child. At menstruation a woman is not only unclean but dangerous and must not come into contact with certain things; for example, she should not sleep in her husband's bed but on the floor, she should not cross a field of crops, brew beer, or climb above others as she might if she were to fetch goods from a roof storeroom. Stakes of the *msane* tree, which exudes a red sap, are sometimes placed in gardens to ward off the baneful influence of menstruating women who might pass nearby. Kaguru believe that were a man to touch menstrual blood he would contract leprosy, or some serious skin disease. This idea also seems the basis of two euphemisms for menstruation: *nahasi* (be under) and *nhama* (sick, unclean, but also menstrual flow). The association of red with dangerous passion may be seen in a well known Kaguru song: *Wadodo nyenye musame ukilawa mwija fikamisa, mhela mukahembe, sikihoma na kisajangu sikiyonesa kudung' hu wao*; "youngsters, don't go out early or you may meet a rhinoceros with a horn and it will be stabbing and showing their [*sic*] red parts." This admonishes adolescents not to enter their parents' houses without announcing themselves because otherwise they might find their parents having sexual intercourse, which would imply incest and a parental curse toward themselves.

The color red is also sometimes associated with death. When members of a matrilineal group decide to execute a criminal, an inauspicious child, or a leper, this task is delegated to a member of another clan standing in a ritual joking relationship (*utani*) to that matrilineage (cf. chapter 8). Such an executioner was given a string of red beads, which was then cut so that the beads scattered on the ground symbolizing the blood shed in execution. Likewise, a great diviner, circumcisor, or doctor decorates his calabashes of medicine with red and white beads, the red standing for the dangerous powers which he confronts, the white for his control.

The association of the uncontrollable aspects of blood with heat is expressed in Kaguru beliefs concerning menstruation and certain types of incest. The term *kuhosa* or *kuhola* (to cool) may be used to describe the fanning of any hot food or substance.[12] It is also used in the ceremony (*imhosa*) held after a girl's first menstruation when the first hot blood of menstruation is cooled by elderly women through cutting, fanning, medicines, singing, and modification of diet. *Kuhosa* also refers to a cleansing ceremony in which a couple guilty of certain sexual offenses are cooled of this pollution. The name of the plant used in preparing the medicine for this also derives from this cooling operation (*luhosa*, a vine, *Crassocephalum bojeri*).[13]

In contrast to these feminine attributes are the masculine ones of solidity, land, mountains, white, and relative coolness. The association of men with mountains and land has already been made clear through the examples referring to valleys and fluidity; thus mountains–land : valleys–water :: solid : fluid :: upper : lower :: male : female. The attributes of solidity and coolness refer essentially to regularity, so that perhaps the term *kuhosa* would more appropriately be translated as "to remove undue hotness," or "to return to normal." It is an attempt to change a powerful but dangerous condition into a safe and ordinary one. In this same sense, one Kaguru word for health and fitness is *mheho* (coolness, wind, breeze, air).

White also expresses safety, peace, and normality. Thus, white beads figure in the medicinal equipment at boys' initiation and may be pulverized to form a medicine to stanch the flow of blood from a circumcision wound.[14] White beads decorate a renowned doctor's medicinal calabashes. Sperm is also sometimes compared, because of its whiteness, to nourishing milk (*mele*), since, along with a woman's blood, it feeds a growing pregnancy.

Earlier I mentioned that Kaguru believe that long ago they divided into their matri-clans at a legendary place called Chiwepanhuka. I noted that Kaguru consider that *chiwe*, the stone, also represents the female fundament. For reasons I have not been able to determine, Kaguru associate stones with females, at least in some situations, even though one might assume that the solidity of stone would lead them to associate it with males instead. In any case, another possible set of sexually related oppositions should be reported, involving the three hearthstones (*mafiga*) located at the center of a house, and the center-pole (*nguso*) which stands near them. For Kaguru, the association is hearthstones : center-pole :: vagina : penis :: female : male. The hearthstones form a low place where fire is kept and where cooking pots are placed; various containers and food itself have feminine sexual connotations for Kaguru similar to what they have for many Europeans. In contrast to the feminized hearth, the height, shape, and strength of the house-pole reflect masculine attributes. The association of this center-pole with masculinity is clear from this initiation song: *Dinkungu mwelu digosi dititu dikola nyumba ne migamba*; "small black bird is a giant which holds up the house and the poles of the roof." Kaguru say the small bird is the penis, which, like the center-pole, supports the house (*nyumba*, house, household, matrilineage). The color black here refers to the smoke-blackened center-pole, darkened by its close proximity to the fire below.[15]

The symbolic coitus suggested by the center-pole in conjunction with the hearthstones is repeated in other combinations of everyday objects whose shapes and uses take on sexual attributes. These paired objects or tools are often mentioned by Kaguru, both in the context of initiation rituals and in general conversation when euphemisms for sexual intercourse are required. Thus, the penis (*mbolo*) becomes a stick, spear (*mugoha*), stone pestle (*isago*), or wooden pestle (*mtwango*); a vagina (*ng'huma*) becomes a stone mortar (*luwala*), wooden mortar (*ituli*), or calabash, pot, or basket. It is not merely the shape involved, but, as their instrumentality suggests, an equation of securing food with sexual congress, and a conjunction of active and passive elements which together produce nourishment and satiation. This is also clear in the case of firesticks, as already noted. Thus, too, working these tools is a euphemism for sexual intercourse: to pound flour (*kutwanga*), to grind flour (*kusanjila*), to make fire (*kuhegesa*). Other expressions of this nature involve spearing animals, poking sticks into holes to flush out game, hunting, and the like. In terms of shape and use, the more important single material object associated with a Kaguru man is his bow (*uta*).[16] It reflects his adult status and his bravery and dominance. The corresponding object for women is the calabash (*mukomba*) for castor oil. Such oil is used to beautify and as a sexual lubricant and is therefore associated with a woman's sexual desirability and receptivity. A man's bow is handed down to his eldest son, while a woman's oil calabash is, along with her jewelry, given to her eldest daughter. On such occasions the recipient is reminded of the traditions associated with the clan of the father or mother.[17]

These are not consistently contrasting patterns, but then their force and value lie in their ability to take on a wide range of valences, depending on the context in which they are employed. Yet it does appear that where contrasting attributes of the same order are conjoined enormous power and dangers are generated. Two Kaguru beliefs are best explained in such terms: (1) The scales of the pangolin (*nghwasuli*) are placed on the backs of sterile sheep and goats to make them bear. These scales are also sometimes boiled in water and the fluid is then used to wash ailing infants' heads to soften the fontanel sutures if these have hardened prematurely. Such hardening is considered a cause of illness. The pangolin is a classic object of liminality and thus of supernatural power in much of Africa. Kaguru remark that it has scales but is an animal of dry land and not a fish; it is a wild creature of the bush yet curls up so that it may be conveniently carried home and eaten. Its powers enable it to return disturbed fertility and development to their proper routine. (2) The complementary differentiation of male and female attributes accounts for the concept of *chimhenu* (Swahili, *kisukumi, kugwaru, or kinyakuzi*). A *chimhenu* is a growth upon a woman's clitoris or a man's anus, each leading them to be sterile, to produce unhealthy children, or to have unhealthy livestock. Kaguru say these growths interfere with the fertility and health of a household; once such growths are cut away, the couple's normality returns.

These growths confuse sexual traits, a growth on the man's anus being a kind of clitoris and that on the woman's clitoris increases its size to make it a kind of penis (cf. Barley 1983:24).

DISORDER, POWER, AND THE BUSH

The bush is associated with many dangerous, polluting, but also immensely powerful forces. Indeed, all really important contact with powerful supernatural forces takes place in the bush (*nyika*). The further removed an area is from habitation, the more powerfully endowed it is, so that the thick mountaintop woods (*muhulo*), with odd formations of rocks and unfrequented, ominous-looking pools, are the most dangerous locales of all. Rainmakers and powerful diviners are said to visit such remote mountain areas. Children who are inauspicious yet powerful (*vigego*), witches, and those with polluting diseases (such as leprosy or dysentery, where body boundaries are blurred through loss of flesh or bloody exudations) are slain or abandoned there. Propitiation of ancestral ghosts involving the aspersion of blood and the cutting of initiates must occur in the bush, as does the preparation of dangerous medicines, such as those used in making rain. Persons should defecate in the bush, and trash and household dirt are thrown in heaps where the bush adjoins a settlement. Conversely, proper sexual relations should not take place in the bush; they should occur within the safe and constraining order of the house. This prohibition is, however, often flouted in adultery. Kaguru also explain restricting boy initiates to the bush as separating them while they are in a disordered and medial state, removed from village order but also from women, whose proper domain is a settlement, Kaguru explain that girl initiates must be brought back to the cultural confines of a village after being cut in the bush, because women must be hidden and not seen, whereas it is maintained that boys should be seen by their future peers, who test their bravery by exposing them to the rigors of the bush and the simulated threat of wild animals.

Kaguru divide many plants and animals into two opposite groups with masculine and feminine connections. It is said that long ago God gave men and women plants and animals which they could domesticate and tend. Women, lacking discipline, neglected theirs and these became wild and unusable. Men, being orderly, tended theirs carefully. Hence, there are wild plants and animals which resemble those which are domesticated; for example, women : men :: guinea fowl : chickens :: zebras : donkeys :: elands : cattle :: wild grasses : grain :: wild plantains : bananas. This association of the bush and wild animals with disorder and the settlement with order is well illustrated in Kaguru tales about baboons, tales which relate the blurring of such distinctions between humans and animals with confusions of other categories regarding diet, etiquette, and body grooming. Wild animals are associated with destruction and also with excessive sexuality, which itself is disorderly. I noted that the *ng'hanu* (wildcat) is associated with genitals. Sexually voracious women are sometimes referred to as *makala* (man-eaters; cf. chapter 10). Kaguru tell children that persons who have died were devoured by a beast (*dikoko*) of the bush. The dead themselves are the epitome of potential disorder, yet they are also immensely powerful and are the ultimate source of fertility and life (cf. chapter 7).

DUALISM OF GROUPS AND THEIR CEREMONIES

Kaguru apply their categories of right (male) and left (female) to the major social groups and to many of the activities, rights, and obligations which these involve.

Kaguru consider their own matri-clan and matrilineage (*kungogo* or *lukolo*, possibly from *kolo*, root or source) to be of the left (*kumoso*); their father's matri-clan (*welekwa*, from *kulekwa*, to be borne) of the right (*kulume*). Appropriately, a mother's father may thus be referred to as *kumoso kwangu* (my left). The reason for this association of clan group with handedness is that one's matri-clan derives from a female (left) and one's father's matri-clan from a male (right). This does not mean that Kaguru consider affiliation to one's own matrilineage to be weaker or less important than affiliation to one's father's group, even though they agree that the left hand is physically weaker than the right. Quite the reverse is true, even though to an outsider this may seem an inconsistency on their part. Kaguru are agreed that the left hand and women have no physical strength (*ngufu hechaka*, there is no strength), but also say: *awang'ina munhu mu wakagulu weja wapata singufu kusume webaba munhu*, "among the Kaguru, persons' mothers have got strength more than persons' fathers"; *kosoko iyo weja wakong'haga iminyiko yose yo lwandi lwa wang'ina munhu*, "because they followed all the prohibitions of their mother's side."

In precolonial times, before current disintegrative factors intruded to accelerate change, Kaguru society was primarily organized about matrilineages, which in turn composed clans. Paternal kin were of secondary, supplementary importance. Kaguru term their own matri-clan *lukolo lwe ng'ina* (clan of the mother) but a father's clan is *ulwandi lwe baba munhu* (a person's father's side), the contrast between centrality and laterality being clear. No terms are employed to refer to one's father's clan or matrilineage using physiological imagery, whereas these allusions are prominent for one's own matrilineage, which is termed *itombo dimwedu* (of one breast) or *itumbu dimwedu* (of one womb). Both *ikungugo* and *welekwa* are matrilineal groups; the distinction between these is based not upon their internal recruitment but upon the way in which a group is related to a person, maternally (left) or paternally (right).

Membership in a matrilineage is so basic that it is achieved automatically with birth; paternal ties, derived through socially acknowledging fatherhood, must be attained through payments and services. Kaguru say: "If a bull enters your herd, the owner of the bull does not own the calves produced." Consequently, payments and services determining obligations between kin reflect the oppositions but also the complementarity between matrilineal and paternal kin, between women and men.[18] When Kaguru speak of these various payments and obligations, they often stretch out first one hand and then the other, as they mention the right and left obligations, making absolutely clear what is meant. This division is especially clear at payments at marriages and funerals, two occasions which Kaguru consider to be the most important events in anyone's career.

The most important concern in contracting a marriage is the collection, transfer, and distribution of bridewealth. That paid by a youth's matrilineage is said to be of the left hand, that paid by his father is of the right. Kaguru carefully differentiate between these payments, which are deposited in separate containers, for wealth of the left and right should never mix. Wealth by the left (groom's matrilineage) goes to the left (bride's matrilineage); that paid by the right (groom's father) goes to the right (bride's father). Payments of the matrilineage (left) involve *wegasi*, *bulai*, or *kolo* (alternate terms for mother's brother); those of the father's matrilineage (right) involve the *webaba munhu* (fathers of the person). The payments, distinct for the two groups, are:

left	right
mukowa (cloth for carrying the child, *viz.*, the placenta)	*chibanyo* (payments for transfer of rights to a woman)
mulomo we kolo (mouth of the matri-clan)	*mhena manyemba* (breaker of the castor stalks)[19]
	itundu (chicken-coop, the payment initiating the arrangement, usually paid before the final ceremony)

There are other payments besides these, and those too are divided into left and right portions, which must be combined to form a total payment. For example, *ndama ndafa mwana* (the calf taken for the child) was, in one marriage which I witnessed, a cash payment in which 150 shillings were paid by the boy's father's matrilineage and 120 shillings by the boy's own matrilineage.

Funerals display a similar division of property. Kaguru wryly observe that the favorite conversational topic at funerals of men tends to be marriage, because inheritance involves the reallotment of any bridewealth collected and held by the deceased from the marriage of his kinswomen. This concerns members of both sides of the deceased's kin, and representatives of both these groups must be present. In the same sense, both sides should contribute the burial cloth (*sanda*, nursing cloth, womb) that wraps the corpse (womb = carrying cloth = shroud), thereby not only expressing the past contribution of both the mother and the father in creating the person, but signaling their accord in reaching final disposition of their relations to the dead. The most serious problem confronting Kaguru at funerals is the division of property of the deceased, and this includes far more than bridewealth. While Kaguru women may possess property, it is more usually held by men. Most funerals for women are therefore not complicated. Like bridewealth, inheritance is divided into right and left. Property associated with a matrilineage is said to be of the left; that with paternal kin, of the right. Political rights to land and to the conduct of rituals associated with the land are inherited matrilineally, and are described as of the left. Kaguru say, "Land is of the left," meaning that political rights to economic use of the land are inherited through women. On the other hand, property such as livestock, planted crops, beehives, and cash may be distributed paternally. While these may be given to a man's children, this need not be the case and such goods may be given to the deceased's father's eldest daughter or some other kin to hold until the son is adult. If there is no son, the bow of the father should be destroyed and the other goods go to the eldest daughter, or, more likely, to more distant kinsmen. Other personal possessions are classified as *chipe*-wealth of inheritance and should be divided into left and right portions, although there is a tendency here for favoring the deceased's matrilineage. Thus, a man's shotgun or other important tools might be successfully claimed by one of his sisters' sons, although the deceased's own son might resent this. In the past, division into right and left payments also involved the collection and distribution of bloodwealth (*chimba*) made for homicide of a neighbor. The nature of such payments cannot be clearly understood since they are no longer made.

Both right and left groups figure at initiation. When a youth returns to his home from his confinement in an initiation camp, he is greeted by representatives of both his own and his father's clan. He is given small gifts and then his father or one of his father's matrilineal kinsmen rubs castor oil onto the boy from the top downward, applying it with his tongue or chin. This is done first to the left side, then to the right: up : down :: right : left. After this, a member of the boy's own matrilineage does the same to the boy's left side.

Kaguru names are divided into the categories of right and left (cf. chapter 6). Kaguru receive several names at birth and again at a ceremony held after initiation, the latter especially in the case of males. These names are given by both matrilineal and paternal kin and sometimes by others as well. Some of these names must be of ancestors of one's own matrilineage; others, of one's father's matrilineage. The former are called names of the left, the latter, of the right. In the same sense, names of ancestral ghosts are divided into left and right categories. These names are invoked as part of certain rituals related to fertility and illness. Most rights concern matrilineal kin and therefore concern names of the left, and Kaguru themselves state that names of the left are more important in ritual. Yet there are important names in both these categories, which should be used on different occasions for seeking supernatural aid in times of crisis, just as the right supplements the left in the creation and growth of a child. In these ceremonies, sheep are sometimes slain and their blood is sprinkled as part of the rites of propitiation to the ghosts of the ancestors and to God. The ritual joking partners (*watani*) who perform these rites cut the sacrificial animal's hide into small rings, which are then worn on the left wrists of the members of the matrilineage for whom the ceremony has been held.[20]

CONCLUSION

The imagery of male and female sexuality permeates every aspect of Kaguru lives. The ordinary aspects of motifs based on sexuality, alimentation, and familiar topography enforce these concepts as they are encountered by Kaguru at every turn. The quotidian round of activities perpetually and subtly sustains such dualism at work, in village and household affairs, and at play. At the benchmarks of life—births, initiations, marriages, and funerals—clusters of motifs come into dramatic prominence, and again at crises where the dead are propitiated. Even the antitheses of social life, witchcraft and sorcery, are cast as perverted caricatures of ordinary aspects of Kaguru life.

The power of such sexual symbols and metaphors in Kaguru thought derives only partly from the primary qualities they evoke. It also stems from their diffuse, ambiguous natures. None of these symbols, whether of fire, water, eating, wilderness, or even birth and death, may be reduced to a single valence or meaning. At any occasion, particular facets of a symbol's meanings and affect are singled out, while even other meanings and feelings arise from a Kaguru's memory of other experiences and occasions. These tinge and expand a symbolic message in broader, more ambiguous ways. Memory and imagination are inextricably linked.

This makes the meanings of formal symbols negotiable. While a symbol's general fund of meanings is recognized, the particular facet to be emphasized depends upon both the situation and the actors who are involved. At times, several readings may be entertained at once, by men and women, by young and old, by paternal and maternal kin. In part, Kaguru interaction may be

understood as the constant attempts of individuals to promote their particular
symbolic readings in social relations, though economic and political aims
often lie at these strategies' roots. To underscore the pervasive, everyday
character of such symbols as well as to illustrate their polyvalent character,
I next describe the ways this imagery is reflected in households and in everyday
village affairs.

Cosmology, as evinced in dualistic systems and associations through metonymy and metaphor, provides an idiom for the construction of categories
of space and time, or for judgment of persons, things, and experience. I have
chosen to use aspects of space and time as points of analytical entry into
understanding in fuller detail how Kaguru beliefs and values are lived out.
While exotic concepts of space and time are complex, their quotidian aspects
are certainly less elusive than notions about kinship, the supernatural, or right
and wrong. The next chapter begins with a consideration of space in its most
palpable, ostensible sense, the house, and then explores how the bodies of
those who inhabit it are socialized. Our dwellings and our bodies are the
primary models by which we try to imagine more complex and elusive aspects
of our beliefs and society. Furthermore, it is in our homes and through our
bodies that we are initially socialized, that we are related to other beings and
things.

NOTES

1. This chapter represents a greatly changed and shortened version of 1973a, which
in turn is a revised and expanded version of 1961e.

2. *Kulume* derives from *-ume* or *-lume*, which is a masculine stem, e.g. *mwan-
alume*, man (Swahili, *mwanaume* or *mwanamume*; *mulume*, husband). The prefix *ku-*
denotes place. The term *kumoso* appears to have a relation to words in other Bantu
languages (cf. Werner 1904; Wieschhoff 1938; Stapleton 1905). The Kaguru terms I
cite are slightly different from those used in Last's study of this language. He gives
mkono we kulumi (right hand) and *mkono wa kumuno* (left hand) (1886:123, 133).

Many Kaguru use Swahili words for right and left rather than Chikaguru ones. The
Kaguru language is being rapidly replaced by Swahili through schools, courts, and
trade. These Swahili words are often similar in both sound and meaning to Kaguru
ones and often seem to involve similar attributes and associations to those had by
Kaguru words for right and left: the right hand is called *mkono wa kulia*, hand for
eating; *mkono wa kuume*, male hand. The left hand is called *mkono wa kuke* or *mkono
wa kike*, both meaning female hand, and *mkono wa kushoto*, an obscure expression
of undetermined origin. One Swahili-speaking Kaguru derived this last from *kushota*,
to drag one's buttocks on the ground when in a crouched position. I am told that such
a derivation is not accepted by Swahili scholars.

Since the theme of this chapter is the pervasiveness of dualistic imagery among

Kaguru, I should note that Kaguru imagine God beyond dualism, having one leg, one foot, one eye, one arm, one ear, and so on; cf. also Wood 1908:121–122; Needham 1980:17–40. I could not determine whether these were of the right or left.

3. Unfortunately, I could not secure further details on divinatory techniques. In a tale which I collected, a Kaguru is instructed to turn to the right in performing what appears to be anti-witchcraft magic (1963c:746). It seems implied that in this magic, involving healing the man's injured hands, his right hand should be treated before his left.

4. A similar account of such positions in both coitus and burial is reported for a number of geographically widely dispersed peoples in Africa.

In actual practice, of course, Kaguru use other positions as well. The right-left position related here is only an ideal one mentioned to me by male informants. Lévi-Strauss (1963:190–191) cites this point but gives an incorrect meaning counter to the facts I reported. Kaguru women do not, as he suggests, use the right hand in sexual play because that is their impure hand. As I have stated, they are sometimes forced or maneuvered by their lovers into using that hand, the pure hand for them as well as for men. Men try to do this in order to demean women.

5. The Kaguru sometimes distinguish between the blood of the body (*sakame* or *sakami*) and the blood from menstruation or from a circumcision wound (*nhamu, tamu* or *nhumne*), but it is not clear to me how these are distinguished in terms of forming a pregnancy. Kaguru relate menstruation (*kutumika*, to be involved, taken up with something) to female fertility yet it is clear that blood which leaves the body during menstruation is considered unclean, hot, and dangerous and plays no part in forming a child. The Kaguru concept of blood is complex and I have discussed it further elsewhere, especially as it deals with blood-brotherhood (1963b).

6. The Ngulu term *mutumbe* is used here rather than the Kaguru term *bulai* or *kolo*. Perhaps this term is used to rhyme with *mwitembe* (on the *tembe*, house).

The reason for the choice of mother's brother's wife in this song is unclear. It may be worth noting that such a woman is a potential threat to the members of her husband's matrilineage, since it is to her own interest to encourage him to provide for his own (their) children rather than for the children of the women of his own matrilineage. In this sense, perhaps we should not be surprised that such a person is mentioned in this negative context. Thatching and repair of roofs are household chores which women should not undertake. Their impurity, due to menstruation, makes it bad for them to have been above men.

7. Similarly, the term *ng'hanu* (wildcat) sometimes refers to the genitals of either sex. The association of fierce feline animals with sexuality and initiation appears to be common in East and Central Africa.

8. It is said that an initiated Kaguru woman would refuse sexual relations with an uncircumcised youth. In many cases this is probably true though I know instances of Kaguru women having intercourse with men of tribes which do not circumcise, although it is said that these women would not be married to such men unless they were first cut (see chapter 5).

A striking illustration of a similar mode of association may be found in the dramatically pivotal section of Ferdinand Oyono's novel *Houseboy* (1966:35) where the African hero loses his awe and respect for his white employer when he sees him naked and finds him to be uncircumcised.

9. For the Kaguru origin of circumcision as a cleansing act see Beidelman 1963e (758–760); the text is similar to an Ndembu tale reported by Turner (1962a:165–166).

10. This negative aspect of the sexual relations is associated with joking relations

(*utani*) and, indeed, a euphemism for sexual intercourse is *kutania* (to joke, to abuse, to insult); cf. chapter 8.

With regard to the "badness" of sexual relations, Kaguru sometimes employ Swahili slang for genitals such as *ubaya* (badness).

11. Although redness and fluidity suggest the uncontrollable power of femininity, the attribute of left itself does not seem to be used by Kaguru to express this.

Some idea of the concept of sex as dirtiness may also be seen in certain Kaguru riddles in which a grandmother (a person with whom one has a sexual joking relationship) is associated with stench and uncleanness (Beidelman 1963h: riddles 15 and 17).

12. I secured more explicit examples of the association of fire-red-blood-menstruation in my work on Ngulu female initiation. I cannot discuss these here but note that Kaguru are aware of many Ngulu customs and find these very similar to their own (cf. Beidelman 1964d).

13. I am grateful to the East African Herbarium, Nairobi, for identifying this.

14. It is also reported that hyena's or hare's feces are used, but I could not learn why. A hyena's feces are unusually white but a hare's are not. Later chapters of this study indicate complex parallels between hyenas and hares.

15. I collected further data concerning the symbolism of the center-pole and hearth-stones among the Ngulu, who resemble the Kaguru and also have the Chiwepanhuka legend (1964d:379–390).

As far as I can tell, the color black does not have sexual associations. It is related to witchcraft, rainmaking, and supernatural powers in general.

16. This is even more true among the Gogo, the Kaguru's neighbors to the west. Rigby relates many such instances for these people (1968 *passim*).

17. It appears likely that the bow and oil-calabash figure prominently in Kaguru female initiation, but my data are scanty. I do possess extensive data on comparable ceremonies for the Ngulu, where the bow and calabash are used in combination and are recognized as male and female.

18. Although matrilineages are the most important corporate groups for Kaguru, this need not mean that they are regarded with unmixed feelings. Kaguru associate matrilineages with certain attributes of left and thus possibly with powerful forces that could lead to disorder. This in turn may reflect their attitudes about the "matrilineal puzzle," *viz.*, their contradictory evaluation of both virilocality and settlements formed around matrilineages. Turner has commented aptly on a situation among the Ndembu which is very similar to the one among the Kaguru (1959:67, 77–78, 228–230).

19. The terms associated with the matrilineage symbolize feminine attributes; those associated with the father's matrilineage are more difficult to interpret, although there is some indication that the castor stalk is associated with males because of its upright shape and strength.

20. I could not obtain such information for Kaguru, but the neighboring Ngulu wear such leather on the left wrist if their own clan has sacrificed, and on the right if their father's has done so and they have attended.

CHAPTER 4.

Moral Space: The House, Settlements, and Body Etiquette

> . . . the house is one of the greatest powers of integration for the thoughts, memories and dreams of mankind.
>
> Gaston Bachelard, *The Poetics of Space*

> The family is thus centre and source, the hearth that maintains the flame of life, the 'vital force' which increases and intensifies as it is manifested in the living bodies of a multiplying and prospering people.
>
> Léopold Senghor, *Éléments constructifs d'un civilization d'inspiration négro-africaine*

This chapter considers some ways Kaguru imagine themselves in social space, how they think of their homesteads, their settlements, and the everyday ways they congregate and encounter one another within them.[1] I refer to space in terms of its social qualities, and by that I mean its moral determinants. Kaguru, like people in all societies, order space into different spheres which convey a moral focus for acts and things associated with them. This ordering of space may be considered from two different yet interdependent perspectives.

In the first sense, the very location of certain actions or things determines how these are judged. It reveals the quality of the motives behind them. For example, sexual acts are appropriate within the house, but are antisocial in the bush; similarly, proper persons consume food in front of others and not privately inside their dwellings; and highly dangerous contact with supernatural forces is made outside a settlement and not usually within it. The particular space in which actions occur should indicate whether these should be considered public or private, sociable or egoistic, safe or dangerous. Yet these categorizations are more complex than this illustrative set of contrasts indicates. Some powerful expressions of moral judgments and even secret suspicions and fears derive from blurring the way acts, persons, and things are allocated in space. Thus different sectors of space determine how actions may be judged. In this sense, Kaguru manipulate space, gauging and modifying behavior according to where it occurs.

Yet, in a second sense, Kaguru themselves are manipulated, forced to perform in space in certain ways, both by the nature of how their social and natural environments are constructed and, more important, because Kaguru society is the kind of small-scale, ambiguously knit collection of settlements that it is. For these reasons, Kaguru are constantly under pressure to present themselves for judgment to their kin and neighbors so as to affirm their sociability, goodwill, and trustworthiness. However much they might prefer to act covertly and alone, they are drawn into the public arena to earn co-operation and support, at best, and, at least, to be afforded escape from accusations of selfishness or witchlike behavior. Kaguru must enter public space to enact their proper social character. Conversely, while Kaguru retreat into the privacy of their dwellings or the obscurity of the bush or to distant settlements for many purposes, such removal from local public scrutiny and judgment must never provoke undue questioning of the motives behind it. Kaguru are drawn in and out of moral spaces, whether they like it or not. The ways Kaguru balance their conduct between public and private space, settlement and bush, community and outsiders, greatly determine the ways their acts and persons are judged by others. This counts a great deal for Kaguru, who depend so much on kin and neighbors for help and security.

I begin this chapter with an account of how Kaguru think about their homes as embodiments of domestic and moral order; from there I then consider some of the ways Kaguru from different homesteads think of settlements as public spaces and how they contrast these with space lying outside the communal order. Finally, I conclude with a brief consideration of the etiquette and grooming by which Kaguru repeatedly assure themselves and one another that they are proper cultural beings fit to be seen in the space they occupy. Thus, the analysis commences with things (houses) and how these govern the ways individuals interact. It then moves in two opposite but complementary direc-tions, considering first the broader reaches of space and their relations to assembly and quotidian life, and then individual expressions of identity, ci-vility, and association, the assertion of self and respect for the person as manifest in etiquette.

HISTORY, SETTLEMENT, AND HOUSE TYPES

Kaguru have two different traditional forms of houses, *misongi* and *tembe*. The *misongi* is circular and has a conical thatched roof. It varies from twelve to fifteen feet in diameter, and has a wall-base over five feet high. The commonest type has an inner area (*nyumba*, house) with the house-post (*nguso*) at its center. This inner area holds the hearth, consisting of three hearthstones (*mafiga*) and cooking utensils. Nearby are the residents' beds and under them wooden chests for storing clothing and valuables. This center area is where all private homelife occurs. A shelflike loft (*ikano*) where food is stored is constructed near the roof in this central area; this and the beds constitute the space farthest removed from outsiders. Where a house also has an outer section (*iseto*), this consists of a concentric ring around the central core. Sometimes this is entirely or partly walled in, while at others it is more like a porch consisting of posts and overhanging eaves but no walls. A Kaguru extended family will occupy a cluster of such houses.

The *tembe* is a rectangular building about five feet high, about ten feet wide, and about twenty feet in length. This has a flat roof constructed of beams and sticks and plastered over with earth. The central focus remains the hearth and food-storage and bed areas, which are secluded. *Tembe* are often constructed to form compounds through a series of accretions. A man may construct a single unit and then, as he takes new wives, attracts kin, or as his sons mature, other units may be added, each woman with her own house and hearth. What begins as a single unit may next assume an L-shape, then a U-shape, and finally become a full enclosure. This final form is best for protecting livestock, which are kept in the center space (*ikumbo*). Sometimes a fenced cattle-byre (*idewa*) is built, either to free part of the center space for human activities or because a full enclosure has not been attained.

Some Kaguru describe the circular house as their most traditional dwelling, yet early European travelers described *tembe* dwellings.[2] Kaguru say that their ancestors changed from circular to *tembe* houses because the latter were more easily defended against raiders. It was easy to set the thatched roofs of circular houses ablaze, driving the occupants out to be slain or captured. It was difficult to fire earth-plastered *tembe* roofs. Likewise, it was more difficult to rustle cattle from a *tembe*-enclosed compound than from the byres built alongside circular houses. Early travelers report a mixture of circular and *tembe* dwellings in the central plateau and lowland areas. Today the mountains and western Kaguruland favor *tembe*, and the plateau and lowlands favor round houses or rectangular houses (*banda*) with thatched roofs. These last appear to be a more recent introduction, easier to erect than round houses or *tembe*, and allowing more scope for partitioning than round homes. This last feature is important since it allows some Kaguru to house several adult women or parents and mature, unmarried children in one dwelling. This practice offends traditionally minded Kaguru who believe that separate dwellings, not mere partitions, should separate such people.

HOUSEBUILDING

Housebuilding (*kusenga*) is usually undertaken during the dry season. The greatest wear on buildings is during the heavy rains, but Kaguru are too busy then to make any but the most urgent repairs.

Construction of a house often takes three or four weeks, sometimes even longer, depending on the skill of the builder and on whether he can secure assistance. Today some Kaguru hire themselves out as housebuilders, but it is thought that any able-bodied man should know how to build a house. It is, of course, prestigious to hire others to do it.

Clearing the site and erecting the frame are done by one or two men. The frame is held together by barkcloth fibers, and gathering and preparing these is a time-consuming task. The frame is roofed with thatch before it is plastered. Securing the grass or palmfronds for this requires considerable effort. Thatching should be done only by men; since women are polluting, they should not become associated with thatch, which will be above the heads of those who will dwell within. This may also explain why bits of thatch, associated with male protection, are used to asperse a house and inhabitants with water when it is polluted by mourning.

In general men build houses, but only thatching is expressly forbidden women. If men do most building, it is probably because they are stronger and because women's chores, such as cooking, gathering firewood, drawing water, and childcare, continue throughout the seasons whereas men's tasks diminish at the dry season, giving them free time to build. Construction of the frame and thatching are usually done by the owner and a few helpers. The final task of plastering with earth is a neighborhood affair, usually done in one day at a building party (*lusigi*, bonds, tying cords). The builder's wife and kinswomen prepare many gallons of beer and invite neighboring men and women to work. Local women bring many jars of water to be mixed with earth. The men and some women plaster, sing, and drink through the day. It is considered neighborly and enjoyable to take part in such work. Plastering usually consists of filling in mud between the wooden wall-lattices. A few Kaguru carefully plaster their houses smooth inside and out so that little or no wood shows.

Despite the simplicity of the Kaguru house, expenditures in time and funds, especially if one is inexperienced and employs others, inhibit many from building. Fathers and uncles often keep married sons and nephews dependent by aiding them in housebuilding, provided that the houses are sited near them. When a house is finally completed, it stands as an embodiment of one's kin's and neighbors' labor and concern.

KAGURU SETTLEMENTS

Kaguru settlements are said to be smaller than in the past, when the need for defense led most to reside in fairly large, stockaded settlements of several dozen adults. Then Kaguru often dwelt atop ridges where they could defend themselves, whereas today many now build on lower ground. Today lone homesteads inhabited by a couple or even by lone women are not uncommon. Few settlements contain more than four or five married couples and most are homesteads of one family and its children. With the decrease in livestock theft and serious violence there is little reason for people to remain closely together. Even so, from any Kaguru settlement one can easily sight six or seven other settlements at a distance.

Kaguru term any settlement a *kaya*, the word meaning both settlement and home. *Kaya* can thus refer to a cluster of houses or to a single homestead. Settlements often appear to contain more persons than they actually do, because custom requires that each adult woman should have her own house and hearth and that initiated boys and girls are forbidden residence in their parents' house. A man with two wives and some initiated but unmarried sons and daughters would require at least four dwellings for his home: a set of houses (*nyumba*) for the wives, a house for unmarried boys (*isepo*), and another for unmarried girls (*ibweti*) who have not had children. The houses for the unmarried children are often older, run-down houses, converted from previous residences of the parents. In addition, there may be a roofed or unroofed platform (*itanda*) for drying grain, rarely a shelter for quartering sheep and goats (*suli*), or a cattle byre (*idewa*). Sometimes the entire settlement is enclosed by a fence, perhaps a stockade of posts, sticks, and thorny branches, or a living hedge of cacti or euphorbia. Such a fence is called *iluwa, mululu* or *ikinga* (a Ngulu word). Today an educated and affluent Kaguru with two wives may build a single large frame house with two separate cooking and sleeping quarters under one roof, divided by a hallway, or he may have separated rooms for children, each leading onto a connecting hallway so that no one invades the other's sleeping quarters. This shocks conservative Kaguru.

Earlier (chapter 3) I showed how the house represents an ordered conjunction of male (house-post) and female (hearth) attributes, the former associated with shelter and stability and the latter with nourishment and warmth. The house encloses a bed, a hearth, and a food-storage loft, all associated with domesticated human appetites. Food and offspring derive from within a house but are ultimately presented to an outside, public world through various exchanges of goods marriage, feasting, and hospitality. The house contains these individual appetites and the potential to fulfill them, shielding egoistic impulses and desires from communal scrutiny. Later we shall see (chapters

9, 10, and 11) that the control of food and sexuality provides the primary means by which Kaguru express and judge their moral worth. Egoistic greed in either area, to the detriment of sharing, exchange, and constraint, is antisocial and its worst forms become witchcraft. The house shields its inhabitants from the community's scrutiny regarding their possession and consumption of goods. In its proper sense, a house facilitates respect between different segments of an extended or polygynous household. Yet a house's walls also conceal the true dimensions of the dwellers' appetites, so that those outsiders who are envious and suspicious may wonder and question what really goes on within and how many resources are actually concealed. The house, then, may be considered as turning both outward and inward upon the community. As the next section shows, the foreground of a dwelling forms the margin between these two spheres, the house's stoop or porch providing a stage on which inhabitants bring forward and enact those aspects of the interior they are willing to subject to public judgment and regard.

SOCIAL AND COSMOLOGICAL CONTEXTS OF HOUSES AND SETTLEMENTS

Kaguru settlements may be seen as moral space, an aggregate of moral centers, each focused on the hearth of a particular household. From these extends a gradient of spheres of social and moral responsibility and safety ending in the dangerous disorder of the bush or wilderness (*nyika*). The house, more particularly the hearth, is the epitome of Kaguru notions of society and culture. The nearest thing in the Kaguru language to our term of "custom" or "culture" or the Swahili term *desturi* (custom) with its associations of ancestry (*jadi*) is *umoto* (hearth; *u*-, locative prefix; *moto*, fire). Indeed, Kaguru themselves often speak of how humans may be distinguished from baboons and other monkeys, which are conceded to resemble humans, by the fact that humans cook (*kutiga*) their food, a point long appreciated sociologically (Bachelard 1964:103–104).

The Kaguru house is sometimes seen as a metaphor for the social ordering of human relations through marriage. The hearth, with its associations of warmth, nutriment, and comfort, is woman's domain, and terms for fire, hearthstones, and cooking pots are sometimes used to stand for women and their qualities, both warming and nourishing yet potentially dangerous if uncontrolled. One euphemism for brideservice is *kulima difiga* (cultivating the hearthstone). Kaguru even compare the vagina to a cooking pot. To function properly the hearth itself must be sheltered within a house, under a roof, and thus the center-post (*nguso*) in a circular house or the main posts in a *tembe*, all supporting the roof, epitomize men in that they rise above, both confining and protecting, women. Some Kaguru say that men should hang their hunting weapons from such posts in order to express the gender of this domain. Male associations with the center-posts are further shown by the custom of sometimes tying a bone from the key bridewealth payment to the pole since it is the male of the house who is the key person in negotiating and approving the receipt of such payments.[3] The house represents a conjunction of male and female principles where material substances such as earth and wood and dangerous forces such as fire and fertility are productively united, ideally controlling the danger that this union of opposites might pose.

Kaguru speak of the house (*nyumba*) in both a physical and a social sense. It is a dwelling of a person, of a family, and it is also a term for a social group; thus *nyumba* may also mean a lineage segment. The term *mulango* (doorway) is also used in this sense, in a way parallel to the use of the term *tumbo* (belly, womb). The essential aspect of the house is that it has a hearth and therefore a woman tends it, cooking meals and feeding its residents. The house contains and refers to women, who are the crucial building blocks of Kaguru social organization. The most important Kaguru domestic activities, cooking and sexual intercourse (which are often equated), take place within a house. A home represents a bulwark against the dangerous, relative uncontrollability of relations outside, in terms of fellow humans and of the hostile wilderness. As a result, Kaguru have many devices protecting their spatial domain from intrusion by others. In the past houses had no windows but only small chinks (*chinyesi*) in the walls. Today some modern houses have small windows, but these have shutters to prevent witches from looking in at night. Many doors have strong, store-bought padlocks. Sometimes protective medicine will be conspicuously buried under a flat stone set at an entryway, though such use of magic within a settlement is antisocial. Most houses have outareas that contrast to less accessible sleeping and food-storage space. These resemble porches or verandas where visitors are entertained and fed, and it is improper for strangers to go beyond these.

In general, eating areas are segregated by sex, which is hardly surprising since sex and alimentation are closely associated. Adult men should not eat with women or children, especially outsider women. Unless a couple is alone, men, older boys and male visitors are fed in the area near the outside facing the entries of other houses and the central plaza of a hamlet. Women eat apart, either behind the house or in the cooking area. Today some educated Kaguru build separate cookhouses behind their houses. Women still eat apart there or nearby, behind the house in the yard.

A few educated Kaguru build latrines and walled bathing areas behind their houses. Traditionally, Kaguru bathed in streams during the wet season and within their houses during the dry. By day Kaguru defecate in the bush outside the view of a settlement; at night people urinate, defecate, and bathe in a low corner (*chaisi*) of the house having a gutter outlet allowing water to flow outside. This avoidance of bush areas at night is on account of fear of witches rather than of wild animals.

Grain is dried on a roof platform (*itanda*) near the house, but people fear theft and so foods are soon concealed in a storage loft (*ikano*) inside the house or in large wicker storage containers (*fidong'a*, sing. *idong'a*). There is a rich folklore about these areas, and it is said that witches conceal their familiars there. These are the most private areas of a house, and it is improper for anyone to be curious about another's food resources. Association of these areas with witchcraft and deviancy is due to the fact that suspicions and accusations about witchcraft and disloyalty stem from alleged deceit over food, especially during famine. If the hearth represents the positive aspects of domestic food consumption, then food lofts embody its secretive, unconvivial sides.

Around each dwelling extends a series of spheres by which external and domestic relations are fused. The porch or veranda is an area where visitors and neighbors eat and chat with the residents of a house without violating the household's integrity. It is the space where inhabitants of the house present themselves to public view. Beyond that is the *luga*, the space immediately in front of a house, where nonintimate household chores are performed. Here women shuck maize cobs, winnow, flail, and soak grain, pound and sift flour, and sort and clean vegetables. Sometimes one such area is especially smoothed and hardened for threshing and is then called *chuga*. Both men and women may sit in the *luga* shelling beans, shucking maize, weaving, or working on handicrafts. It is an area where people can sit drinking, smoking, and gossiping, although as a rule drinking should not be done within a woman's house lest the woman acquire the reputation of being loose, but at a club outside a settlement or in a special building constructed mainly for that purpose, and often managed by an old woman. In general, Kaguru associate being within a house with night. During the day, people spend most of their time outside, even if only propped against a wall protected by overhanging eaves. Even sick Kaguru usually lie or sit outside during the day rather than within, unless very ill indeed. Similarly, one should eat outside, not only because the inside may be smoky or dank but to show that one is eating ordinary and proper fare and has nothing to conceal. The outside *luga* of various houses in a settlement face inward, toward one another, converging to form one plaza which unites a village through display of sociability.

HOUSES, SETTLEMENTS, AND THE BUSH

Each household is responsible for keeping the clearing around its dwelling neat and clean. Ideally a housewife sweeps the area clean once a day, so it is a common sight at dawn or evening to see women sweeping and sprinkling water over their *luga* to set it in order. Households also have a trash-pit (*dikusisi*, pl. *makusisi*) at the side or behind the dwelling; this is often the excavation from which earth was collected for plastering the house. A few settlements are bounded by a fence, but where livestock are kept, a wider clearing has been eaten and trampled beyond this. While the bush and thus disorder commence outside the settlement clearing, in a sense a settlement's domain extends as far as the next intersection of paths leading to other villages. This is not firmly stated by all Kaguru, but it is clear from two facts: (1) During the dry season Kaguru are expected by their local headmen to clear the paths leading from their villages. Usually a village clears only to the next crosspaths. (2) In the past when illnesses or difficulties beset a village, polluting agents were magically gathered into water, beer, or a slain animal which was then cast upon crosspaths, that is, upon the liminal space betwixt and between social areas (cf. King 1921:76–77; Puhvel 1976). An abandoned housesite (*inhagale*) has a similar ambiguous status and is often avoided, the assumption being that some misfortune led to its desertion. Such sites are neither bush nor society, having attributes of both and being thought frequented by witches.

Kaguru build simple, unwalled shelters in their fields where they stay while guarding crops from wild animals and birds and where they cook and shade themselves during a day of cultivating. These too were neither strictly part of the bush nor of any proper communal sphere. Rules about comportment and segregation by age and sex, such as sleeping and eating, are not strictly observed there, presumably because no proper domestic activities occur.

One way to appreciate the significance of the house for Kaguru is to indicate its features in various rituals. For example, its hearth often is used to mark important points of ritual transition. At mourning the fire inside a house is extinguished (or, at the least, not used for cooking) while a fire is kindled outside the house where men sit to inform visitors about details of the death. In the past, when each owner-clan undertook local rites to purify the countryside and its inhabitants, each hearth was extinguished and new ones were rekindled from a special fire made by the owner-clan and their joking partners at special cleansing ceremonies held in the bush. Fires were put out and rekindled to mark a year's time. Fire from the wilderness, from land associated with spirits and therefore great supernatural power, is domesticated into the home.

Similarly, in the four basic Kaguru *rites de passage*, related to birth, initiation, marriage, and death, the persons involved are controlled in relation to domestic space. At birth a mother and child are rigorously confined within the house near the hearth for the first four days after delivery. The house becomes a kind of womb. When the infant and mother are finally brought out to confront the hostile world, a special ceremony is held in the doorway. Similarly, when a couple is married and the union consummated, the pair is compared to newly born infants and are again, at least in the past, confined indoors for four to seven days, *majuwa mifungata* (days locked up). The house has no hearth fire and the couple's food is brought from outside. Traditionally, the couple should have no autonomous household (hearth) until a child is born or until they have reaped their first harvest. Their subordinance is expressed through being fed from another hearth. At crucial *rites de passage* Kaguru revert to a status resembling young people (*wali*) or children (*wana*) and must be coached back to ordinary adulthood.

The house protects nascent, fragile social statuses. The spatial principles at work at initiation and death appear more complicated, varying in terms of sex. Men are intitiated outside the settlement, in the bush at a camp (*dilago*) termed *ikumbi*. The youth are divested of the qualities and activities with which they are normally associated. They are disgorged from their households and settlements and placed in the wilderness, harassed by threats of wild animals, to be reintegrated only after their recovery and symbolic rebirth. Even then they remain in a somewhat anomalous state, residing in a bachelor's house (*isepo*), a peculiar residence where people sleep and fire may be kindled but where food is not cooked, since that is the prerogative of women. In contrast, women (though cut in the bush) are initiated within a house and within their settlement; indeed, in the past they were often confined for many months. They were put into contact with many feminine duties they would perform during the rest of their lives, especially those connected with preparing food. They were fed and treated as though they were infants, the house serving as a kind of sustaining womb for growth. Nubile women are thus encapsulated by society, and their enclosure is seen as a period of domesticating growth, of restraining their wild and less orderly natures. The house then is here not only a kind of womb but a place where the young girls are nourished, groomed, and domesticated. Afterwards, girls reside in special houses for unmarried girls (*ibweti*); they can cook there, if they so desire, since they are now mature women. Men then are cleansed by circumcision in the wilderness; women are controlled by confinement in settlements, but their fertility, and hence power and danger, is never expunged until menopause. Male initiates are separated from the hearth. The campfires of initiation are tended by men and, unlike hearths, are not used to prepare basic Kaguru foods. These are prepared by women at home and brought to the camp. Men regain full access to a hearth only when they marry. If widowed or divorced, they depend upon the hearth of a mother, daughter, sister, or other kinswoman. In contrast, female initiates are drawn ever closer to the hearth throughout their careers. Similarly, during mourning a hearth fire is often put out and the wife or kinswomen are confined indoors around its ashes, unable to pursue the task that best defines them, cooking. In contrast, male kin remain outside the house during mourning, but with a special nonhearth fire related to warmth and protection but not to cooking and domesticity. Mourning men are separated from those associations with women that would define a house or hearth as domestic. Such divisions in mourning are observed regardless of whether the deceased is the man or woman of a house. At the end of mourning the entire house and its objects must be ritually purified; like children, the inhabitants are retaught their social roles, and only then may social life be reconstituted.

That initiated boys and girls must reside apart from their parents does not relate so much to the separation of a hearth from competing controls as from the separation of a marital bed from knowing children. All overt aspects of sexuality, even the most discreetly allusive, are forbidden between parents and offspring, who may not even touch the bed of their parents.

The central space of a settlement serves as a stage on which Kaguru present themselves to their fellows. Village residents present a public version of their affairs to one another as they conduct matters in their space (*luga*) before their doorways. Furthermore, the settlement as a whole presents itself to outsiders at periodic ceremonies. Thus, a wedding, funeral, or initiation draws in kin and neighbors from outside, so that all the settlement's members are encouraged to present it and themselves in as attractive a manner as possible to their guests. At such times the settlement as a whole becomes a kind of larger household. While actual sexual relations and cooking of food should take place inside a house and indeed epitomize a domestic unit, at such public ceremonies transformations of these key activities pervade the settlement as residents and outsiders, kin and neighbors, mingle in the plaza. Drinking and dancing are public enactments of private attachments, broadened and thinned in their affectual aspects. For Kaguru, dancing and drinking are modified extensions of sexuality and alimentation, which in turn are often equated. Indeed, to dance (*kufina*), to eat (*kudia*), and to play (*kuchesa*) are euphemisms for sexual relations. Assembling people beyond the scope of a household devaluates loose behavior and therefore permits it. What would have been obscene and improper within an intimate gathering between households becomes permissible in a crowd of hundreds, many unknown to one another. While dancing does represent a relaxation and expansion of ordinarily constricted sexual conduct, it still exhibits basic Kaguru contrasts between the sexes. Thus, women take on a role of encouraging, judging, and, ultimately, praising or rejecting male performance. Women form a circle drumming, clapping, and singing to inspire men, who in turn enter their enclosure, singly or in pairs, and compete with one another for the attention of the crowd, especially the women. As in sexual relations, for Kaguru the burden of performance lies with men, while it is women rather than other men who provide the key estimation of these performances. Men conspicuously separate themselves off, competitively from one another, for the approval of women who, unwilling to differentiate themselves or stand out, form encircling ranks.

Dancing and drinking, far more than feasting, are essential for defining a proper Kaguru *rite de passage*, which, to be complete, must be "danced" (*kufinwa*). As such, celebrations mark public enactments of otherwise private, domestic passions and pleasures, which are potential sources of conflict and envy. In their watered-down forms these passions and pleasures may be shared and dissipated, whereas ordinarily they divide people. In this, most Kaguru ceremonies take on a similar character, thus tending to repeat the same form. Kaguru themselves are keenly aware of this and often stress this reduplicative nature of *rites de passage*. At weddings they chant *cheleko* (birth), and at funerals they repeatedly refer to birth and marriage. The images of death and rebirth are repeated as one moves from one status to another at each such ceremony. Death and regeneration are, after all, merely two aspects of one process of social and natural reproduction.

In contrast to such agonistic group sociability within the spatial heart of a settlement, other forms of dancing and drinking are excluded from the center of a village. In the dry season young people often hold nighttime dances to flirt and let off energy. These are always held outside a settlement. Similarly, commercial drinking occurs either at clubs outside a settlement or indoors or at the edge of a settlement of brewers, never in any kind of central, public, open manner. Outside the protective rubric of ordinary developmental ritual, dancing and drinking are viewed as potentially disruptive and sometimes sordid though pleasurable activities, and consequently are pursued in areas removed from the moral confines of a settlement.

THE CULTIVATION OF THE PERSON: ETIQUETTE AND GROOMING

The smallest social space in Kaguru (or any) society concerns an individual as she or he strives to assert and retain a certain definition of the person. This is a never-ending task, varying with space and time, from the intimate exchanges within a domestic group to the casual greetings between neighbors and strangers who encounter one another on a path. Yet etiquette, as Norbert Elias (1978) observes, lies at the heart of how a people imagine themselves as cultured beings. It provides means by which we persuade ourselves that we as humans are superior to other animals, that we are not beasts. The word *etiquette* derives from a term for label, for the attributes we stick upon others, and hope they stick upon ourselves. Yet this sounds misleadingly limiting, for etiquette also has roots in terms for embroider, as in stitch, and, true enough, it provides means not merely for labeling but for a wealth of elaboration and shading, depending upon the protagonists' means and training. Above all, as Elias well appreciates, etiquette creates culture through bodily discipline, through modulation and repression of our appetites. As Durkheim would say, it embodies the fundamentally altruistic impulse underlying social being.

The following brief discussion of Kaguru comportment and etiquette repeatedly touches on the care and uneasiness with which Kaguru handle sexual and alimentary etiquette, with the two spheres repeatedly resonating upon one another. For Kaguru, the rigorous social regulation of these impulses constitutes the very essence of culture and sociability. For them, also, the loss of such control leads to pollution and danger, but also to power and freedom transcending social constraints.

The most basic attributes affecting Kaguru interpersonal interaction are age and sex. It is very difficult to argue that either takes absolute precedence over the other. Youth should defer to age, and women to men, Yet a very old and forceful woman may receive deference from mature or young men. What makes it difficult to rate such attributes is the fact that men and women rarely interact in any public, formal manner, other than dancing. Elderly women, especially one's mother or one's father's sister, merit exceptional respect; yet grandmothers are figures of intense familiarity and mutual indulgence. The only instance I encountered where Kaguru expressly contrasted age and sex was where a firstborn child in a key lineage group was a woman and there were no males of proximate age to her. Kaguru remarked that it was unfortunate but necessary for the woman to assume ritual tasks more properly conducted by men. Even here, Kaguru noted that once males reached adulthood they would still replace their female kin in such roles. Yet some Kaguru traditions relate that in the past some Kaguru areas were at times ruled by women, presumably older ones. For Kaguru a central force of life springs from the ordered conjunction of the sexes in domestic life; conversely, unregulated sexuality, dangerous in promiscuity and horrific as incest, epitomizes the worst possible immorality.

Proper relations between kin invariably stem from the model of domestic relations within the household, and in these women should defer to men. We have seen earlier that men should control as well as protect women, standing between them and those outside the domestic group, even while within that group it is women who provide the most crucial social and affectual links. Men form such links chiefly with other men and in doing so never elude the limitation that all such jural relations involve competition for domination. Ironically, their extensory relations between groups consequently take on a difficult, divisive quality even though they are aimed at joining people together. Men and women should present themselves separately at most occasions where they are viewed by others. They should eat separately, sit separately at ceremonies, and today worship seated separately in church.

The potential conflicts and ambiguities of sexuality, its hotness (*moto*), should be controlled through people preserving a sense of *chinyala* (notions of shame and respect). Such control indicates that a person is sociable and therefore reliable; exercise of *chinyala* varies with groupings in space. Such restraint is most demanded at the gatherings of kin in public, where various relatives assess how they stand toward others and where neighbors and outsiders judge the cohesion and strength of the group. What occurs inside one's house is not nearly so important as what occurs in the *luga*, the plaza, or at public gatherings. For these reasons verbal abuse and disrespect may be judged to be as serious as physical assault if done before others.

If sex propels life through time, accounting for succession and continuity of names and lineages, then food sustains life at present. Kaguru repeatedly equate sexual conjunction and alimentation, imagining one in terms of the other. Food, like sex, also has the ability to suggest disorder and immorality as well as dependence and sociability. Gluttony and stinginess are nearly as forceful as sexual transgression in eliciting images of selfishness and inhumanity.

Both animals and humans need food (*chakudia*), but only humans have cooked food (*fidyo*). Many Kaguru stories tell of animals disguised as humans but which are exposed through their inability to control their appetites, their repulsive eating habits, and their inability to postpone their craving to eat until their food is cooked. It is such imagery that makes the hyena, a devourer of bones and carrion, a witch. Cooking, then, is a shorthand expression for the restraints which culture places upon the appetite.[4]

Kaguru consider no day properly complete without an evening meal when residents of a settlement gather to eat and later visit in front of their doorways. For food to constitute a proper meal at such times it must consist of both *ugali* (starch such as maize, millet, rice, plantains) and a sauce of meat (*nyama*) or vegetables (*mboga*). While meat is not available for every meal, it is the ideal complement to *ugali*, so that the vegetable garnish is actually a surrogate for meat. These two components of a meal epitomize Kaguru domesticity: the *ugali* is exclusively a product of women's endeavor; the garnish may, of course, be a vegetable from a garden or even wild herbs, but the ideal garnish is meat, either from domestic stock or poultry or from game. Most meat traditionally derives from men's labor as herdsmen or hunters, roles that characterize their attributes of domination and aggression as subduers of the bush. The proper meal is a complement of masculine and feminine, assertive and supportive elements.

For Kaguru eating at mealtime is an enjoyable but serious business. The food merits full attention. The best-mannered people, therefore, do not talk idly when they eat. Nor do they stare at others eating, since that might imply that they begrudge the eater food. If there is an honored and respected guest, no one should cease eating until the guest has finished. Otherwise the guest might think it was being suggested that he or she not eat so much. Men are served before women and elders before juniors. On very formal occasions where animals are butchered, certain male kin are singled out for certain cuts. Thus the tongue or the area around the throat (*fonango*) is given to the advocate who spoke for one at a meeting (often a paternal kinsman). The breast (*chidali*) is often given to one's father, while the heart (*moyo*) or liver (*itoga*) is given to the mother's brother. It is not that these cuts are especially valued as delicacies but that they express the giver's recognition of certain attributes of those who receive them. For example, the heart and liver are centers of feeling and hence express the close ties of matriliny; the breast is said to call discreet attention to one's father's coupling with one's mother (he lay on her breast).

One further aspect of Kaguru oral behavior merits comment, though I am not sure whether to characterize this as eating or grooming. Kaguru express intense affection and care by licking the openings of another's face. Thus, a concerned mother licks mucus and dirt from her infant's eyes, nose, and ears. In imitation of this, elder kin lick anointing oil onto an initiate or newly married relative. Such licking is termed *kulambita*. In a number of Kaguru stories old women (grandmothers) bestow supernatural powers on young people (grandchildren) who lick the filth from their faces.[5] Such behavior evokes a powerful sense of equivalence between alternate generations, those standing nearest the spirits of the dead. It is one more instance of the pervasive and powerful oral, nurturative imagery pervading Kaguru thinking about social solidarity and reciprocity.

How one appears, how one is groomed and what one wears, figures deeply both in what we try to say to others about ourselves and in how others judge us. In this Kaguru seem to be no different from others. Some are well known for neat and attractive appearances; others are slovenly and careless. Cleanliness, tidiness, nicely oiled bodies, and clean and well-mended clothing are all, hardly surprisingly, features Kaguru parents try to inculcate in proper children. But there are a few features of Kaguru grooming and body etiquette that underscore some of the cultural features repeatedly stressed throughout this study. I limit myself here to two related sets of attributes, both related to parts of the body considered repellent or sufficiently peculiar to merit special treatment of precautions.

Kaguru prize a smooth, oily, glistening skin. A hairy body is not attractive. They recognize that human beings and baboons and other monkeys are very similar, but that humans are superior can be readily discerned by their not being hairy. Kaguru say that baboons originated from intemperate, careless

Kaguru who did not observe proper constraints on feasting at initiation and whose children consequently became monkeys (Beidelman 1965a:22–23). In keeping with such views, traditionally Kaguru shaved body hair, especially pubic hair (*ujoya*). In contrast, head-hair (*madosi*) was cut short or even braided by young people. Proper head-hair grooming expressed attention and moderation. The two extreme departures from this mode signify abnormal moral states. In mourning and at initiation, the head is shaved. All body hair is also shaved at initiation, purportedly to facilitate the operation. Conversely, at mourning, pubic hair is untended, since one should then be uninterested in appearing sexually attractive. Long, unkempt hair, then, denotes a slip from cultured conduct; that pubic hair is downright repellent relates to the fact that Kaguru have negative views about the pudenda. Common euphemisms for the genitals are *mwasi* (what is covered) or *mumwika* (forbidden). This is especially so for women. Thus little boys often play naked in public, but by five or six girls invariably wear small pubic aprons of fiber (*isegele*) or beads (*iguni*). Women's genitals are especially dangerous since they involve the possible pollution of menstruation. Some of this negative tone is caught by the term *ifuli*, which translates both as vagina and anus and which relates to *kufula* (to fart). Kaguru initiation ribaldry credits women's genitals with making supposedly repulsive sounds in sexual relations. Yet when bathing together, even men show shame toward one another by covering their genitals with their left hands or by hiding them between their legs. To be naked outdoors and by day is to be like a witch. Still, Kaguru are far from prudish and enjoy dirty jokes and horseplay as much as most people. What these data suggest is deep concern for those features of the body involving generation, which, of course, is the source of all enduring social power.

There are two further bodily areas which should be respected, though it is not possible to relate them to grooming: the navel and the top of the head. These two are linked in that both connect persons to birth and thus ultimately to the land of the dead. These represent the last body sectors to coalesce after birth—the remains of the umbilical cord do not fall off immediately and the fontanel hardens only slowly. One should avoid touching others in these spots. Interestingly, the misuse of the umbilical cord is related to witchcraft. If the cord touches a child's genitals, it causes sterility. If a person could steal an umbilical cord and boil and drink its soup, that one could cure his or her sterility, though at the cost of the cord's possessor's own.

CONCLUSION

I began this chapter with a discussion of Kaguru houses and settlements, yet the discussion went considerably beyond physical space to consider its moral implications. Houses and settlements provide stages on which Kaguru assert basic ideas and values about themselves and their society. The house provides a useful point of departure for considering the implications of relations between persons and things, those relations that constitute the supposed trivia of everyday life. This involves the complex and ambiguous processes of sexual reproduction and nurturance, which span domains of material culture, biology, and morality in provocative and powerful ways. The deepest forms of Kaguru moral metaphor are embedded in such quotidian affairs.[6]

Kaguru hold formal beliefs and symbolic terms of expression, but how these are interpreted depends upon the occasions and the protagonists involved. This indeterminacy is essential in that it draws Kaguru into continued negotiations as to which tones and meanings will be stressed at various encounters, and what they will mean. Yet formal symbols rest on a more constant, implicit base. What remains pervasive and unnegotiated is the tenor of everyday activities, Kaguru modes of work, cooking, alimentation, play, grooming, and sexuality. These routines are molded not only by etiquette and habit, but by the very forms of Kaguru settlements, housing, and landscape. Kaguru say that their teachings about initiation convey the essence of their culture, but this is misleading. Such teachings are self-consciously voiced pronouncements of how they see their social world and its relation to the cosmos. As such, these pronouncements are subject to disquisition. But the style of Kaguru quotidian activities is not subject to such ideological embroidery, because that style is unquestioned, is assumed as naturally given and therefore beyond reflection.

Next to space, time in its quotidian sense is the most accessible sphere to consider when trying to enter into the thinking and experience of another society. It is through time as much as through space that Kaguru imagine themselves related to one another. Time, however, is more difficult to apprehend than space; consequently, I will devote the next two chapters to a consideration, first, of the relationship of time to the social collectivity and, second, of the meaning of quotidian time to the individual.

NOTES

1. This is a revised version of 1972b, adding sections from 1973a. My thinking owes much to Mauss (1979a) as well as to Dumont (1954:67–81), who was inspired by him. More detailed, illustrated information on houses is available (Beidelman 1972b).

2. Good descriptions of early Kaguru housing appears in Watt (n.d. 42–43, the late

1880s) and Stuhlmann (1894:81). Reports on early housing and settlements are numerous: Last 1878:645; 1881:555; 1883:592; Rees 1902a;1902b; Meyer 1909:198; Stuhlmann 1894:817.

3. A further point may be significant regarding center-poles. The one portion of a house which Kaguru sometimes decorate is the center-pole, which may be elaborately carved in an abstract design. While no Kaguru offered any explanation, they explicitly describe the center-post as a kind of penis. Perhaps the carving represents a kind of circumcision. If so, this may be a further triumph of women. Kaguru see circumcision as making men attractive to women; they also say that the pain altruistically taken on by men undergoing the operation was originally inflicted at women's demand (Beidelman 1963c:758–762).

4. Readers may want to consult a relatively unknown but pioneer work, Middleton 1961, which first alerted me to the great socially symbolic functions of food.

5. Beidelman 1964a:18; 1966b:76, 80; 1975b:543–546.

6. After completing the manuscript of this book, I read two essays by Jackson (1983a, 1983b) which advocate considering the bodily activities of everyday life as keys to understanding culture.

CHAPTER 5.

Legendary Time, Clans, and Ethnicity

Should you ask me, whence these stories?
Whence these legends and traditions?
W. W. Longfellow, *The Song of Hiawatha*

When thou must home to shade of under ground . . .
Thomas Campion, *A Book of Airs*

Kaguru as a people have had to work at constructing their ethnic identity. They have done so through two basic modes of thought involving time and space. While these concepts define Kaguru as different from their neighbors, they also separate various Kaguru groups one from another.[1]

Kaguru have a traditional history which explains their present society. Not surprisingly, the past is viewed as a powerful validation for the present and therefore it is subject to dispute as well as consensus. Legends or history account for how Kaguru reached and settled their land and formed one people, and also explain why they are divided into competing matri-clans and lineages within different home areas. The force of these accounts of time lies in artful employment of key symbols and values of Kaguru thought. For Kaguru, historical time or legend is imbued with metaphor, so that one repeatedly feels that if matters did not happen that way, they should have.

Kaguru also have a kind of anthropology, their own set of ideas about the character and customs of humankind, especially their neighbors. By describing these outsiders' ethnicity, Kaguru define what they themselves are, in terms of what they are not. What Kaguru select for ethnic stereotypes reveals some of the attributes and beliefs central to their culture. Again, as with legends, these stereotypes sometimes separate Kaguru from one another as well as from outsiders.

Kaguru concepts of societal time (legend and history) and societal space (ethnicity and land) are steeped in metaphor. In the first section of this chapter I examine some symbols about ethnicity and their relation to society and culture; in the second, I consider these symbols in terms of legend and history.

ETHNICITY

Kaguruland forms a natural, mountainous, hilly haven rising to the north, west, and southeast from the broad plains of eastern Africa. A series of river valleys form clear boundaries with the hill peoples to the south. The land may be well defended against raids from the plains, and although the rains may be capricious, it is far better watered and more fertile than areas to the north and west. As a result, Kaguruland long served as refuge for a succession of peoples fleeing raids and famines, and has itself also suffered from raids by neighbors seeking to replenish their losses by seizing livestock, grain, and women and children. Furthermore, since Kaguruland straddles one of the main trade and caravan routes from the East African coast to the rich region of the inland lakes, it long endured the passage of a wide range of aliens, a flow reaching hundreds of thousands annually during the decades before the establishment of colonial rule.

Kaguruland is thus an exceptionally heterogenous ethnic region. Even among Kaguru themselves there are considerable variations in dialects, clothing, customs, and housing; these contrast as one moves westward from the lowlands and the rainier plateau and mountains toward the drier upland plateau. At the first European contacts in the 1870s people now called Kaguru were often described as several related but different ethnic groups. Kaguruland bridges a number of radically different cultural regions: to the north are the Paranilotic, pastoral Maasai, whose language, culture, and even physical appearance sharply contrast with Kaguru. On the other three sides are sedentary, Bantu-language-speaking peoples practicing a mixed economy. To the west are the Gogo, and while their language is somewhat similar to that of the Kaguru, their customs sharply diverge, for they are patrilineal, take a deep interest in livestock, and imitate some Maasai practices. To the south are other Bantu-language-speaking, patrilineal peoples, including the warlike Hehe, all considerably different culturally from Kaguru. Only to the east and southeast do the Kaguru's neighbors closely resemble them in customs; these related matrilineal peoples allow considerable exchange and even mixture of population, though not without some ambivalence. Finally, within Kaguruland itself there have long been significant settlements of unabsorbed outsiders, migrants, and refugees (and their descendants) who have sought to amalgamate with local people. Thus, in 1961 the chiefdom where I worked (two-thirds of Ukaguru) had nearly 2,000 Ngulu, nearly 2,000 Kamba, over 1,500 Baraguyu (an offshoot of the Maasai), and over 1,000 Gogo, as well as nearly 50,000 Kaguru.

In Kaguruland, labels of ethnicity are important, both in uniting people, by defining culture and setting boundaries, and in facilitating relations between these different groups. By briefly examining these broad labels one can discern a few important attributes lying at the center of ethnic identities, as well as a number of labels in which the history of past relations is embedded and recalled.

Kaguru (Wakagulu) themselves derive their name from *gulu* (hill, mountain), since they consider the essence of their culture to derive from the Itumba Mountains which form the heart of their country. In this they resemble the related matrilineal Ngulu and Lugulu to the east. Kaguru also term themselves Megi (from *kumega*, to break something such as food with the fingers or teeth). This refers to the daily Kaguru meal, where all sit about large containers of cooked maize or millet flour and break off pieces to dip in meat or vegetables. Kaguru are grain eaters and stress this in contrast to the Maasai and Baraguyu. Kaguruland itself is broadly divided into mountains, surrounding plateau, and eastern lowlands. Lowlanders are referred to as Wasika (*sika*, low) and uplanders as Wetumba (*itumba*, mountain), and while these terms appear to be merely descriptive, they may be spoken in a manner implying disdain by one group to the other. Uplanders also sometimes speak disparagingly of lowlanders as Wamangaheri (probably from *kumanga*, to eat food without relish), implying that at times in the past those Kaguru from these less favored areas had to seek food from those in the hills.

Kaguru have absorbed many peoples but underplay past differences in public. They generally avoid drawing attention to the fact that neighbors may descend from outsiders, but they may point this out, by allusion or bluntly, when annoyed. Kaguru like to believe that only native-born people speak their language properly, and refer to border people and outsiders who do not as Wandubu (garblers); while this literally refers to speech, it implies improper observation of customs as well. Yet some outsiders do speak Kaguru fluently. They are called Wandiyesi (dissemblers), implying that these are particularly unreliable because they appear to be true Kaguru but in fact probably have hidden beliefs and loyalties that set them at odds with their neighbors.

Some Kaguru descend from those aliens who passed through in caravans from the precolonial era; some were traders (largely Nyamwezi) while others were freed, escaped, or abandoned slaves taken from distant lands to the west. Even though Kaguru ordinarily speak of such people as Kaguru, everyone knows who descends from outsiders or slaves, and allusions to this constitute serious insult. Such people are sometimes referred to as Makonongo (Konongo, a people in Mpwanda District to the west), the insult lying in the prefix *ma-*, given to things, rather than *wa-* or *we-* for people. A further insinuation of this usage is that people to the west probably did not circumcise (or this was not done properly), and thus were not fully moral beings. To make this point, Kaguru sometimes use the *ma-* prefix for any alien people. The same insult is applied to peoples to the south. A more brutal insult would be to term outsiders Wafungwa (those who are tied up) or Watumwa (Swahili, slaves). A more indirect aspersion, difficult to counter since it is ambiguous, is *watani* (joking relatives). Since Kaguru can be joking kin to one another, the term can be used among true natives, but its other implication is that joking involves insult and aggression and that *watani* are potential ememies.

Kaguru have highly ambivalent relations toward the matrilineal peoples to the east, especially their immediate neighbors, the Ngulu. These people have a similar language, similar clans and customs, and have intermarried and settled with Kaguru. Nearer the coast and more involved in trade, Ngulu were longer exposed to the influences of Arabs and then Europeans than were Kaguru. In Arab times they secured firearms before Kaguru and raided them to sell as slaves to Arabs. Today a large number of Ngulu hold important positions in trade, teaching, and even in Kaguru local government. Kaguru both envy and distrust them, often crediting their success to witchcraft and sorcery. When Kaguru want to emphasize positive relations with them, they seek out Ngulu clan names, especially where these parallel those of Kaguru. When they intend more ambiguous relations, they call them Wajumbi (Swahili, *jumbi*, pawpaws) referring to Ngulu Arabization or Swahilization of diet, their sophisticated status as not proper upcountry Africans. Or Kaguru may call Ngulu Wegeja (*kugejageja*, to trade), noting not only Ngulu prominence in commerce but their status as strangers drawn into Kaguru midst for profit; Wegeja also signals the crafty, deceitful nature which Kaguru associate with all traders. For out and out insult, Ngulu are called Weyombo (*mwiyombo* tree, *Brachystegia* spp.), from the tree whose bark made ropes with which prisoners could be bound; here Ngulu are pictured as perfidious, betraying their neighbors and selling them into slavery. Yet even insults thrown at Ngulu partake of begrudged admiration, for traders, sophisticates, and successful slavers are all cleverer than their victims.

Kaguru have no special terms for the Gogo to the west. Where relations are amiable, Gogo clan names are employed. Where not, some Kaguru say that the term Gogo itself is abuse enough. Indeed, when Kaguru tales or jokes describe a bumpkin or yokel, the character is often portrayed as a Gogo. Gogo posed no threat to Kaguru; where exchanges occur, especially during trade and famine, it appears that Kaguru are at advantage over Gogo, much as Ngulu are over Kaguru.

A number of Kamba settlements have existed in the midst of Kaguruland for nearly a century, yet Kamba retain their own language and customs, although they also speak Kaguru and are subordinate to Kaguru headmen (Beidelman 1961d). Kaguru have no special terms for Kamba, but characterize them as licentious, thieving, and cunning. Kamba women are said to be promiscuous, in part because of certain customs required of brides and widows (cf. Lindblom 1920:81–82, 85, 109). Men are suspected of bestiality, of rustling livestock, and of dubious skills in medicine.

Of all peoples with whom Kaguru come into regular contact the Baraguyu are the most different in language, social organization, custom, dress, and appearance. Kaguru and Baraguyu profess mutual contempt and dislike yet are involved in complex economic interdependences (Beidelman 1960; 1961b). These prolonged, uneasy relations prompt various terms of insult by each group, yet such abuse holds no sting for the insulted, only self-confir-mation for the abusers. Baraguyu call Kaguru (and other agriculturalists) Il-mek (from Megi), calling attention to their eating grain (yet, as Kaguru them-selves observe, Baraguyu themselves depend on Kaguru grain to supplement their diet). In any case, Kaguru are proud of being cultivators. For Baraguyu, however, Kaguru dig because they are poor in cattle. Baraguyu also call Kaguru Il-kiposo (diggers), and view all digging up of the earth's surface as both demeaning and sacrilegious. They also consider Kaguru cowardly, not manful warriors such as they. In turn, Kaguru call Baraguyu Wahumba (from the Maasai term for Baraguyu, Lumbwa). Baraguyu would like to be termed Maasai, and Kaguru are aware that the term Wahumba calls attention to the fact that Baraguyu are too poor in cattle to carry out the ideal Maasai life-style. Kaguru also describe Baraguyu as "half-circumcised," because they do not remove all of the foreskin at initiation. To Kaguru this represents a failure to achieve total morality, as is reflected in Baraguyu unconcern over male nudity, the sexual freedom between warriors and unmarried girls, and, worst of all, the fact that warriors sleep in their mothers' houses, which for Kaguru is tantamount to incest. Kaguru profess no interest in the details of their neighbors' customs, yet quickly single out any practice that, in their eyes, sustains the judgment that their neighbors are more savage than they.

Kaguru emphasize their cultural unity and integrity in terms of language. Their morality is seen by them as quintessentially expressed through circum-cision and its concomitant moral instruction at initiation. They do not speak directly of matriliny as a key feature of their cultural identity but put this in terms of customs and attitudes about sexual conduct, as it relates to spouses, rules of exogamy, residence patterns, and the etiquette between elders and juniors. Where Kaguru's neighbors resemble them in such manners, Kaguru call attention to more ambiguous or ambivalent qualities: cunning, knowledge of magic and sorcery, ill-gained or ill-deserved wealth. In doing so, Kaguru view these threatening peoples who most resemble themselves through the same stereotypes they employ for their exploitation.

LEGENDS AND HISTORY

The legends and histories recounting the origin of the Kaguru and their clans represent a complex blend of the mythic and the historical. The first half of such an account is couched in Kaguru visions of space, sexuality, and the tensions between sociable humanity and the wilderness in which they dwell. The second appears more historical, more factual, yet, on closer consideration, this too reveals a traditional idiom: appeals to leadership against outsiders, boasting of livestock and raiding, and respect for acuity, knowledge, and eloquence. Those fit to lead speak best, are shrewd, promote their followers' interests as well as their own, and have detailed knowledge of topography and genealogy that validates claims to the land. For Kaguru, then, history and legend cannot be separated. Their recounting of events through time is bent to the needs of ethnic and group solidarity and exclusivity, to territorial and political ambitions, yet always within the broader metaphors that link their culture to cosmic constancies. The word *legend* itself derives from *legere*, to gather up, and for Kaguru the legend of their origin gathers up key themes of how they define themselves as cultural beings.

The following Kaguru legendary history is typical of the kind of moral charters I propose to analyze. I first present this as Kaguru recount it and then discuss the ways it sustains traditional Kaguru notions of continuity and legitimacy. To conserve space, I have abridged part of the text. The first, legendary half is presented complete. The second half, relating events during the German and British colonial periods, is presented in highly condensed form since it does not closely relate to the problems addressed in this study. The complete text has been published in both Kaguru and English, along with copious ethnographic comments (Beidelman 1970a:78–88).[2]

History (*Usimo*) of the Mukema or Mphene of Talagwe

The Mukema clan (*lukolo*) is among the clans (*singholo*) which came from far away into the land (*isi*) of Ukaguru (*Ukagulu*).[3] The Mukema came from Irangi.[4] They stayed there for many years along with other clans. Later that land of Irangi was entered by two other groups (*ngholo*) and those were fierce, the Maasai (*Wamasa*) and the Little People (*Fimbwiji*).

Because of their fierceness those people made others afraid to stay in that land, so they departed group by group (*matewatewa*) and went down from out of the north. They marched slowly until they reached a certain land in Ugogo called Ifunda.[5] They stayed there at Ifunda for a long time and then they slowly went further [south][6] until they reached the Ruaha River. There many groups (*matewa*) of people failed to cross the river while others succeeded, so then one group (*ditewa*) that failed returned back from where it had come. During that journey the group was led by three female elders (*wakulu*), for even though there were males, those were youths.

The first of those leaders was Old Woman (*mudala*) Lugode.[7] She
was the eldest (*imukulu*) and was with her younger sister (*mfuna*)
called Nechala,[8] but the name of their third comrade is not known.
They marched together back to Ifunda. When they left Ifunda, they
reached Chimagai Swamp and then Igombo. There at Igombo they
settled for some time. Then they climbed up into the Itumba Mountains and crossed through Munyela Pass.

When they left Munyela, they reached Munhindili in Uponela.
They did not spend much time there but continued with their quest for
a good land to settle. Then they entered Itungo in the land of Maundike. From Itungo they went to Maundike itself, but they did not like
that land, so they soon left and went to Ikonde in the land of Mam-
boya. They stayed there for five years and while some of their comrades remained, all of that Mukema group left and passed along the
way to Chimhinda at Mugugu until reaching the land of Talagwe.

At that time no other clans had yet reached the land of Talagwe, so
Old Woman Lugode and her comrades climbed Talagwe Mountain
and made a fire to show that they themselves were the first to arrive.
Thus the clans that appeared later had to go ahead to find other lands
on which to settle.

Old woman Lugode had reached a cave in the rock on the west side
(*ulwandi lo uswilo we dijua*) of the mountain near the trail at the pass
to Iwale and Ngutoto. There that younger one named Nechala and the
others said goodbye to Lugode so that they might go on ahead to find
more land at neighboring Mukundi, and that land pleased Nechala
very much, so she made a fire on top of a hill to show that she
herself was the first and therefore the owner (*mwenye*) of that land.[9]

The others who appeared later passed through to go ahead to find
lands to settle. So even today the land of Mukundi is the land of the
Mukema. Old Woman Lugode and others had settled there and she
was the leader (*mundewa*) of all the lands which stretched around
Talagwe Mountain.

Long ago when a person or group of people were the first to enter a
land they made a fire so that their fellows who came later would
know that they would be their subjects (*wekalisi*) in case they also
wanted to settle the land.

Now when Old Woman Lugode stayed in that land she was
followed later by Gweno people.[10] Those just passed on ahead for
they wanted a land to settle, but they failed, so they returned later to
Talagwe and told Lugode that they wanted gardens to cultivate, so she
gave them some and later many other clans arrived in that land and

they also failed to get their own lands for settlement, so they too
became residents of Talagwe.

Lugode stayed there in the cave for years and then one year six
hunters came from the land of Itumba. They hunted animals in
Talagwe and then one on them was lost on the mountain. He was an
uncircumcised person [viz., a minor] (mulajoni). His five comrades
returned to Itumba and announced that their friend was lost (kaga).
Then his kin despaired and ate the mourning-feast (matanga)[11]
because they thought he was dead (kafa).

That youth who was lost on the mountain had seen a rock cave
from which smoke was coming, so he went there and found the old
woman alone outside the cave. She had a garden of fresh ripe maize.
He greeted her, and that woman responded and took him to the cave
and gave him food, which he ate. So he stayed there for many days.

That youth told her his home was at Musongwe in Itumba and that
his clan was Njewe. Many days passed and then one day Old Woman
Lugode saw some travelers on the path to Iwale, and those were
coming from Ungulu (Uyombo). She called to them and asked them
where they were going. They told her that they were going to Itumba.
Then she told them that when they reached Musongwe in Itumba they
should tell people, "There is a child who may be seen at Talagwe
Mountain."

Those travelers kept on with their journey until they reached the
land of Musongwe in Itumba, and there they told them as they had
been instructed. When the youth's kin heard, a group of men and
women set out for Talagwe. When they got there, they saw Old
Woman Lugode and that boy. They were welcomed nicely, even
though they had come weeping.[12] They stayed there for many days
and then they circumcised (wamufina) that boy there in the cave.
When he had recovered, they returned home to Musongwe in Itumba
so that he could be anointed with oil (kubakwa mafuta).[13]

Later those people returned that boy to Old Woman Lugode and he
became her husband who married her. When he married her, he
stayed there, and then she bore her first son, Segala; the second,
Sembaya; the third, Mulunguwafula. And then there were two girls
and those were Malagala and Muhaima. This Malagala bore Maluta
and others and Muhaima bore Mfundo.

At that time the first white people (awanhu wajelu) arrived and
found Sembaya in his land of Talagwe and those people were Arabs
(Walabu) who were trading for elephant tusks and also catching
people to make them into slaves (watumba). Up to that time no other

clan was known there but the Mukema, who held the lands of
Talagwe, Iyogwe, Makuyu, Chinyolisi, Chikunde, Masimba,
Makutwi, Luseka, Ngutoto, Diola, and others around the mountain.[14]
Sembaya and Mulunguwafula were known even before the English
(*Wangelesa*), Germans (*Wadachi*), and Arabs arrived in this land, but
they were first known by outsiders then.

The seat (*digoda*, stool) for Sembaya and Mulunguwafula was
Talagwe, and all the inhabitants obeyed the leader (*mundewa*) of
Talagwe when he summoned them to the seat of his eldership (*ukulu*)
or leadership (*undewa*).[15]

*The rest of this history relates events after the Germans and British arrived.
What follows is a highly condensed version of this.*

Sembaya was the acknowledged leader of the Mukema at the time
the Germans arrived. That was a period of great turmoil because the
Maasai were raiding Kaguru, killing many people, burning villages,
and seizing livestock. The people of Talagwe did not suffer as much
as many other Kaguru because they retreated to Talagwe Mountain,
from which they could successfully defend themselves. At that time
the Mukema had a fierce warrior named Mulunguwafula who was
very successful in fighting the Maasai. Not only did he drive those
raiders from the Talagwe area, but he pursued them eastward into
Ungulu. Although the Mukema were now rid of the Maasai, those
raiders continued to ravage Ungulu.

The Germans sent a very fierce officer to Ukaguru to restore order
by subduing the Maasai. That officer went north from the German fort
at Mpwapwa (on the southwestern border of Ukaguru) and made the
rounds of Ukaguru to gather Kaguru allies to help defeat the Maasai.
He enlisted an elder from Rubeho in west-central Ukaguru, another in
Chibedeya in northwestern Ukaguru, and finally Mulunguwafula at
Talagwe. All three of these leaders were renowned for their bravery.
The German and his Kaguru allies defeated the Maasai in Ungulu and
drove them northward, back into Maasailand. In these battles the
Kaguru and Germans seized much livestock.

When order was finally restored, the German announced that he
would appoint local leaders to help him rule. These were to be the
descendants of ''those people who came first to their land long ago
before others.'' They were given badges of office and Mulunguwafula
was one of these. Because of his help to the German, that Mukema
was also rewarded with livestock.

*The history then recounts the various landmarks that signify the boundaries
of the Mukema's land of Talagwe. Then various Mukema who subsequently
led the people of Talagwe are recited.*

When the British came, another officer arrived to determine which
Kaguru should help rule the land. He sent an African assistant to
Ukaguru to interview people to learn who the proper leaders were. At
Talagwe this was disputed by several people, but only the matrilineal
descendants of Sembaya and Mulunguwafula could recite the true
genealogy and boundaries of the land and therefore prove that they
were the rightful rulers.

THE METAPHORS OF LEGEND AND HISTORY

Kaguru resemble other matrilineal peoples in this area, the Sagala, Ngulu,
Zigula, Lugulu, and much of what they recount of their past parallels the
narratives of their neighbors. This may, however, only indicate similar cultural
beliefs and values and not any actual shared historical experience. The plausi-
bility of Kaguru legends of origin may well not be due to factuality so much
as to conformity with ideal Kaguru values: if it did not happen that way, it
should have. A comparative survey of Kaguru clans shows that they share
many common names not only with their matrilineal neighbors but even with
the patrilineal Gogo to the west. A few of these clans have tribal names—
Hehe, Bena, Sagala—the first group explicitly tracing its origins to the Hehe
people to the south (Beidelman 1967c).

Most Kaguru say they originated to the west and north, from the Kondoa-
Irangi area. Yet the languages and customs of that area are strikingly different
from anything found in Kaguruland today.

Kaguru assert that the main body of their ancestors arrived *en masse* in a
great trek; yet they also admit that Kaguruland took in waves of immigrants
over a fairly long period. Only by this second argument can they explain how
some clans are dominant in an area while others have less right to these lands.
The notion of successive waves of immigrants is far more credible, of course,
but both explanations express social truths independent of historical facts.

Kaguru associated the west with death, the land of the setting sun. They
also associate it with birth, the two processes being in one sense similar, for
children are born from out of the land of the dead. As Kaguru express this,
the west is an inauspicious direction, but it is whence Kaguru originate. Bodies
are therefore buried with their feet pointing eastward in continuation of their
progress from out of the west. The spirits of the dead, however, return to the

land of the dead from which they came. Marching with their backs to the west they faced eastward, with their inauspicious sides, their left, toward the north (see chapter 3). Following through this logic it seems consistent for Kaguru to consider the northwest (Kondoa-Irangi) as their origin if they see history as conforming to moral directions.

In all Kaguru clan legends (excluding the Hehe one) the founding ancestors wander widely, often far to the south, before returning to climb the Itumba Mountains, which form the heartland of Ukaguru. In so doing they describe an arc covering nearly all directions from which present-day Kaguru are likely to have come. The Ruaha River is the crucial geographic boundary at which wanderings southward were redirected back toward the Kaguru's future homeland. While this river is an obstacle, it is not impassable, especially in the dry season. It does form a convenient natural boundary approximating the difference between the Kaguru-Gogo to the north and the Hehe-Bena-Pogoro to the south, two broadly different cultural groups. It may be these ethnic-cultural differences that Kaguru are trying to describe by this allusion, rather than any physical obstacle. Although the clan legend recorded here might be a true account of this particular clan's history, the pattern is nearly the same for all clan legends; it seems more likely, therefore, that legends are presenting a more general cultural rather than particular historical truth.

By describing clans wandering over a wide area the legends separate Kaguru from their place of origin and explain the present considerable differences between Kaguru and those peoples to the west and south. Although Kaguru once dwelt together in one land of origin, and though they set out together, the vicissitudes and varying fortunes of the long trek led to current differences. The most radical are due to groups originating from clans different even before their trek southeastward, yet their common trek indicates shared sentiments and interests on which clans base a tribal consciousness. Kaguru believe that such "unity is the strength of Kaguru" (*umwedu no lodole lwa Wakagulu*). It is shared culture that provides the "understanding" (*nimanya*) and "harmony" (*malagano*) that allows "them to show respect to one another" (*wakiyonelaga soni*). Lesser differences, such as those between different clans within one phratry, between clans linked in ritual joking relations, or between important lineage segments within a clan, are often explained by events which took place toward the end of the trek when groups were seeking proper areas for settlement. Thus, these clan legends provide a rationale both for the unity of Kaguru and for their various degrees of differences, for tribal endogamy and associated ethnic loyalties, yet also for divisive clan loyalties consistent with exogamy and on which local allegiances are founded. Most important of all, they provide scenarios legitimating the identity of different clans and their claims to certain lands.

In all such clan legends (except those involving the Hehe, who are reputed

to have entered Ukaguru as warriors) the founders of Kaguru clans are women.
This is consistent with Kaguru emphasis upon matriliny, but does force Kaguru
to hold to clan legends which are implausible in terms of what we know of
conditions in early East Africa. The original group is described as led by a
woman because there were no mature men in the group. Like all matrilineal
peoples, Kaguru see authority as properly held by men of a matrilineage and
any matriarchal tendencies are considered odd: female leadership is here explained away through an abnormal lack of adult males. We are then confronted
with the unlikely picture of a band led by a woman and without mature men
to protect them as they wander for hundreds of miles over warlike wilds.
While Kaguru emphasize women at the founding stage of a clan, once these
bear offspring, women are relegated to the background for the rest of the
legendary account.

In the legends, distinctions in authority within lineages are expressed
through age. While this is not always followed in practice, it is ideal Kaguru
behavior. Thus the eldest ancestress founds the settlement at Talagwe, while
her younger sister founds a subordinate lineage and settlement at Mukundi.
The storyteller is a member of the Talagwe branch and would certainly favor
an account giving his branch ritual and political precedence. Unfortunately,
I did not secure a comparable legend from any member of the Mukundi group.

In all clan legends there is careful recitation of place names as the clan
ancestors wander over the countryside. This is not explained further by Kaguru, to whom, of course, this simply reflects historical events. Regardless
of any historical truth, this attention to place names adds credibility and
vividness to a legend that otherwise may appear questionable. It also explains
other social peculiarities. For example, if members of a certain clan settled
at a particular place, how is it that today members of such a clan are found
scattered far and wide throughout the country? Can this simply be due to a
clan's giving men and women out in marriage and to difficulties subsequent
to original settlement, such as battles, raids, and famines, which dispersed
the population? This may be so, but if, as is implied, some faint and tired
comrades dropped off and settled at stipulated spots along the way, an even
simpler explanation is built into the original legend.

The main issue in any Kaguru legend of clan origin revolves around establishing that clan's primary rights to control its country. Such lands are
described as empty until settled by a clan. These initial pioneers become
owners (*awenye*) and one of their members becomes the leader (*mundewa*)
of the group or flock (*idewa*), while subsequent settlers become subjects
(*wekalisi*).

Ukaguru has probably always been relatively underpopulated. Settlement
in the mountains rather than the plateau was probably an attempt to escape
the raids so common in less easily defended areas. From the earliest recorded

raide

historical accounts we have reports of almost continual raiding of the less
defensible lowlands and plateau areas by Hehe, Kamba, Maasai, Baraguyu,
and later by caravaners and slavers. Those settled in any area were keen to
attract as many fellow settlers as possible for defense. As a result, the position
of those not of a dominant clan remained rather favorable vis-à-vis the dominant group; manpower was scarce and prized but land plentiful. This, of
course, hardly accords with some features of the legends which present land
rather than manpower as the organizing factor. This accords with Kaguru
beliefs about the supernatural ties between land and founder clans as well as
with Kaguru formal minimization of the shifting exigencies of alliance and
search for manpower as bases for ordering society.

The land itself does not change and can therefore serve as an enduring grid
of reference in which to place those sociopolitical relations between Kaguru
which do alter. Kaguru try to discount these fluctuations in their depiction of
social ties of kinship, alliance, and neighborliness. Instead, they affirm the
enduring nature of matri-clans by expressing those bonds in terms of links to
land itself. Accordingly, it should not appear surprising that legends connecting clans to land express this bond through women as founding mothers.
If land is viewed as the most immovable of objects, the most inalienable
possession, so too do women occupy a comparable position within social
organization. Women's affectual commitment as mothers to the offspring
continuing a matrilineage is of an uncompromising and enduring nature. This
contrasts to men's contradictory or ambivalent commitments both as fathers
and as mother's brothers. Women of a matrilineage may be bestowed in
marriage to men of other matrilineages in exchange for goods and services,
yet women remain ultimately inalienable from their matrilineage. It could
hardly be otherwise, since they form the integral core of that group in terms
of their and their children's deepest loyalties, which are axiomatic to what a
matrilineage is defined to be in the first place. Women are bestowed in marriage, but they are never truly given away, nor are women's children. In a
like manner, an owning matrilineage may bestow access to its lands upon
guest kin and neighbors and even reciprocate ritual duties toward the land
with outsiders (*watani*) (see chapters 6 and 8). To bestow land or women is
to create important reciprocal ties; yet these bestowals remain negotiable and
temporary and in no way abrogate the owning clan's enduring identity with
both land and women. The modes in which Kaguru clan legends are couched,
linking land and women, underscore this.

In the legend, the founding ancestress settles on a mountainside within a
cave and shows her ownership by kindling a fire on top of the peak. Kaguru
traditions associated stones with women and caves with wombs, and the upper
sides of mountains with the spirits of the dead. A mountainside cave may
well suggest imagery of the continuity of a matrilineage. That the foundress

settles on the west side of the mountain certainly suggests an association with
the ancestors and also with birth and origins. The kindling of a fire clearly
denotes the foundation of a more ordered society. The word "custom"
(*umoto*, hearth) suggests cooking, softening and modifying raw nature. Yet
despite the fire, true culture is not yet wholly achieved, for the ancestress
dwells alone in a cave, not in a house with a husband and children.

The cooking of raw foodstuff parallels the transformation of the youth which
follows. The legend describes an uncircumcised youthful hunter who becomes
lost in the bush and who is befriended and fed by the ancestral woman. Later
he is circumcised, goes home, returns, marries the woman and resides with
her and her people. They produce children, from whom the clan descends.
One possible explanation for this passage is that it is the necessary complement
to the earlier account of the woman's settling down. Thus, the wandering
ancestress in search of land initiates an aspect of culture by settling a homeland
and founding a hearth but not a house. In contrast, a wandering' uncircumcised
youth engages in the purely masculine quest of hunting for wild game. Only
with circumcision (rebirth) is he, too, fully settled and made aware of his
responsibilities. Kaguru credit the invention of circumcision to women, both
because the operation was accidentally discovered by women and because
women urged that this become a custom (for the text of this legend, see
Beidelman 1963c:758–762). The general theme of this legend is in keeping
with the view that men are socialized or domesticated in order to complement
women and that initiation not only differentiates men from women but allows
men to dominate them jurally. Male circumcision is followed by separation
from parents and sisters and by eventual marriage, which in turn here leads
men to replace women as leaders of the matri-clan. Finally, the youth seeking
wild food is lost but succored with agricultural produce; later, he himself is
both "cooked" and "reborn" (circumcised) so he is fit to join his benefac-
tress. Terms for eating have explicit sexual connotations for Kaguru whenever
these occur within the context of the two sexes.

It is at this point in the legend that Kaguru society assumes its full dimensions. Regulated commensality and regulated sexuality (marrying, initiation,
and combining agricultural and hunted food) legitimate a person's moral and
jural responsibilities and fix her or him within a social frame. Alliance between
different corporate groups commences here, where the legend loses its mythic
attributes and begins to relate conventional affairs in terms of Kaguru society
as we know it. Here mythic legend is transformed into historical narrative.
Up to this point, Kaguru are epitomized by the Mukema clan living in a
manner inverted from proper Kaguru life. The clan is a woman who cultivates,
dwells in a cave, and has no offspring and no men to oversee her. Similarly,
the only readily available male is uncircumcised and seeks food in the bush.

Yet the male hunter does not entirely shed this initial role, for Kaguru liken the domestic prowess of men to the hunt, for orderly males are thought of as husbands who subdue dangerous females as well as satiate their sexual appetites just as hunters subdue wild animals and provide food to satisfy hunger. Circumcision and marriage put two modes of domestication into an uneasy but specified relation. Only when their various complementary features are joined is there any possibility for regulated fertility and sociability, albeit these require constant effort to maintain.

The account of the arrival of the Arabs and later the Germans and British is clear enough. Recorded history is consistent with this version of how various ambitious Kaguru leaders competed for these strangers' favors in order to secure arms, ammunition, and other goods with which to impose their authority and influence on their neighbors. During this time the spheres of political influence exerted by local leaders increased far beyond the crucial factor.

The account of how Germans with Kaguru allies raided Baraguyu, Maasai, and Ngulu seems accurate. Reports by German administrators and British missionaries bear this out, although the legend fails to mention the more uncomplimentary reality of the many raids which Germans undertook against Kaguru as well. Yet even where the Kaguru legend approaches a Western form of history, those elements stressed by Kaguru embody Kaguru modes of validating authority. First, the legend cites ability to organize people against outsiders as the main basis for acknowledged leadership. Traditionally, this involved defense against predatory Hehe, Kamba, Baraguyu, and Maasai; less often it involved skill in allying one's own group with some of these potential enemies in order to attack other Kaguru (we know this too was sometimes done). Second, the validity of the account is thought to be provided in part by the recitation of detail, by lists of names of ancestors and, even more important, by names of places that may still be seen in the countryside. These place names convey a sense of immediacy and vividness; they are also recited as validations of claims to land, office, or ritual rights. What passed as the proper account, however, was a matter of continued dispute previously settled by the force of opinion among those leaders or groups with the most clout.

The concluding remarks about clan boundaries and clan rights to political authority reflect current clan politics (1950s and 1960s). With the colonial authority's policy of Indirect Rule and its interest in basing this on traditional social forms, Kaguru became especially sensitive to ways they might cast such accounts so as to appeal to colonial administrators. Competing versions were even transcribed and edited so as to be transmitted to colonial government centers. At this point, the legend enters in the new phase of rationalizing the status quo of delegated colonial power.

CONCLUSION

The legend discussed above reveals social or cultural truths outside the sphere of the historical. The first half of the legend accounts for (a) the solidarity of the Kaguru people and how this may be resolved with the clan divisions of that society; (b) the primacy of matrilineal descent in a world dominated by male authority; and (c) the association of matrilineal clans with certain localities, yet the distribution of members of these clans over all of Ukaguru rather than only within their respective clan areas. The basic symbolic processes by which men and women are socialized and domestically linked are expressed briefly yet memorably as a set of primal events marking the onset of society as Kaguru know it. Thus Kaguru legends of clan origins merge expressions of political legitimation of domination through monopoly of land with central features of cosmology and domestic organization. The patterns of tensions, assertions, and dependencies between men and women are shown to be replicated in the patterns linking lineages, kin, and neighbors in local communities, so that the metaphor of political rhetoric is enhanced by even more deeply engrained sexual and cosmological imagery.

When asked to describe their past, Kaguru nearly always begin with clan legends, usually of their own clan. In the telling, the initial mythic aspects of the legend are never clearly separated from the concluding, less fundamental struggles of men involved in more recent lineage politics. Kaguru see such legends as all of a piece. Yet to us the two kinds of truths they relate are of different orders. The latter may be questioned or even replaced with competing, alternate accounts; the former are moral, unchanging cosmological verities that provide coherence to how Kaguru imagine their society. These do not alter and are structurally the same in nearly all clan legends, even though particular details may vary.

Having considered time in the broader sense of its relation to Kaguru culture and society, I will now consider it in the narrower and less enduring sense of how it relates to personhood, as reflected in the quotidian passage of routine, in the events of special occasions, and in those odd situations where occurrences seem out of place.

NOTES

1. This chapter represents radical reworking of 1962a, 1964c, 1968, 1970a, 1971d, 1978a. In 1970a I discuss Kaguru traditional oral history in terms of criticizing the ways historians have employed this to construct Western-type histories of African societies. In 1978a I indicate some of the ways modern colonial rule led to new ways

of manipulating traditional history. Here I confine my discussion to how oral history and notions of ethnicity and cosmology reflect Kaguru images of their culture and society.

2. In my initial publication of the text (1970a) a map is provided indicating the area discussed. I also comment on many of the names of persons and places recounted. I omit these here, since they are irrelevant to my interpretation. For comparable texts of legends of other Kaguru clans see Beidelman 1967c, 1968, 1971d, 1978a.

3. Kaguru speak of the members of the Mukema matri-clan as Wamukema (sing. Mukema), from *kukema* (to bleat), referring to the sounds of goats. They also sometimes refer to it as Wamphene (sing. Mphene), from *mphene* (goat). Names associated with the clan also refer to goats. In another legend in which Kaguru explain how the Mukema and Fugusi clans are related, the term *kukema* is interpreted as "making noise": the Mukema arose early making noise and went on their journey, leaving the Fugusi behind (*kufugusa*, to be late).

4. Most Kaguru believe that their ancestors came from this area now inhabited by the Rangi of Kondoa-Irangi, a people culturally very different from Kaguru.

5. At this point in most Kaguru clan legends the group passes through a place called Chiwepanhuka (the breaking of the rock). I could not determine why this is omitted here. This is worth noting because Chiwepanhuka marks the point where Kaguru begin separating into different clans. The people are thus compared to a solid stone, breaking into various fragments (clans). Kaguru emphasize this incident by referring to Chiwepanhuka when reciting clan traditions during initiation.

6. Like many other Bantu-language-speaking peoples, Kaguru are vague in expressing compass directions (cf. Doke 1956). East-west orientation presents little difficulty because of the rising and setting sun, but north-south is less clear. Usually these latter directions are indicated by "up" (*kuchanya*) for northward and "down" (*hasi*) for southward. East and west have moral associations, death being associated with the west.

7. *Mudala* means "old woman" but here is a term of respect.

8. Normally, relative age of siblings is significant only with reference to persons of the same sex. Here, relative age justifies the seniority of one potential descent group over others.

9. In the colonial period Mukundi comprised two headmanships, dominated by the Limbo clan in the northwest and the Nyafula in the southeast. The Mukema narrator is claiming kin ties for rights to these areas, including them as subordinate to Talagwe.

10. Gweno is a Kaguru clan (*kugwena*, to discuss). These people contend lands claimed by the Mukema, which this version attempts to weaken.

11. Some time after a Kaguru is buried, a feast is held which settles his or her estate and ends public mourning. Kaguru sometimes refer to someone dead (*kafa*) by the euphemism *kaga* (lost). Some ambiguity seems intended here.

12. They wept because they assumed he was dead.

13. In the past important Kaguru ceremonies involved anointing with castor oil.

14. Although all these areas are here claimed for the Mukema, these are claimed by other clans as well.

15. Talagwe became the seat of the Mukema headman and the site of a local school, church, and trade center. A stool is a sign of office, but there was no special stool associated with an office. Officeholders were entitled to sit in the presence of others, since seating is an important measure of respect at a Kaguru gathering.

CHAPTER 6.

Persons and Time: Seasons, Names, and Omens

We have no sense for empty time.
William James, *Psychology*

Why should it not be possible that a man's own
name be sacred to him? Surely it is both the
most important instrument given to him and also
something like a piece of jewelry hung around his
neck at birth.
L. Wittgenstein, *Remarks on
Frazer's Golden Bough*

Today no Kaguru imagines time in an entirely traditional manner. Instead, Kaguru speak of days, years, months, and dates by referring to calendrical systems introduced first by Arabs and then by Europeans. Although few Kaguru read clocks (much less possess one), all are familiar with Swahili reckoning of a twenty-four-hour day: twelve hours of daytime, twelve hours of night. After over a century's contact with Europeans, Kaguru have absorbed further alien concepts of time, what with Western education, wage labor, Christianity, and governmental schedules for taxation and labor.[1]

In this chapter I do not consider Kaguru time reckoning as it exists today, for at present this is a hodgepodge of traditional and modern beliefs held in different amalgams by each individual and in different social contexts. Instead, I here try to present some of the ways that Kaguru traditionally imagined the connections between different natural and social sequences of events and activities, and how these patterns relate to the other sides of Kaguru life and beliefs recounted elsewhere in this study.[2] To accomplish this, I consider three different ways that Kaguru think about time.

First, I consider the ways Kaguru speak about aspects of time which closely correspond to our everyday thinking about the same topic. In this I include ways they sort out and keep track of events over relatively short periods with reference to work, household, and village affairs, and the lifetimes of individuals. I then note how Kaguru try to comprehend longer expanses of time, embracing events even beyond the experience of living persons. These temporal expressions are grounded in the pace and pattern of physical environment, the sequence of days and nights, seasons, and the passage of heavenly bodies, as these relate to human activities. This is hardly remarkable in a society utterly dependent upon seasonal agriculture. In the course of this discussion I also try to show how changing environmental conditions, such as day and night and the seasons, take on contrasting and complementary effectual and moral qualities imparted by the social ideas and activities which Kaguru associate with such changes. While such notions do not correspond with Western abstract ideas about time, they do resemble how most of us ordinarily think temporally about our daily routines. In all these areas Kaguru do not grasp time in any abstract and nonmoral manner such as we occasionally claim to do.

Second, I consider two facets of Kaguru temporal conceptions that differ sharply from our own thinking today, though not with the thought of our European ancestors who saw names as manifestations of our socioreligious identities, and who believed omens and signs did indeed presage events. For Kaguru the bestowing of names reflects complex ideas about the temporal existence of persons in society. Names both express and contain features of change, isolating individuals from and also merging them to their matrilineages, depending upon which temporal perspective is assumed. Names express complex and important junctures between the social person and his or her group over time.

names

Finally, Kaguru view some special events as standing in complex interrelationships that reflect a system of causation and dependence spanning different domains of experience which they usually consider unrelated. In short, Kaguru believe in various portents and omens. They believe, for example, that phenomena in the sphere of the bush and outside the ordinary realm of settled social life may sometimes reflect inevitable and incipient sequences of events within the social and human realm. To us, this is perhaps the most alien aspect of Kaguru temporal thinking. This is an area where we can readily discern the considerable differences separating Kaguru investment of temporality with moral and inclusive implications, as contrasted with our own more compartmentalized appraisals. These are events revealing time out of joint, departures from the ordinary passage of temporal sequences.

TEMPORAL RECKONING

Kaguru have two terms for "time": *ugele* (or *ngele*, *gele*) and *daha*. *Ugele* refers to a span longer than a day. When a storyteller refers to a period in which conditions such as famine or warfare prevailed, he says *ugele uya* (that time); or when Kaguru wish to stipulate a long span of time, they say *kwa gele wa minyaka* (for a span of years). *Daha* refers to a relatively short period, usually less than a day. If a boy is sent on an errand and loiters, returning late, one may ask where he has been *idaha dyose* (all that time). If Kaguru wish to express quickness, that it "took no time at all," they may say *ng'halonda idaha* (it didn't take time). This may also be expressed negatively: *siludaha* (no time, soon). Refinement of the meaning of *daha* is made by adding the prefix *i-*, indicating large size, or the diminutive prefix *chi-* (*chidaha chidodogi*, a little time). Kaguru are imprecise in not limiting *ugele* to periods of over a day and *daha* to shorter periods, but within any context *ugele* involves longer periods than *daha*.

Kaguru never speak of events occurring "so and so many years ago." Instead, they refer to what events mark the period. These are kept in sequence but need not be assigned precise points in time. The Kaguru past is relative. Kaguru speak of the last arrival of Halley's Comet (*ugele ya nyelesi*, time of the star); the last severe rains (1962); the last great famine when the government distributed American food supplies (1961–62); the rule of Chief Yustino (the 1940s); the Germans (the 1880s to 1916); when someone's grandfather was circumcised or someone's father was newly married or someone's mother died. These times are not confined to a specific year, but to a general context centering around the event. Kaguru seek common points of experience between themselves and others, so time becomes less delineated as one goes back and ever fewer events hold common importance to the living.

One way Kaguru place past events is by reference to those people from whom they trace descent. Kaguru rarely reckon genealogies beyond three generations of the dead.[3] Within this scope, time is meaningful in terms of explaining changing social relations and allegiances, distribution of bride-wealth and bloodwealth, loyalty to kin, responsibility and obligations for paying and receiving property. Outside specific reference to kinship Kaguru speak of a person's birth (*cheleko*) within a certain generation (*isika*, pl. *masika*).[4]

Except for reckoning particular economic and social obligations toward genealogical kin, there are no occasions for considering past relations or sequences of events with precision. Beyond this, Kaguru speak of "long ago" (*katali*).[5] Under this term Kaguru categorize their legendary past when they arrived in their land. Legends and stories are set either in this "long ago" or in a vague time which is not clearly present or past.

The most frequently used terms of everyday time-reckoning relate to days. One of the commonest expressions for a long period of time refers simply to many days (*majua mengi*). Kaguru have no traditional week or names for days, but locate days by reference to the present:[6]

dijusi dia, three days ago
dijusi, day before yesterday
digulo, yesterday
diyelo, today, or *hambiya*, now
nosiku, tomorrow, or *nosiku yakwe*, its tomorrow or the next day
chisindo, day after tomorrow
sindocho, three days from today
chamiagwe, four days from today
ifia, five days from today

A day commences with sunrise, day (*ijua*, pl. *majua*, sun).[7] Day is divided into daylight and dark, and daylight is divided by the progress of the sun. Unlike the moon, the sun is eternal; it disappears each evening, entering the west, but returns each morning in the east, unchanged. The daily regularity of the sun (contrasted with the varying phases of the moon) is emphasized. Concern for solar regularity is illustrated by disturbance over a solar eclipse (*dijua koligwa*, the sun is caught), a period of jeopardy when ancestral spirits and God are invoked to free the sun from darkness.[8] Kaguru show no such concern for the moon's eclipse.

Day begins with *kucha* (to dawn), when "the sun comes out" (*dijua kulawa*). Once dawn's colors (*mugingu*) fade, real morning (*nosikusiku*) begins.[9] From about 10:00 or 11:00 in the morning until about 4:00 p.m. is *nemisi* (midday). Sometimes late afternoon is termed *duswa* or *kuswa* (to go down), because "the sun is lowered" (*dijua siswa*).

In contrast to day, night (*usiku*) has no gradations. It is also called *ichilo* (dark). Kaguru speak of *digoingo diusiku* (the middle of the night), when everyone should be safely abed because then the sick are in most danger of dying and witches wander about.

Kaguru mark the months by phases of the moon (*mwesi*). At the end of each month a moon dies, supposedly eaten away by the dark, and a new one is formed, grows to fullness, and, in turn, is gradually eaten away. (I could secure no explanation of why the metaphor of devouring is employed.)

Waxing and waning are points of reference within expressions for phases of the moon. Waxing is described as *mwesi weagwe umlaolao* (the moon's emergence), or simply as *mulao* or *mlao* (emergence).[10] The moon waxes until reaching fullness (*mwilenga*) and then wanes (*kushisa*), when "the moon dies" (*mwesi ufa*). *Mulao*, *mwilenga*, and *kuchisa* subdivide the lunar month (*mwesi*). Kaguru also refer to a month as *nyesi* (pl. *minyesi*). In the past, months or moons were counted by knotted cords, each with thirteen knots, one space for each month. These intervals would be further subdivided into days by adding pegs. Whether this was observed before Arab contact is un-

certain. Today this practice has died out. Kaguru also refer to the moon's
corona (*iuta*, the bow) to indicate that the rains have arrived.

Kaguru mention few other heavenly bodies to indicate time. One is Venus.
As the morning star (*itondomanga*) it announces the day. It is also called
mukowa (killer), because it "slays the moon," which disappears after it
shows. As the evening star (*nhembelega*) Venus helps the moon shine and
marks the beginning of night.

The most important constellation for time-reckoning is the Pleiades (*chil-
imia*, Swahili *kilimia*, from *kulima*, to cultivate). This appears about the end
of December or in early January when maize is first planted; it disappears in
late April or early May when maize planting ends. The Pleiades epitomize
and demarcate the time of cultivation during the rains. Other constellations
are *chikusi* (cloud nebula), *mihini wa magembe* (bundle of hoes, the Southern
Cross), *mudimi na mhene* (the dog, shepherd and sheep, probably Orion),
and *magembe* (hoes, Ursa Major and Ursa Minor).

Today most Kaguru refer to the year as *miaka* (pl. *minyaka*; Swahili,
mwaka, pl. *miaka*). This is gauged by the arrival, progress, and cessation of
the rains, from November to June. The rainy and dry seasons provide the
fundamental contrast in Kaguru social life, comparable to what Mauss and
Beuchat (1979) reported for the warm and cold seasons among the Eskimos.
Kaguru orient their time around the rains (*mfula*) because these are the central
determinant of their labor. Since the rains' arrival, duration, rate, and distribution are never assured, each year fixes anxious attention of Kaguru to
this schedule. An alternate and perhaps more archaic term for the year, *di-
gembe*, pl. *magembe* (hoe) underscores the agricultural cast of Kaguru
seasons.

Once the first showers arrive, "another year" (*ikonga miaka*) begins and
the preceding dry period of five or six months is relegated to the "ended
year" (*miaka musha*). First showers usually arrive in mid or late November
and are light, usually lasting less than an hour. They are called *ng'hokola
some* (sweeping away the ashes). This refers to the accompanying winds which
blow away the ashes of grassfires common at the end of the dry season. These
fires mark the nadir of fertility, while the damp winds extinguishing them
initiate a new cycle of growth. The fires themselves are sources of renewed
fertility and are sometimes set to encourage regrowth of grass for grazing and
to clear land for cultivation.

Kaguru observe that God's seasons parallel human ritual. The act of sweeping away debris, of tidying up, is a Kaguru expression for ritual, social order.
(That our English words *time, tide,* and *tidy* derive from common roots makes
sense to Kaguru.) Setting fires and sweeping mark a new year in a cultural
as well as a seasonal sense. Kaguru value fire for cooking food and as pro-

tection and warmth against the hostile world outside the home. To set the seasons on their annual course, Kaguru elders of the clans which own the land end and then re-create social time through fire. All hearths in Kaguruland are extinguished and sexual relations cease while elders ascend to the sacred groves or ancestral burial sites on the mountain slopes. There they clear and sweep holy spots and rekindle fire using firesticks, with all their sexual significance. Ideally, all hearths should be rekindled from flames of this annual rite.[11] God and Kaguru reassert an orderly process at the beginning of every year, so the rains' advent is a social and moral as well as climatic event.

The first showers of the new year, confirming that these rituals were proper, are usually followed by several rainless weeks. The first heavy rains fall in early December and are called *ifula ididime* (the trembling rain) because of accompanying thunder and lightning. Final clearing of the fields is done then and hoeing begins. Up to mid and late December Kaguruland is subject to irregular but frequent heavy downpours, heralded by masses of dark rainclouds building up over days. By late December these give way to sudden storms. Because quickly rising rain drenches even the wariest person, this time is called *mhinga* (unexpected); with its onset, planting commences. January brings heavy, regular rains, sometimes accompanied by spectacular thunder, lightning, and hail. Then Kaguru plant larger fields of staple cereals. This marks the second phase of the rains and is called *mhili* (second). In February and March rains are heavy, but often several days pass between. The weather becomes increasingly hot and humid. Kaguru start weeding and complete planting cereals. This time is called *chifuka* (weeds). Soon some trees shed leaves and gain new ones, which at first have a reddish color. This time is *luhungu* (reddish hue). The heaviest rains come in April, *sangila* (downpour). This is the the time for planting second crops, such as beans, peas, tomatoes, potatoes, and groundnuts. In May the direction of the rains shifts. Previously these came from the north, from the mountains;[12] now they are from the lowlands to the south and the time is *masika* (monsoons, but also lowlands). By June the rains cease and cool winds blow across the drying landscape, called *inyota* (coolness) or sometimes *manyani* (baboons) because the undulation of windblown grass is said to resemble loping baboons. By late July the dry season, *chibahu* (dry), is in full force, and almost no rain falls again until late November. Brief, light showers rarely occur once or twice during late July or early August. These may cause damage if they drench ripening millet. Now the shrub *muluati* (*Abutilion zanzibaricum*, Swahili, *mbiha*) flowers and its name is given to this brief initial period of the dry season.

This dry season, from late June to November, is time for visiting, for male initiation, and for other ceremonies requiring stocks of beer and food. It is time to repair houses, shuck maize, refurbish tools, and engage in handicrafts, all either group labor or at least work which people can undertake while sociably gossiping together in their front yards. It is also when paths connecting hamlets are cleared by group labor. While people marry at any time, most prefer to do so now when harvests guarantee readier hospitality. Now, too, people congregate at beer clubs and the young hold dances.

SEASONAL AND QUOTIDIAN
DICHOTOMIZATION OF SOCIAL LIFE

At a broad level, the Kaguru tendency to dichotomize experiences and ideas into dualistic modes falls into line with two sets of natural contrasts, the rainy and dry seasons and, at the quotidian level, day and night. These subtly govern a wide range of social experiences and activities that contrast communal and more individual pursuits and, less distinctly, contrast public and private aspects of households.

In the rainy season life is organized around domestic and personal affairs. It is a time of intensive labor from dawn to dusk where each household is absorbed with assuring its future food supply and income. Kaguru are then too busy to socialize, unless this in unavoidable, as for a funeral. Most settlements are empty during the day while people are off in their fields, together with their children and even food and cooking utensils for worktime meals. Kaguru agriculturalists must respond closely to the dictates of the rains, and for four or five months they are caught in an inflexible climatic, not social, timetable.

In contrast, the dry season draws Kaguru back from their scattered fields to their homes and villages. It is a time for social or cultural work, not agricultural labor, for building and renewing social ties, for ceremonies, fun, and gossip. Whereas during the time of cultivation settlements are places where people only sleep and eat at night, now, in the dry season, when people mend houses and tools, process food, drink, and visit, go to markets, or attend ceremonies, life is overwhelmingly within settlements and among neighbors.

The other important aspect of Kaguru dualistic perceptions of time contrasts day and night. Day is a time for work and sociability, while night is for retiring to the safety of the home, for shutting out the negative forces epitomized by immoral and dangerous night creatures—hyenas, owls, nightjars, and witches. Yet night has its seductive features, and fire, especially the hearth, makes these possible. At evenings a family and neighbors gather to eat and later to gossip. They also assemble to hear stories. At night some of the most fetching and exciting dances are held. There people can be seen only dimly by flickering fires and some do what they might not do by day, such as flirting, making obscene gestures, or even initiating adulterous relations. Night is a complex, ambiguous time, a social frontier dangerous yet full of covert possibilities, antisocial yet seductively convivial and tolerant (see Melbin 1978 for an interpretation of night as a social frontier).

The seasons also determine some varying qualities of night. During the rains Kaguru are usually too exhausted by night to consider anything but rest; in contrast, during the dry season, when no strict work schedule demands rising by dawn, night assumes its more flexible and inviting attributes. It loses some of the enclosing and exclusive qualities of the rains, becoming a cloak for permissive, irregular contacts.

In contrast, regardless of the season, day is time spent outside one's house. Even sick Kaguru are unlikely to stay indoors but lie in the public area under the overhanging roofs of their houses. One goes inside the house at night; by day one confronts the outer world sociably.

Both these daily and seasonal features are filtered through the demands of sexual roles. While all Kaguru, men, women, and children, experience the contrast between the laborious rains and the more leisurely dry season, the latter brings an accentuation of the differences between the lives of men and the lives of women. First, while all adults partake in dances and ceremonies, men come into ritual and leisurely prominence during the dry season. Women may sell beer, but only men spend endless hours sitting around drinking, visiting, and gossiping at beer clubs. Furthermore, the male initiations held after harvest are the exclusive concern of men. Women's initiations are tied to the individual onset of menstruation and may thus occur any time. Finally, women experience a year with far less seasonal variation in their work schedules than men have. Regardless of the season, women spend many hours daily cleaning, washing, and soaking, pounding, and cooking cereals. They alone gather firewood, collect water, and tend children. These essential and time-consuming tasks make all women's days remarkably similar throughout the year.

NAMES AND TIME

One of the first problems I encountered during fieldwork with Kaguru was determining names. This stemmed from my ethnocentric assumption that someone would have only one proper name. Instead, each Kaguru has several names, not only because he or she interacts with different groups but because new names may be taken throughout one's life, marking changes in status or the vicissitudes of endeavors.

For Kaguru, names indicate how a person is set into social time. A woman or man is tied to kin, both living and dead, and to tradition; and that person is moved through time, through her or his career as a human, taking on fuller humanity, responsibilities, and individual identity by means of names bestowed, assumed, and shed. Every Kaguru has many names, depending upon the time and place she or he is encountered. By such names Kaguru indicate their recognition of the different roles and statuses which the same individual may bear.

Like most people, Kaguru take considerable interest in the names (*disina*, pl. *masina*) given a person. These are enmeshed in time. They convey the double nature of a Kaguru's existence, indicating affiliation with groups in both the present and the past, and also denoting the individual, changing character of a person's experiences, personality, success, and misfortune.

Each Kaguru is a complex aggregation of social statuses with corresponding names. These change with time as one passes from infancy into mature responsibility and authority toward others. Each time one addresses someone by name, one makes choices about what role or status one seeks to evoke. A person is a field of concentric social circles. The most intimate and dangerous access to the person is at the center, the most formal and neutral at the periphery. Different names reflect these varying degrees of accessibility. Unwarranted use of a name thus represents invasion of a person's social space, esteem, or dignity and is therefore abuse (*maligo*). When abuse of names is public, it constitutes an offense as serious as physical assault and may lead to litigation and fines. The brief preceding discussion serves to underscore how integral names are to a Kaguru's notion of self. Names are a complex topic meriting considerable attention, but I confine myself here to how these relate to time.

WELEKWA NAMES

The most basic and enduring name which a Kaguru holds is one automatically gained at birth. This derives from a father's matri-clan (*welekwa*). Each matri-clan (*ikungo*) has a pair of names, male and female, which are given to the offspring of its men, but not to its own members. Such names express the powerful complementary bonds between children and their fathers and their father's kin. These are the most readily used names between Kaguru. A Kaguru receives no such automatic name from his or her own matri-clan. When I asked why matri-clans did not also have such associated names, some Kaguru told me that these clans were already so important to a person that they did not need further reinforcement.

A *welekwa* name distinguishes a Kaguru and his or her siblings from all other members of the matrilineage, since a woman is forbidden marriage to a man of any matrilineage from which one of her living lineal kinswomen has already found a husband. Thus members of any matrilineage have many different *welekwa* since their fathers come from different matrilineages. Since a *welekwa* name is shared by siblings with one father, it sets members of a household apart from other matrilineal kin. Where a man is polygynous, the *welekwa* name expresses the common moral and jural obligations that all his children hold toward him, in contrast to their different matrilineal allegiances.

Besides expressing enduring patrilineal allegiances, *welekwa* names signify ties to the future. There is a renewal in intensity of this tie at life's end, when men of one's father's lineage officiate at one's inquest and funeral, defending one's interests against possible inroads and cover-ups by one's matrilineal relatives. This earlier *welekwa* bond thus serves to protect a subsequent one in that those survivors most needing protection against inroads from one's matrilineage are one's children.

Usually *welekwa* names derive directly from the names of one's father's matri-clan. For example, a child of a father who is a member of the Wedongo clan (from *kudonoka*, to bend) is, if a boy, called Mwidongo; if a girl, Mamwidongo. The son of a man of the Welimbo clan (from *mlimbo*, birdlime) would be Mulimbo, and his paternal sister Malimbo. Sometimes such names derive from synonyms and metonyms. As an example of a synonym, a son of the Waganasa (*ganasa*, a dog with spots over its eyes, like a Doberman) would be called Chadibwa (*dibwa*, a large dog). As examples combining synonym and metonym, a son of the Wanyagatwa (*nyagatwa*, brown ant) is called Mwanakadudu (child of a *dudu*, insect) and his sister is called Madisemo (*isemo*, anthill). There is no simple or consistent principle accounting for how such names derive.[13] As we can see from the preceding chapter, these names refer to details in the legends relating the origins and legitimacy of Kaguru matri-clans. As such, these names evoke all that the past stands for in terms of traditions, rights to land, and rights to ritual powers.

In poorly defined social situations Kaguru may safely refer to one another by *welekwa* names. These are the names I was most often given for people when first introduced. It is of course possible for Kaguru to lack a socially acknowledged father and thus a *welekwa* name. That would be unfortunate since it would indicate that the child had no complementary kin to pit against demanding members of his or her own clan. If a Kaguru woman marries a non-Kaguru, a *welekwa* name is often manufactured by the parents or other kin. This is easy if the father comes from a neighboring matrilineal people with clan names similar to Kaguru: then the Kaguru parallel is used. If there are no obvious parallels, as when one's father comes from a really alien group, a *welekwa* name is constructed either from the father's tribal clan name or from the name of the tribe itself. Some traditional Kaguru clan names apparently originated in this fashion.

DOMESTIC TEKNONYMS

Kaguru often refer to one another by mentioning spouses, parents, and children. Such teknonyms stress the domestic group, the person's integration into the jural building block of Kaguru life. In contrast to *welekwa* names, which are rooted in the long and enduring history of one's father's clan, teknonyms are the products of the immediate events of a present-day, ephemeral household. Thus one may refer to a woman as mother of Musulwa (*nina ye Musulwa*) and a man as Musulwa's father (*baba ye Musulwa*). Parenthood is the final seal to adulthood, establishing lasting ties between affines through the child linking them together. Parenthood binds both men and women to the past and future—the past because these offspring perpetuate the names and identities of those ancestors now gone, at times including a parent's parent, and to the future because parents' children's children may one day assume these parents' names as well.

In another sense, teknonyms stress the inferior, vicarious status of those who bear them. While both parents may be so addressed, teknonyms are specially favored for women and children. Child teknonyms have special significance for women because they are taught that it is through offspring that they meet their duties to perpetuate their clan and fulfill their husbands' desires. Kaguru often speak of women as men's wives, but never of men as women's husbands. In western Kaguruland, some husbands also give names to their new wives, apparently in imitation of the neighboring Gogo people (cf. Rigby 1968:272).

Just as women are more often subject to teknonyms than men, so too children are more often mentioned as offspring than adults as parents. Yet I should not overstress this subordinating aspect, for teknonymy also signifies that for Kaguru it is women, not men, who are the supremely important transmitters of group identity and tradition through time, as embodied in matriliny.

PERSONAL NAMES

Kaguru names are often tied to the activities of the ancestral dead. Names mark changing relations between the living and their ancestors and signify how time alters but cannot efface these ties. The living and the dead constitute one enduring moral community. Kaguru venerate the ancestral dead (*musimu*, pl. *misimu*), who inhabit a land of their own (*kusimu*). Death in this world constitutes a birth there and a time for ancestors to celebrate. Children are born from out of that land, and thus there is perpetual exchange between these two spheres. Each sphere therefore has its own time, yet, viewed from a greater distance, both conjoin to stand eternal, beyond such temporal processes. The concepts involved are complex, for Kaguru do not believe in literal reincarnation so much as in replication of particular qualities and character. These are embodied in names, which, along with sacrifices, guarantee the dead their link of remembrance with the living. Thus names repeat themselves, establishing ties between dead and living and, since so many have passed before, constituting multiple strands linking innumerable generations. Names both individuate and generalize, depending upon which perspective one considers.

When a Kaguru child is born, it has a precarious foothold in the land of the living. The dead miss the child and try to draw it back. A child's career, from birth and infancy, is modulated by detected influence of ancestors, determined through divination (*maselu*). By determining which ancestral dead are disturbed at any particular crisis, especially at the illness of a child, divination reveals which names need to be evoked. Bestowing these names of the dead assuages their vexation, so that ancestral rituals become recitations of the names of those now gone. Names are like cords binding the disorderly present to a settled and refined other-world where the dead are troubled by our failure to live up to obligations which they are better aware of than are we ourselves. Thus a sick and cranky child may stand doubly for some disturbance between these two spheres. First, such an illness implies that the dead long to draw the child back to where it came from; second, it suggests that the dead may aim to punish the child's kin for neglecting them. A child with a long history of illness may have a wide assortment of names, representing myriad attempts to locate the ancestral source of difficulties.

None of this means that traditional Kaguru names serve only to placate and memorialize ancestors. One can give a child a name after a living kinsman, though that name too would inevitably also belong to someone dead. One can also give a name because of circumstances surrounding birth, childhood character, events at initiation, or on account of later acquired traits. One may coin new names to fit a person, though chances of such a name being truly new are slight. No Kaguru lives who does not possess some personal names linking her or him with the dead, whatever name he or she may publicly prefer.

A child's birth marks a slow process by which it becomes a full human being. An infant receives no name at all until its fourth day. Until then it occupies a precarious position between life and death. (Four is an auspicious number in Kaguru belief and many processes are regulated in terms of it.) Only gradually are additional names bestowed, usually on a trial and error basis to see which suits the ancestors. This is deduced by a child's remaining well and happy, not sick or constantly crying after a name is given. At this stage an infant is not even a full human being and it has no truly lasting name. Were such a tentatively named minor to die, it should not even be mourned or be given a formal funeral. The names intoned at proper funerals are those also intoned for ancestral propitiation and those are ones given only to properly initiated adults. While no name every given is entirely lost, different names come to the fore as one's life develops and assumes a more stable form. Lasting names are received (or confirmed, if earlier ones are retained) only at adolescence after initiation.

Traditional names are bestowed by both maternal and paternal kin, and on such occasions one witnesses the pervasive, complementary dualism of Kaguru kin ceremonies. Kaguru names tend to be given in maternal and paternal sets, forming an onomastic microcosm of the broader social organization. Maternal names are bestowed before paternal ones, reflecting the matrilineage's primacy in social life, though never at the exclusion of paternal kin as well. Some Kaguru say that the midwife (usually of the child's matrilineage) bestows the first name; others say it is usually a maternal grandmother or other elderly kinswoman. The names selected often derive from the alternate generation, that of the child's grandparents. Finally, the child might also receive a name from a doctor or diviner if such an expert's services were required to facilitate conception or delivery. Some key forms of Kaguru address using kin terms (and related conduct) are rationalized through such names. For example, Kaguru act unconstrained, even bawdily between alternate generations (grandparent/grandchild). They say this is because these persons may have the same names and are consequently equivalent. If a grandparent has my name, then I can call the grandparent's spouse "wife" or "husband." Hence, the term grandparent is often a form of sexual flirtation.

Kaguru boys become truly adult only after initiation. As newly initiated novices they lose prominent use of their old names and indeed even what little social status they may have had. Upon recovering, they are "reborn" and require new, adult names. Returning from the initiation camps, boys receive such names from both maternal and paternal kin. In contrast, girls are not always given new names after their initiation, since initiation for girls does not fundamentally alter their jural or moral character in the way that marriage and motherhood do. (They are not given new, personal names then either.)

The precise connection between a particular ancestor and the current holder of that ancestor's name may be unclear, except that divination has revealed that some tie exists. We should keep in mind that names are not always bestowed to describe their holders, but rather to placate the dead, though obviously names were originally coined with various personal traits or circumstances in mind. There is no simple pattern in deriving Kaguru traditional names, yet tendencies are evident. Some names indicate valued personal attributes, either attained or sought, while others reflect events associated with one's birth. Names may refer to one's being obedient, handsome, aggressive, or eloquent; others may refer to being first-born, last-born, first-initiated, last-initiated, delivered while one's parents were traveling, born during a famine, or conceived by help of magical medicines.[14] Yet, in striking contrast to our society, many Kaguru names reflect negative qualities and experiences. Kaguru see the public iteration of adversity as a way to avert it. Conversely, mentioning good fortune is often a sure way of losing it. Kaguru are therefore likely to disparage their children and stress their poverty, difficulties, and unattractiveness, especially to strangers. To do so, names such as Disappointment (Majuta), Unwanted (Musulwa), or Scabious One (Chauhele) are often employed. Kaguru say that if the dead heard children praised, they would strive all the more to draw them back. Similarly, boasting of success or possessions might prompt a witch or a sorcerer to do harm, and, of course, numerous and healthy children are the highest form of success. If one is to thrive, one should do so unobtrusively.

Names link one both to the ancestors and, eventually, to those yet unborn. They denote individuals yet aso evoke group identity, continuity, and solidarity of kin. What a particular name means often tells us little about what its present holder is like, but rather that she or he is part of a longer, broader moral system.

I have indicated many functions of names, especially as they reflect changing (temporal) attributes of persons and their relations within social organization. Earlier in this chapter I discussed notions of time as modulated by days and seasons; these give a rhythmic pattern to Kaguru communal organization and everyday social life. In contrast, names draw attention to a much deeper, more changeless aspect of social life, even as names also focus on the relatively ephemeral. On the one hand, names identify an individual as a social being, as a person, a unique element in a constellation of changing roles and statuses through that person's life. Names change with occasions and the course of one's career. On the other hand, in a broader sense names reflect a time cyclically changeless, since, from a longer perspective, names circulate between the spheres of the living and that of the yet unborn and the ancestral dead. Few if any names are either added or lost. In these two senses names reveal a double aspect about a Kaguru person in time: in one sense, a person is individual and transitory, changing and jockeying for advantage and alliances through varying situations and time; in another sense a person is categorical and changeless, embedded in a lineage and clan, forever linked to land, legend, and rituals that perdure beyond the experience of any single individual.

OMENS, EVENTS, AND TEMPORAL DISORDER

In the preceding sections I considered Kaguru temporal imagery in terms of sequences of events or acts that reflect the expected order of experience, ordinary daily and seasonal changes and their reflections in people's activities, or in terms of names and their relation to the regular course of human development within the social order. In contrast, this final section considers time out of joint, the temporal frame in which events are viewed by Kaguru as being out of everyday order. In its fullest sense, this problem would involve all departures from the ordinary, including those due to the influence of God, the ancestral dead, and sorcerers and witches. I delay discussion of those influences, however, until the chapters which follow. Such aspects differ from the material at hand here in that they reflect the influence of some sentient being, albeit supernaturally endowed. In contrast, the events I consider here stem from no such motivated force. Their cause is unknown and unsought by Kaguru, who are more concerned with what these events portend. By briefly considering these situations, I believe we can better grasp a general principle of Kaguru temporal thought that has been implicit in all that preceded: Certain sequences of events embody an assumed order of things and place, and where a disturbance in these events occurs, so too is there disruption in proper sequential processes. What is significant here is that these disturbances lack any real moral evaluation. Some set the stage for desirable events; most portend unwanted or even dreaded ones. Yet in no case are sentient moral or immoral agents necessarily at work. What is crucial is that a temporal frame is discerned which indicates that certain outcomes are likely while current prevailing conditions continue. There are varying degrees or intensities to which this temporal frame is focused. The greater the crystallization of this set, the more determined is the course of events. Thus, some omens merely indicate that certain things may happen; these usually allow for some alternate course, such as not pursuing some plan until later. It is the time and place that are auspicious or inauspicious and not the act. Other omens indicate a set of conditions so fixed that nothing can prevent what will happen, which is usually threatening. Even here, and even where the signs may involve creatures associated with evil forces, such as owls or nightjars, these omens are not the causes of misfortune but merely reflect that mode.

The rest of this chapter considers the four different types of signs that inform Kaguru of these out-of-the-ordinary temporal frames: *ndege*, *kwinja*, *mauliso*, and *ugego*. Kaguru have no terms which subsume all these. The first three lie on a continuum in which *ndege* is a minor deviation from order, not necessarily negative in its implications, *kwinja* greater and invariably negative, and *mauliso* horrible. *Ugego* is different, a perversion of human development, very dangerous to others but rectifiable.

OMENS (NDEGE)

In both Kaguru and Swahili *ndege* (sing. and pl.) means both "bird" and "omen." All feathered creatures are *ndege*, but only some may be omens;

furthermore, things other than birds may be omens.[15] Omens are not creatures or objects but events or appearances. For example, Kaguru meet people daily on paths and are unconcerned about the combinations in which they appear. Yet if they set out on a trip, they are concerned about the numbers and gender of those met en route as omens of the outcome of the journey. Similarly, Kaguru take no notice when they see or hear a woodpecker, unless they are embarking on an important task, in which case the woodpecker may take on considerable significance. Omens are phenomena selected by Kaguru as clues about the nature of times when they are highly sensitive to making decisions, worried about certain matters, or performing certain acts.

This is not the place for a lengthy list of Kaguru omens.[16] A few examples should suffice, here, to indicate their character. For example, repeated noise from a nightjar or a blue monkey may signal death; repeated tapping by a woodpecker means a successful journey; meeting a lone woman while setting out on a journey indicates an unsuccessful venture, but meeting one man or a man and a woman means success; stubbing one's right foot on a trip means success, stubbing one's left means misfortune; repeated injury away from home means there is danger that one's spouse might commit adultery in one's absence. Obviously omens may be either good (*luswamu*) or bad (*fiha*), but, in any case, they are far from conclusive.

PERVERSITY (KWINJA) AND TIME

Kaguru sometimes compare *kwinja* (to depart, i.e., from normal behavior) to perverse human behavior, but strictly speaking it most commonly refers to phenomena outside the sphere of human (adult) action. Perverse adults risk being punished as witches or, at the least, thought mentally odd. They are accountable if they persist. If *kwinja* is sometimes applied to describe their acts, it is merely to underscore their uncanny, nonhuman side. Yet odd sexual behavior, if not blatant, usually incurs no violent reaction.[17]

Domestic animals may *kwinja*, thereby creating a situation dangerous to humans in their vicinity. When a dog howls continually for no accountable reason, "it departs from the normal" (*dekwinja*). So too does a cock crowing at night. Animals of different species or of the same sex having sexual relations, or a hen laying eggs on a bed also represent departures from the ordinary. Severely malformed offspring, whether domestic animals or humans, are also considered cases of *kwinja*.[18] In all these cases the source of *kwinja* must be eliminated. The domestic animals involved are slain. In the very rare case of humans who *kwinja*, these would be slain. Yet we must remember that since this refers only to truly monstrous births, these must be fairly rare and unlikely to live anyway. In any case, newly-born children are not regarded as fully human. The owners of such domestic animals or the parents of such infants are thought to be in considerable danger, as are all those in the vicinity of such departures from the ordinary.

The state of *kwinja* represents a gross departure from the normal sequential processes manifested by living things. It is restricted to the sphere of settlements, for domestic animals and newborn infants are the most likely to deviate. The deviant being is destroyed and diviners are consulted to indicate what further dangers might ensue. Yet the owners of deviant domestic stock or the parents of monstrous children are never considered bad; they are to be pitied and helped to regain a position of order. The central feature in *kwinja* is that it indicates a departure from the ordinary and proper on-going or developmental sequences of settlement life. It could signal that more extensive and dangerous deviance is in store; it could also indicate that something further is amiss that also should be corrected. In any case, *kwinja* is more a cause than a sign of disturbance. As such its removal and the employment of prophylactic or corrective medicines should restore the regular temporal pace of activities.

DISASTER (MAULISO)

Whereas omens (*ndege*) suggest some possibility of a departure from the ordinary, good or bad, and perversion (*kwinja*) represents a likely but amenable divergence from proper order, *mauliso* indicates unequivocal disaster. One sophisticated Kaguru informant told me that *kwinja* is like a letter warning of possible trouble; *mauliso* is like a telegram letting you know it is about to occur. *Mauliso* portends occurrences utterly out of the ordinary and inescapable. Here are a few examples: a wild animal which would not normally enter a house or cattle-byre does; thus, if a lion or leopard enters to steal livestock, this is not *mauliso*, but if a zebra, giraffe, or antelope does, it would be; a nightjar or owl enters a house; one sees a tree or branch fall for no reason. Upon seeing such things, one consults a diviner, but only to see if one can learn what is coming. It is hopeless to try to ward off the coming disaster; one can only prepare oneself. The sheer unusualness of such a phenomenon as *mauliso* indicates that for the present and for oneself it is a time of unresolvable danger and disorder.

SUPERNORMAL DEVELOPMENT (UGEGO)

The final instance of a disturbed temporal sequence considered in this chapter involves precocious or abnormal infants. These are termed *figego* (sing. *chigego*) and include twins, breech deliveries, those born with teeth, those who cut their upper teeth first, and all infants born after them and before corrective medicines have treated the parents involved. *Chigego* does not refer to a malformed child; even harelipped, albino, and crippled children are cared for and usually marry, though Kaguru agree that these may be repulsive. These latter are unfortunate but in no way dangerous, whereas *figego* are.

Kaguru cannot account for why a *chigego* is born, but see such an infant as an extremely disruptive being in the normal temporal sequence of things, departing from the gradual pace of child development, or as confounding births appropriate for animals (multiple) with those proper for humans (single). The parents of such an infant are in no way blamed for the calamity, though they would be blamed if they allowed such a creature to live or if they failed to seek divination and medicines to rectify the situation that led to it. The condition producing a *chigego* persists until formal steps are taken to amend it.

The reasoning behind the idea of *figego* rests on the assumption that there is a fit and ordered sequence of development for all human beings. Emerging from the sphere of the dead, Kaguru infants undergo a long and precarious transition into true humanity that is completed only at adolescence. The most problematical period in this transition spans the time from birth through cutting the first teeth when the child begins to eat proper food. It is some disturbance in this ordered process that accounts for the *chigego*. Producing such an infant is not inevitable, and if an expectant mother suspects anything at all out of the ordinary about her pregnancy, she and her husband will consult a diviner for advice and medicine to keep the infant developing in the proper order. Parents continue to be wary and watchful until after the child cuts its first teeth. Sometimes they even cut the child's lower gums to encourage proper sequence in teething. The child's maternal grandmother may string beads which a diviner treats and which are then tied around the infant's waist. These are combinations of red-white-yellow or red-yellow, colors preventing dysentery (yellow) or denoting danger (red) and normalcy (white). This is replaced by a celebratory necklace when teething ends successfully.

When I asked informants further about what characterized *figego*, one sophisticated Kaguru compared them to motorists passing down a highway in the wrong lane. This is a danger to everyone, although it may allow the offender to get ahead. What I think was meant here is that *figego* are abnormal and dangerous because not only is their temporal development different from that of ordinary people but they may also be abnormally precocious. Kaguru say that kin kill *figego* because they are endangered by them. *Figego* are said to develop into extraordinarily clever, strong, and vigorous persons, but at the expense of their kin about them, whose strength is correspondingly sapped; that is, their developmental processes are correspondingly inverted. *Figego* thrive, and while they are not intentionally evil in the way that witches are, they resemble witches by inevitably causing harm to all in their midst. I recall the first time I was made aware of this. During a sudden and violent thunderstorm, I and a large group of Kaguru scurried for protection under a beer-shelter hardly large enough for all of us. Lightning began to strike alarmingly near. One of the Kaguru shouted, "Who's the *chigego* in our midst? He'd better get out of here or we'll all die." It was a joke, but for a dangerous situation.

The phenomenon of *ugego* is to temporality what witchcraft is to moral action, an expression of the inversion of proper temporal sequence. It pertains not to just any sequential sphere but to that which is most important for Kaguru in expressing the temporal nature of meaningful life, the ordered and predictable passage of persons (and consequently kin groups) through the proper phases of development from birth to maturity and death. *Ugego* exemplifies a temporal frame that distorts this process, crazily accelerating the pace for *figego* and destructively inverting it for their kin and others around them. Kaguru try to think temporally in an ordered, measured sense; in the case of people, they even try to iron out any discrepancies in the "natural" sequence by imposing a social form to such processes through *rites de passage*. *Ugego* represents a conception of temporal sequence or frame outside and opposed to normal development, a time out of joint.

CONCLUSION

Kaguru imagine time not in any abstract sense, such as Western intellectuals project for it from time to time. Rather, and quite sensibly, they view it in terms of the events that fill it and the space in which these events take place. Kaguru temporal thinking can be considered in three aspects. First, the natural or physical sequence of events, the passage of day and night, the round of seasons, figure in how Kaguru picture time, or, rather, how Kaguru think about the things they do that make reference to temporality meaningful in the first place. These natural images of temporal thinking, although highly modified by culture, are roughly familiar to all of us. Their significance lies in the ways they impress an entire community, drawing all its members into similar rhythms and patterns, although for Kaguru there are significant differences in how these affect women and men. Second, time is modulated and even surmounted through naming, especially as this relates to the constitution of kin groups and to the constructed profiles of individual life spans. Naming expresses particular and changing facets of persons, yet also subsumes these changes within a broader, timeless matrix of enduring clanship rooted in land and ritual to the ancestors. All of these features of Kaguru imagery about temporality embrace and describe sequences through modes of continuity and cyclical replication that provide a sense of constancy and stability. There is also a deviant side of temporal sequences, one outside the order characterizing most Kaguru thinking about events and change. Kaguru like to envision life as an orderly, predictable procession of events and to picture a lifetime proceeding along a measured, well-paced course. When such sequential order is disturbed, time itself is thought to be awry. Considerable effort is made to reassert order in the face of such a challenge. Deviation in spheres outside what is responsive to social or cultural manipulation and contouring is alarming. The physical world and biological processes sometimes seem to defy human influence and reason. Extreme deviation of this sort confronts Kaguru with a vision of disorder that they find especially alarming and requires immediate repression through destruction of all such threatening contradictions to the ways they need to imagine how things act and develop.

So far I have been writing about Kaguru imagery in the sense that it challenges my imagination as an analytical ethnographer. Kaguru themselves employ these images as means to grasp the very world about them, a world of landscapes, settlements, plants and animals, and other Kaguru, as well as the thinker himself or herself. In this sense, this imagery deals with what is relatively apprehensible even to the curious and patient stranger, the anthropologist. In the next chapter I begin to consider how Kaguru imagine what they themselves admit they cannot readily perceive—the spirits of the dead and those as yet unborn. Here not only is Kaguru imagination more fully exercised, but its findings remain, even for Kaguru, more ambiguous and undetermined.

NOTES

1. This chapter represents radical revisions of 1963d, 1963e, 1974a. Obviously, it owes much to Evans-Pritchard (1939), as well as to Dumont (1954:372–403).

2. In my earlier version of this section (1963d) I stated that Kaguru have some abstract notion of time, whereas Hallpike criticizes this, noting that this would more properly be termed a period encompassing a sequence of events: "Rather than being '*time*-reckoning' it is really 'process-classification' and 'processing-marking' " (1979:345). This chapter emphasizes that aspect as the most relevant to the problems at hand regarding the relation between time and other forms of imagery.

3. Early colonial governments encouraged the paramount chief's clan to record genealogies, which now extend beyond this length (cf. Beidelman 1978a).

4. Apparently this word is not related to its homonym, which refers to "late rains" and to "southward." The Kaguru's neighbors, the matrilineal Ngulu, employ *lika*, pl. *malika*, for generation.

5. This is related to *kutali* (far away), the root *-tali* meaning "long," e.g., *munhu mutali* (tall person).

6. Today Kaguru often use a modern seven-day Swahili week.

7. Today Kaguru know the Swahili custom of reckoning days from night to night.

8. Kaguru do not cite solar eclipses as points of reference in time.

9. A reduplication of the word *nosiku* (tomorrow).

10. *Mulao* also refers to the emergence of an adolescent after initiation.

11. I use the ethnographic present. Such rituals have not been fully performed in the Kaguru plateau for many decades, though Kaguru maintain that these are observed in the mountainous northwest.

One early missionary implies that this liminal ritual period should be a time of no quarreling; otherwise the rains may be held back (Spriggs 1910:32–33).

12. I collected my data in the plateau of Kaguruland. There this distinction is meaningful, since the rain descends from the peaks which stud that area, the highest to the north. This association makes no sense if Kaguruland as a whole is considered.

13. For a list of these, see Beidelman 1971d, 1978a. Kaguru also sometimes give special names associated with membership in a patrilineal group (*mulongo*, pl. *milongo*) and whose only apparent function today is prohibiting contact with certain substances, usually foods. I found such naming only for men. What little importance such names may hold lapses with the birth of one's own sons, who then assume whatever names and related restrictions these require. Despite over three years' intensive fieldwork with Kaguru, I secured little data on this, presumably because these groups have no present importance. Such names are applied to men only during a period while they themselves lack sons (likely to have no households of their own) and therefore, in a sense, are likely still to stand in a particularly subordinate position toward their own fathers.

14. For a list of Kaguru personal names and their meanings, see Beidelman 1974a.

15. The term *ndege* (bird) is difficult to define. Ostriches do not fly but are *ndege* because they have wings, but bats and airplanes are *ndege* as well. Many Kaguru omens involve birds, and Kaguru folklore has many instances of birds with magical powers; see Beidelman 1974c.

16. I provide a list of Kaguru omens (*ndege*) elsewhere; see Beidelman 1963e:47–49).

17. In a modern case of bestiality no mention of *kwinja* was made (Beidelman 1961a).

18. I provide a fuller set of examples of *kwinja* elsewhere (Beidelman 1963e:49–51); comparison of that paper with this chapter reveals that I have considerably altered my views about the significance of this belief.

CHAPTER 7.

Death and the Ancestors

We have left undone those things we ought to have done;
and we have done those things which we ought not to have
    done;
And there is no health in us.
                    General Confession, *The Book of Common Prayer*

Is it not strange that sheep's guts should hale souls
out of men's bodies?
                    Much Ado About Nothing II.iii.

For Kaguru a matri-clan or matrilineage is composed of inumerable beings
extending in both directions of time. This includes the living, the dead, and
those yet unborn, forming a moral entity with common concerns and one fate.
The conduct and thought of the living affect the well-being and peace of the
dead, and, conversely, the disturbance and neglect of the dead trouble those
alive. Proper and sustained relations between these two spheres ensure the
future by maintaining the birth of future generations. Kinship is couched both
in quotidian exchange and respect and in remembrance of past and future
relations. The ways these relations toward the dead are imagined appear
perplexingly different from how we think of ourselves, and Western analysts
have pondered this problem of interpretation as much or more than any other
aspect of thought among many African peoples (cf. Temples 1959:73–74;
Fortes 1961; Kopytoff 1971; Brain 1972).

This chapter provides a view of how Kaguru express these relations. The
modes for doing this are common to the ways Kaguru imagine other facets
of order, society, and time; how could it be otherwise? The concepts involved,
however, remain the most difficult to clarify of those considered in this study.

Considering this difficulty in conveying these ideas, due both to their distance from our own thought and to Kaguru's reservations about discussing
the dead and their world, especially with outsiders, I organize my inquiry
around the ways Kaguru express this in texts.[1] In the first half of this chapter
I present three Kaguru accounts about the relations between the ancestral dead

and the living. In the second, I provide a social and ideological context for these accounts, and then discuss each text in some detail. In this way the reader should be able to view these relations as Kaguru themselves express them, and then consider the kinds of metaphors and images which Kaguru employ to fathom influences and beings remote from immediate experience.

The First Tale: The Return of the Dead[2]

There was a man who cultivated his gardens, and out of all his gardens one of maize had been planted earlier than the rest. The maize sprouted nicely, and when it reached weeding time, he weeded it. He stayed near home and continued to plant other gardens. When it was again time for the garden of maize, he went to weed it. He weeded it until he finished. Then when that garden of maize was ready for the second weeding, he went again to weed it. When he had finished the second weeding, the maize was coming into ear.

That man had more expectations for that garden of maize than for the others which he cultivated. He visited all his gardens, but his heart was in the maize garden alone. The man's next work was to cut poles to build a large granary for the maize which he would put there at harvest. He was also busy preparing beer ahead of time for the people so that they would readily come to help him harvest and not be late, for if the harvesters did not show up the maize would be spoiled in the garden. Then when he was finished, he was pleased because everything was made ready waiting for the maize.

When the maize reached the size of large ears, his wife went to visit the gardens. When she got to the maize, she found that it had started to get ruined by wild pigs. When she returned home and her husband saw her, the first words he started to speak with her were about the garden and how it was getting on. His wife told him that the garden was being spoiled, for wild pigs had entered and had broken about eight to twelve stalks. When the husband heard this, he was displeased that day. The same day he collected the old hoe blades in his house and took them to the blacksmith telling him, "Old fellow, I am your comrade. I have no luck. My maize is being ruined by wild pigs. Make me some spears so that if I go to watch my garden, I can stab the pigs." The blacksmith set to work making the spears. When he had finished making them, he brought them to the man. When that man got the spears, he was pleased. Then that day he slept in his garden because the time that the wild pigs were coming was at night. He slept there for two weeks, but not even one wild pig came into his garden. When he saw that the wild pigs were no longer coming there, he got tired of sleeping in the garden for nothing and went home. At that time the maize had great ears. The maize ears were large and nearly ripe and during all that time no one was sleeping in the garden. One day the wild pigs did come and many of them ate much of the maize.

When the man said, "Let us go see the garden," he found that the entire garden was leveled. When he returned home, he fetched his spears and returned to the garden to lie in wait to hunt. He went to sleep and in the middle of the night he heard the wild pigs coming. Then he hid and in a little while the pigs entered the garden. Then he threw one of his spears which stabbed a pig. Then all the pigs ran away. At daybreak next morning he did not return home but took his spears and entered the forest on the mountainside where the pigs had run. He followed the trail of blood. When he climbed the mountain, he reached a large cave which all the pigs had entered. Then he entered the cave. He entered and followed the footprints one by one. As he continued tracking, he saw the cave widen and then there was light again, and he saw a country with mountains, villages, and gardens. So he hurried toward the light and suddenly found himself out of the cave. At the village where he went, he found the people indoors. He came up to a house which was filled with people and inside there was an ailing person groaning. He was told to enter, and when he did, he found his spear at the head of the bed of the sufferer. That one was that man's dead mother's brother and the person nursing him was that man's dead mother who had borne him. Then that man stood amazed and speechless. His mother told him as he stood there like that, "My child, now look, you have hurt your mother's brother. We are ghosts of the dead. If we stop eating in your garden, where shall we eat? These days all of us have been going daily to your garden, your mother's brother, grandfather, grandmother, and all your relatives who have gathered here. But oh, my child, you did not know that it was we who were in the garden. Look at your mother's brother! Look and see where the spear hurt him!" Then that man saw that truly all the people in the house were his relatives and that this really was his mother's brother. He said, "Mother's brother, I did not know that you were eating there." His mother's brother said to him, "Go home. If you see that your gardens are eaten by baboons, by monkeys, by wild pigs or other creatures such as guinea fowl, crows, small birds, and if you are guarding against this but the gardens are still being finished just the same, then go to see a diviner. Perhaps you will find

that it is the ghosts of the dead. If it is found to be the ghosts of the
dead, make beer and sweep our graves. But now I am getting well.
Here in the land of the spirits there is tobacco seed which you yourself don't know about. Go without shaving until your hair gets long,
and then when you shave put the hairs in the ground to be cultivated.
Then, when the rains come, that which sprouts there is tobacco.
Transplant it in the same way that you transplant tomatoes, and when
it is ripe the leaves are its wealth which you will be smoking or
selling.''

After he was told this by his mother's brother, the man returned by
the same path to the garden. He had grown thin out of fear at seeing
people who he knew had been dead for a long time. He told his wife
and children and relatives, but they did not believe that he was telling
the truth. And yet some said that perhaps it was true. So he shaved
and told them that where he had sown his hair tobacco plants would
sprout. Then when they saw the tobacco which he had said would
truly sprout there, they believed him somewhat. Then when the tobacco ripened, he told the people the many ways that they might use
it. Then after this had gone on for three years, tobacco was known to
many smokers and many persons were using it. Goats, hens, and all
kinds of things were brought to exchange for tobacco. Ever since then
many people have planted tobacco and it is known in every country.
That is the reason why the wild pigs of the ghosts of the dead can eat
not only the outlying gardens but even those in the heart of the fields.

The Second Tale: The Old Lady Who Picked Okra

Long ago there was an old lady (*mudala*) who used to pick okra
(*dilenda*).[3] One day the old lady went to pick okra while she was five
months pregnant. At that time some people were carrying the corpse
of a man who had just died. Then the people carrying the corpse
started talking with the old lady who was picking okra. At the same
time the corpse and the unborn child within the woman's womb were
talking with one another. The people greeted the old lady and then
she asked them, ''How did this man die?'' While she and they were
talking to one another about these things, the unborn child in her
womb and the corpse were also speaking. The corpse asked the
unborn child, ''You, my comrade, who are from the land of the
spirits, is it a good home there?'' The unborn child replied, ''The
land of the spirits is good if you were good in the world.'' Then the
unborn child asked the corpse, ''You, who are my comrade, how is

the world from which you come?'' The corpse replied, ''In the world
there is nothing attractive; in the world laughing is bad; frowning is
bad. It is like that.'' Then the people lifted the corpse up to take it to
the burying place, to its grave.

The child said to itself, ''I am yet to be born. I shall become mute
and not speak with people in the world in order to watch what is
happening which is bad.'' When the child was born, he did not cry;
he was mute. He stayed at his home until he reached about ten years
of age. Then one day his mother and father went to cultivate and told
him, their child who was not speaking, to stay at home. Then two
people came, a man and a woman with a child on her back. Then
these said, ''This is the boy who is not speaking. Let us enter the
house and steal.''

The boy stood aside, and they passed in and took many things.
When they were leaving the man said, ''I'll stab this boy with my
spear.'' But the woman refused, saying, ''Oh, I don't like things like
that!'' But the man seized his spear in order to stab the mute boy, but
the spear stabbed the child on the wife's back instead. The child died
and they were very upset. The woman said, ''You, my husband, you
killed our child!'' The man took the dead, bloody child and put it into
the hands of the mute boy. Then he made a commotion saying, ''The
mute boy has killed our child.'' The people arrived to see what was
happening. When they saw, they felt sorry for the mute boy who was
saying nothing there with the child which they thought he had killed.
Because killing people is a serious matter, they sent for the chief. The
chief was very angry and asked, ''How was this small child killed?''
He asked, but there was no reply. Then the chief told the parents of
the child, ''Go, bury it and return tomorrow.'' But the mute boy
remained at the chief's. The chief told his warriors to put the one who
was left behind into a small hut filled with thorns. The boy slept there
bearing this discomfort until morning. In the morning he called the
warriors and then he said, ''In the world there is nothing good. If you
see something, do not say anything bad, just watch. These people
came to steal. I gave them a chance, but the man took his spear to
stab me. His wife was the one who protected me, but they killed their
child which was on her back.''

When the warriors heard him saying these words, they told the
chief. Then the chief also heard from the boy himself. Then they
called the couple and said to them, ''You are liars. You killed the
child yourselves. Now you are trying to kill this mute boy as well.
Now both of you are fit to die yourselves.'' So they killed them, and
the mute then continued to speak like other people.

The Third Tale: The Jealous Grandmother

Once there was a man and a woman, and the woman bore a child. One day they went to weed in their garden. The woman was accustomed to going with her child to the garden and then while they were working they would keep the baby at the foot of a *musingisi* tree. The *musingisi* is a tree which is eaten by donkeys, which like its bark. There those two talked as they went along hoeing, first talking about one thing and then about another while the child played there at the tree. Then an eagle (*dinumba*) passed by flapping its wings, and when it saw that baby at the foot of the tree, it decided to catch it and take it off. Then the parents of the child heard it crying above, but they were helpless. When the mother reached the tree and found the child gone, she cried. Her husband asked her why she was crying. She said, "The child has gone off with an eagle. That is why we heard wings flapping overhead."

Then her husband gave the war cry. The people gathered and asked why they had been called. The man told them, "I and my wife are crying because an eagle passed by and carried off our child which did not cry out until we heard it overhead. Then we looked for it at the tree and found it gone." Then all the people told each other to take position for a search, because the child could not have gone far. "Perhaps you will find the eagle before it starts to eat the child." Then all the people divided, some going to the bush, some to the forest, some to the ponds. Luckily, those who went to the ponds met the eagle with the child. When it saw them, it entered the water along with the child. Then those people returned home and beat the drum. The people who had been searching all returned. They told them, "We met the eagle at a pond and it had the child with it, but when it saw us, it went into the water along with the child."

Their leader told them, "Now, nine people go into the water." So nine people entered the water. The journey into the water took many days. But on the morning of the third day they found the eagle. But there inside the water it was no longer an eagle but had turned into a human being. Then they asked it how it could travel on through the water like that. Then it told them, "I am not an eagle. No! I am the grandmother of this child. Its mother is my child. When I died, I did not rot, but went here into the water. Then if you want me to come out, I come out as an eagle. When I came out, I saw my daughter hoeing with her husband while they had left the child at the tree. So I said to myself, 'I'll take my grandchild and pinch it so that it cries every day.' But I found that people still did not understand why it was crying. So I took the child off. You go and tell them it was with its grandmother. When you see them, tell them that when a person bears a child, she is to give it the name of its grandfather or grandmother. If it is not given such a name, you will see that it is troubled by the dead so that it is crying every day.'' (cf. chapter 6)

THE RELATION OF THE LIVING
TO THE DEAD

For Kaguru, ideas concerning the ghosts of the dead cannot be separated from those concerning matrilineal clans. They see a clan as a group of men and women descended matrilineally from one ancestress who lived in the distant past (*katali*) when Kaguru first arrived in their present homeland. A clan (*ikungugo*, pl. *makungugo*, or *lukolo*, sing. and pl.) has a beginning but no end, for new members are constantly being born into it. All members of one clan are considered to be of one blood and descended from one womb. In practice, any particular ritual does not involve all living members of any one clan, scattered widely over all Ukaguru. Instead, it involves the members of a subclan or lineage. Kaguru speak about any group within a clan as a *nyumba* (house, sing. and pl.), applying this term to one household, to a matrilineage in which relationship may be traced, or to a group of matrilineages which cannot always trace their ties with one another but which recognize one matrilineage as senior to the rest and therefore entitled to conduct ritual toward common ancestors recognized by all members of this group. This last type of ''house'' is what I term a subclan. All of the members of a subclan recognize a senior matrilineage, but they may not be in full agreement about ranking other matrilineages junior to this. These groups are specified relatively as *nyumba ng'hulu* (senior house), *nyumba yagati* (intermediate house), and *nyumba yasiwanda* (junior house), or are designated by their immediate ancestors or living heads.[4] In some cases, Kaguru can trace genealogical links for such groups; in others, they cannot. These subclans or ritual groups are larger than the groups involved in inheritance of political and economic rights, that is, matrilineages.

In any Kaguru clan there are a number of subclans, each propitiating a different set of ancestors. The members of any one of these may be scattered over all Ukaguru, although the majority tend to be concentrated in one locale. Within any subclan, propitiation for the group is carried out by the senior members of the senior matrilineage, sometimes regardless of sex or age, although an elderly male is the preferred person. Such ritual is prompted by need for rainmaking, expiation of breaches in marriage regulations and sexual prohibitions, and treatment of difficulties which have not been solved through propitiation of more immediate ancestors by those directly involved. In addition to such subclan ritual, a leader of each household and matrilineage may consult diviners and perform small libations to immediate ancestors for minor difficulties.

Although most ritual activities involve groups smaller than a clan, I present Kaguru beliefs in terms of clan units, because Kaguru themselves speak in terms of such larger units, in which they see their social system as ideally functioning, not in terms of these smaller units by which the system at present actually works.

A Kaguru clan is composed of two broad, interdependent categories of persons: (1) those now alive and inhabiting the world (*chilungu*), in lands (*muyisi*) which compose Ukaguru; (2) ghosts (*misimu*, sing. *musimu*) of those no longer alive and those who have not yet lived, both inhabiting the world of spirits (*kusimu*).[5]

Kaguru believe that the energy or substance animating a living person comes from the land of spirits. In a living person this is called *chidoga* and might be translated as "life-spirit."

Kaguru consider the heart the center of feeling and consciousness and, if the life-spirit must be located, it would be there, although Kaguru themselves are not specific about this. Upon death the living spirit is transformed into an ancestral ghost, a *musimu*, which cannot be seen in the world of the living although it may temporarily take the form of an animal or a bird. In being a ghost, a spirit has more strength than when confined in a living body. There is a vaguely defined period between the state of living and being a spirit, a condition occupied by the recently dead and by a fetus (*ingogo*) or child before its umbilical cord has fallen off. These latter are not fully human; they cannot be named, and, if they die, they cannot be properly mourned. A child is considered a living being in the full sense only when certain ceremonies have been performed after the loss of the umbilical cord. Likewise, a newly dead person does not immediately become an ancestral ghost, and is hesitant to leave the world of the living for that of the spirits. After the spirit has left the body (*ifimba*, corpse), the bodiless spirit hovers near its former home before being sent back to the land of the spirits through a postfuneral ceremony (*ng'hungusi*, forgetting). Before this ceremony the spirit of a recently dead person may disturb the sleep or peace of mind of a living kinsman. The negative aspects of this intermediate stage before ghosthood may be seen in such indirect terms for dying (*kufa*, to die) as *kwaga* (to be lost; *kaga*, the lost ones, the dead; *mateto*, the finished ones; *kabanika*, he is put into disorder, dies).

Kaguru ideas about the condition of the ghosts and the region which they inhabit are vague.[6] However, a few points seem fairly clear. The land of the spirits is difficult to reach, is far away, and is above, often associated with mountainsides, or else beneath, in bodies of water. It is associated vaguely with the west, although corpses are buried with their feet pointing to the east because people arrived in Ukaguru after an eastward trek. Some Kaguru also say that the land of the spirits is a dark place. The beings of this land live in villages and conduct affairs similar to those on earth.[7] The most influential persons on earth are correspondingly the most influential ghosts; that world, too, has its leaders and followers. In contrast, children or immature persons cannot become propitiated ghosts since they were not full social beings when alive. Similarly, convicted witches, executed recidivists, and those dying polluting deaths lose fully human status and cannot become ghosts.

Ghosts have some human appetites and depend for nourishment upon the sacrifices made by their living kin. These ghostly appetites are not essentially for material goods themselves but rather because such sacrifices provide proof that ghosts are not forgotten. The ghosts' desire and need to be remembered tie them to living kin. Also, ghosts miss the young who have just left them to be born. Desiring these young to return, the ghosts must be soothed and consoled for this loss. Finally, the ancestors are linked with the living through their desire to preserve traditional morality. Breaches of traditional customs offend and disturb them, preventing rest (*kugoha*, to sleep). In their normal quiescent state ghosts are referred to as *wagona* (the ones who sleep).

Ghosts depend upon the living, but the living depend upon ghosts as well. The newborn come from the land of the spirits, who must be comforted for their loss. It is thus through these spirits that the perpetuity of the clan is possible. The living are further dependent upon ghosts for supernatural aid during trouble. Some misfortunes, of course, are caused by ghosts who are disturbed by the immorality of living kin or by being forgotten. A quarrel between kin may end with the intervention of ancestral ghosts who cause difficulties until the disagreement is settled. Other misfortunes, especially extremely serious ones involving many people, may be caused by God or may simply be considered inexplicable.[8] But just as God's motives are often unknowable, because of his distance and difference from humans, so too God is not directly approached but is contacted through the ancestors. As one Christian Kaguru said, "Our dead are like Roman Catholic saints who take your part seeking help from God. He listens to them even when he will not hear you." One Kaguru told me that only Christians use the second person to address God, rather than referring to him in the third person while addressing the ghosts.

There are two means by which the living and ghosts are linked: through rites of propitiation, held by the living at graves of certain ancestors; and through bestowing the names of certain ancestors upon the living. Kaguru determine this by consulting diviners, who are the crucial means of interpreting

the desires and aims of ghosts. Without divination, certain difficulties would
suggest that perhaps the ghosts are troubled, but Kaguru cannot be sure, for
such difficulties might also be caused by God or witches.

In most cases, Kaguru are concerned with ancestral propitiation only when
troubles arise. Even rainmaking is not performed every year but only when
rain seems unlikely to fall on time or in the amounts desired. As long as there
is no trouble, the ghosts are sleeping peacefully and there is no need to disturb
them. It is best to leave well enough alone. If trouble arises, the ancestors
are a possible source. In some cases, Kaguru do not wait for punishment from
the ghosts; instead, they immediately hold the required expiatory propitiation
in hope of preventing misfortune. Such a ceremony also reconciles the various
persons involved. Yet these account for few rites held to propitiate ghosts.

If a Kaguru or his family is plagued by difficulties, he visits a diviner
(*muganga*), who uses divination (*maselu* or *mulamulo*) to determine the cause.
If the cause of the trouble is divined to be ghosts, it must be determined which
ghosts are the cause, and what must be done to remove their annoyance. Any
ancestral ghost may be a source of trouble or help, but emphasis is upon
matrilineal kin. A Kaguru has perpetual ties with all members of his matrilineage (theoretically, with all members of the clan), and although Kaguru
have heavy obligations to a father, they have restricted obligations to a father's
matrilineage.[9] Unlike some other African societies, Kaguru do not consider
one to have obligations to the ghosts propitiated by a spouse.

Kaguru rites of propitiation (*tambiko* or *mufiko*) involve clearing the graves
of dead ancestors (*kushangila kufilalo*, to sweep a grave) and the libation or
aspersion (*kunyaga*) of beer and perhaps tobacco and flour. Such rites also
may involve the slaughter of a chicken or, in serious cases, a sheep. Blood
of the slain is poured on the grave, but the creature itself is consumed by
others than those needing the propitiation. Kaguru graves are marked by a
few stones and are untended and uncleared except at propitiation. Good Christians try to bury their dead in one place, often near a church, and among them
propitiation is not allowed. Only the most senior person in a group may make
propitiation, and, in serious cases, this involves the senior member of the
senior matrilineage of the subclan. Serious difficulties necessitate propitiation
at graves of long-dead ancestors whose powers are recognized. Today it is
mainly in terms of this common recognition of propitiatory rites that such
subclans are defined. During such rites, it is not necessary for all concerned
to attend, only the senior member performing the rites.[10]

Let us consider one example of a propitiatory prayer:

> Ancestral ghost, the children at home are ill.
> They call Chibaibai's name for good health.
> We give this beer to you and to your comrades.

It is only a little, but you must be like the *chimote*-finches
which cluster on a single stalk of millet to feed.

This prayer mentions the name of only one ancestor, Chibaibai. This is considered sufficient to include members of the entire clan. The ancestor is asked to bring his comrades (*wayago*, your comrades) with him. Sometimes Kaguru prayers mention several prominent kinsmen, sometimes, as here, only one. Sometimes a prayer asks the indulgence of all those ghosts whose names have been forgotten. Propitiations include all deceased members of a clan, not merely a matrilineage. One sophisticated Kaguru compared such ritual to Remembrance Day or Memorial Day services for dead soldiers held by Europeans and Americans: "You put flowers on the graves of a few soldiers who died here in Tanganyika and then shoot rifles over them, but you do this to show that you remember all your dead soldiers everywhere, not just those here in Tanganyika." Kaguru use a symbolic shorthand by which a few represent a large number. Likewise, the sacrifice itself is in no proportion to the number or importance of those propitiated. The dead are compared to many birds clustering upon a single millet stalk,[11] a small portion sufficing for many. Here is a second example of such prayers:

You, along with your comrades! We have come!
We have brought you this sheep.
Our children are sick.
Sleep peacefully so that our children gain health.

Here, too, one ghost is addressed (though not named) to represent the collectivity.

Sometimes a Kaguru child does not thrive, or continually cries for no apparent reason. One likely cause is that an ancestral ghost is disturbed at losing the child from the land of the spirits whence it came. A diviner is consulted and, if this is divined to be the cause, the name of the disturbed ghost is given the ailing child. The disturbing ancestor is often a classificatory (or actual) grandparent. Troubling a child by a ghost is called *ndege* (omen, bird).

When a child first emerges from the confinement house, it is given several names (see the preceding chapter).[12] If it later becomes ill, another name may be given, though the previous ones are not relinquished. Further names are taken after initiation, at puberty. Names of those in one's grandparents' generation are usually selected, and it is almost always grandparents who bestow them. These are the two groups living nearest the spirits, those most recently coming from them and those soonest to return.[13] This mutuality of alternate generations and their relation to the continued round of death and birth give added force and sentiment to perpetuating names.

THE TALES CONSIDERED

I now consider the three tales presented at the outset of this chapter in order to discuss some metaphors used to imagine the dead.

The first tale: The main themes here are the importance of propitiation for soothing ghosts and the benevolent nature of such ghosts once they are assuaged. The tale opens by emphasizing that the man has spared no pains tending his garden and that if it is violated by wild pigs, this cannot be explained as negligence, though he was eventually negligent. His dead mother's brother notes, "If you guard against all this, but the gardens are finished just the same, then see a diviner." The wrath of ancestral ghosts explains the inexplicable.

Although ghosts may assume the shapes of different animals and birds, they are here presented as wild pigs (*igubi*, pl. *singubi*). Such animals have an important significance for Kaguru. The word for the initiation of women into adult life is *igubi*, and in such ceremonies the wild pig symbolizes the womb of a woman, her generative capacities. A related symbol of perpetuity is blood (*sakame*), and it is through a spoor of blood that the hunter tracks his ancestral ghosts. Another symbol is the cave, which Kaguru use to denote the vagina or womb, and it is through a cave that the hunter passes to reach the land of spirits. Finally, the cave itself is located in the mountains, which are traditionally associated with spirits. These motifs of wild pigs, blood, cave, and mountains reinforce the theme of the perpetuity of the matri-clan.

When the man attacks the wild pigs with his spears, he wounds one, which is in reality his mother's brother, the authoritative person within his matrilineage. This may express the man's disregard for the needs of his matrilineage, perhaps his failure to remember the ghosts through propitiation, or even his failure to respect some rules. The attack may express resentment and aggressive, ambivalent feelings which any junior at times feels toward those in authority over him. These two possible interpretations are consistent with and complementary to one another.

The injured ghost's concern with his nephew's conduct may be further indicated by the nephew's spear being placed at the head of his uncle's bed. Traditionally Kaguru placed an object there so that they might dream about it and thereby fathom its significance. Here the mother's brother is concerned with the bad conduct of his nephew, exemplified by the spearing. He wants to understand what happened and to make spiritual contact with the nephew so such action will not recur. The wild pigs feeding on their living kin's maize expresses the ghosts' dependence upon the living. Yet without divination, the man could not have realized that the marauding wild pigs were his kin. His spearing them can only be considered hostile if taken to symbolize some deeper, unspecified grievance toward these ghosts or toward matrilineal duties. Another interpretation would make the uncle's remonstrance ludicrous since it would be only natural for a man to defend his garden against pests. The motif of the spear itself may be important in this respect, for it is a sexual symbol, explicitly used as such by Kaguru. Associating the spear with masculine attributes (and the spears were transformed by the smith from hoes, a form of bridewealth), we may relate it to establishment of a household and fathering children for another clan. These masculine activities eventually set a man at odds with his own matrilineage.[14]

Shaving the hair is a difficult motif. Shaving is associated with most Kaguru rites of passage. In marriage, rebirth is represented by shaving, and Kaguru themselves speak of newly married people being like newborn children. In this tale, shaving is complexly tied to the gift of tobacco, but also to the man's emergence (rebirth) from the land of the dead. Tobacco, along with beer, may be used as a sacrifice to the dead. The gift of tobacco affirms that ghosts, when properly respected and remembered, are sources of good. (I avoid speculation on the possible liminal substantiality of tobacco for want of any supportive data.)

The second tale: The main themes here are the two contrasting aspects of beings as spirits (ghosts and unborn) and as living, and the perpetuity of the clan expressed by cyclic exchanges of unborn and dead. The overriding impression of this tale is pessimism about life and human nature, which seems typical of much Kaguru thought. That the next world is a place of punishments and reward (as mentioned here) may be partly due to Christian influence, but this is consistent with Kaguru belief. Traditionally, Kaguru do not speak of heaven or hell but do say a person socially prominent in life will be an important ghost, whereas one of little account will become an ineffectual one. The worst persons do not become ancestral ghosts at all, since they no longer qualify as fully human. These either cease to exist or wander about as evil spirits.

The division into living and spirit worlds is neatly made by the characters' contrasting conversations. The old woman talks to the men carrying the corpse's bier, while the unborn child talks to the corpse. Each conversation is unheard by the others. The link between the unborn and the corpse is indicated by their addressing one another as "comrade" (*miyangu*, my comrade). Just as ghosts depend on the living for propitiation and remembrance, so too the corpse and the unborn child physically depend upon the living: the corpse is borne on a bier carried by men, and the unborn is borne inside the woman's womb. The word *sanda* can mean a cloth for carrying an infant, a womb, and a shroud.

The muteness of the child suggests the transitional period between its emergence from the land of the spirits and its delayed assumption of an active part among the living.

The third tale: This emphasizes the importance of propitiatory naming in assuaging ghosts and in expressing the solidarity and continuity of matri-clans.

The association of the ghost with a bird is not surprising; in Kaguru tales birds often appear as instruments of fortune (Beidelman 1974c; cf. Werner 1933:87–91). The motif of an eagle (*dinumba*) snatching away a child fits in with Kaguru beliefs that a newly born child is endangered by a bateleur eagle (*chipunga, Terathropis ecaudatus*) until certain rites have been performed. Unfortunately, a larger type of eagle rather than a bateleur is mentioned here. Nonetheless, the motif may relate to the vague and dangerous transitional period between a person's change from the world of the spirits to that of the living.

The entry into the land of spirits through a pool is another Kaguru theme common to many Bantu peoples (cf. Werner 1933:93–95). The mirror surface of a pool reflects another world. Water is interpreted by Kaguru as a symbol of fertility, the matrilineage, and life-giving powers in general. That nine people seek out the child in the pond may allude to gestation.

CONCLUSION

Kaguru can imagine the dead only in terms of what they know of the living; they admit that they cannot really know the full nature of the dead, either in terms of their mode of existence or in terms of their true and manifold wants. Consequently, the dead both resemble the living yet in some powerful and troubling ways differ from them. The dead are a powerful amalgam of the future of both the elderly and the unborn, as well as being guardians of the status quo among the living. They are older than the old, younger than the young, and both dangerous and necessary, like those in their prime. They embody the rectitude and authority (but also the greed) of the elderly, the capricious, demanding dependence of the young, and also some of that com-bination of moral threat and unfathomable deceit evinced by the living with whom one constantly contends. These widely different social attributes are believably combined and sustained for several reasons. The dead often appear to respond to pleas and gifts just as do living kin. The dead are omniscient; no wrong or unfulfilled obligations escape their notice and eventual punish-ment until put right. The dead act this way because their peace depends upon the goodness and justice of relations between their living kin, and in this respect they epitomize moral benevolence and rectitude, although their ulti-mate purpose is their selfish desire to be at peace. Finally, like some selfish adults and many demanding children, the dead become angry if ignored and periodically crave gifts and attention, though the living would be wise to leave well enough alone and steer clear of the dead so long as they remain quiet. These seemingly contradictory and ambivalently felt qualities may all be held for the dead since, unlike the living, they can only make themselves known through episodic departures from everyday order, albeit the living may themselves have set disruption in motion by their own bad acts. Thus each manifestation of the dead has its own social (moral) context. Furthermore, the veiled motives of the dead can be discerned only through divination, which itself is an imperfect searching through signs read by an expert who could at times be wrong. It is through trial and error in myriad situations that the changing aims and feelings of the dead may be known.

Reviewing these qualities of the dead and the means Kaguru have for discerning them, one finds that the dead embody another mode of the same contradictions and conflicts that disturb and absorb the living. Kaguru constantly struggle to meet the conflicting and competing demands of their own kin while faced with a world of limited and unreliable resources. In a society where loyalties and demands have so many countervailing qualities, these are often best expressed indirectly and guardedly. Likewise, the dead's needs and wants involve ceaseless deciphering before the dead may be supplicated and allayed. Kaguru view the dead through a glass darkly, just as their judgment of the living is also often blurred. The price of membership in social life is ever negotiated and redeemed, and one's accounts with the dead are never settled. The dead reflect these strains in their own contradictory and difficult influences, both benevolent and disruptive, which are meant to reinforce social order but at times contribute to uneasiness and recrimination as well.

Having considered how Kaguru picture ancestors, I now consider the ways they attempt to respond to them. I begin to examine ritual as metaphor expressing how social relations, human appetites, certain persons and things, correspond to the ambiguous and ambivalent relations first imaginatively represented by those between the living and the dead. The more tangible aspects of this world are dragooned to manipulate and represent relations to a less palpable one.

NOTES

1. This chapter is a revised version of 1964b; there the original Kaguru texts are provided.

2. This is a popular tale among Kaguru. For another version, cf. Beidelman 1976:47–50.

3. *Mudala* means "old lady" but here is a polite address not referring to age. *Dilenda* (okra) is a creeper collected for edible leaves. A branching creeper may relate to Kaguru images of matriliny, since they compare lineages to decumbent vines.

4. A lineage consists of matrilineal kin who trace their relationships genealogically. A senior lineage is one recognized by other lineages as descending from the genealogically oldest of several sisters. This lineage is acknowledged as holding the exclusive rights to perform certain ritual for its own and junior lineages. An intermediate lineage is descended matrilineally from a sister younger than the ancestress of the senior lineage, but senior to ancestresses of other related lineages. It is therefore recognized as senior by some related lineages but itself acknowledges some lineage as its superior in authority. A junior lineage is one that has no lineage junior to it but recognizes lineages holding authority over its ritual affairs. Senior, intermediate, and junior statuses are thus reckoned in relative terms.

5. Some Kaguru speak of this spirit world as *ahela*, from the Arabic Swahili *ahera* (next world).

6. Kopytoff's (1971) assertion about lack of interest by Bantu-language-speaking peoples is not so, at least in this case. His remarks conflict with material for many Bantu peoples besides Kaguru.

7. Mawinza, a Lugulu, writing of his people, who are closely related to the Kaguru and who neighbor them, states: ". . . the Bantu spirit-world is inhabited not by mere shades but by people who betake themselves to their old pursuits, amuse themselves with their old frolics and beguile the time with gossip and good fellowship of kindred spirits" (1968:246).

8. It is difficult to determine whether Kaguru traditionally worshipped God (*mulungu*) (also called *bode* or *mateke*, soft one), but he receives considerable attention today. To all but the most sophisticated Kaguru Christians, he resembles the unreasonable God of Job, whose actions and wrath remain inexplicable, far more than he resembles the forgiving God of the New Testament.

9. A Kaguru man believes that after he is dead he will gain comfort from the propitiations of both his sons and his sisters' sons, but these persons' children (his grandchildren) will be represented only by his sisters' daughter's children (his classificatory grandchildren), who will continue to propitiate his ghost. Perpetual propitiation is exclusively by the matri-clan. If a matrilineage died out, its members would still be propitiated indirectly through rites of other matrilineages of the clan.

10. In expiation of a breach of sexual prohibitions and in making rain the actual ritual is not performed by the clan, but supervision and organization are controlled by the senior member of the senior matrilineage involved (see next chapter).

11. Kaguru offerings involve small amounts of invariably inferior or damaged goods. It is said this is to make the propitiated feel pity.

12. Paternal kin would never be allowed to assist at birth. This was the exclusive right of matrilineal kinswomen of the mother.

13. Kaguru are not much concerned with great-grandparent and great-grandchild relations, since so few live long enough to hold such status.

14. In this text the spear is fashioned from hoes, metal being a common Kaguru metaphor for bridewealth. In another version of this tale (Beidelman 1976:47–50) the spear belongs to the man's wife's brother. Allusion to affinal loyalties seems likely.

CHAPTER 8.

Kinship, Pollution, and Death

Days and moments quickly flying,
blend the living with the dead . . .
Edward Caswell, *Days' Moments Quickly Flying*

Birth, and copulation, and death,
That's all the facts when you come to brass tacks . . .
T. S. Eliot, *Sweeny Agonistes*

In the preceding chapter I discussed ways Kaguru imagine the dead and their
influence upon the living. Here I consider the ways Kaguru ritually associate
death with other biological and social processes—sexuality, marriage, and
affinity.[1] By making these associations Kaguru fit death into a broader frame
of human and social cycles. They imbue key but problematical social relations
(*utani*) with the same dangerous and powerful qualities which they imagine
about death and dying. These then become both embodiments of those forces
and also means to manipulate and control them. This is possible because
Kaguru culture and society conform to broad principles underlying apparently
disparate features. We see this in rituals of pollution, where notions of kinship
and politics are colored by complex associations with life and death, im-
mortality and mortality, order and disorder.

Each Kaguru stands in a relation of *utani* toward persons called *watani*
(sing. *mutani*). These or similar terms and practices are found over a wide
area of East Africa[2] and are generally spoken of as "joking partners," person
who stand in reciprocal "joking relations" with one another, though jocularity
is only one aspect of the relationship, and not even the most significant.
Watani figure prominently in removing pollution incurred through death, certain prohibited sexual relations, and other misconduct of the living. All these
polluting events require rituals enjoined by ancestral ghosts. The principles
by which *utani* relations are linked relate to patterns of marriage, so that one
cannot fully understand *utani* without understanding Kaguru notions about
affinity. To explicate these matters I first discuss various rites conducted by

watani to show how Kaguru ideas about kinship and sexuality are integrally related to ideas about pollution and death.

RITUALS AND DEATH

As I indicated in the preceding chapter, propitiation must be made to regain order and harmony when the dead are disturbed. In such situations, those whose ancestral ghosts are roused contact their *watani* and request that they make sacrifices. Supervision, arrangements, and payments for rites are the responsibility of elders of the lineages or households involved, but the actual rites are conducted by *watani*, who risk exposure to the uncleanness (*iha*) or disorder of the disturbed dead. *Watani* sweep (*kushagila*) graves clean, removing the overgrowth of weeds. Graves are always in the bush. Tidying graves achieves a corresponding rehabilitation of the abode of ghosts in the land of the dead. *Watani* slay the sacrificial sheep, goat, or fowls, and sprinkle blood, beer, tobacco, or flour over the grave. The creature slain is often black, a color associated with rain, power, and strength. *Watani* eat the sacrifice, which on no account may be consumed by those for whom offerings were made.

Watani stand between the living and the dead, much as the ghosts of the dead stand between their living kin and distant God. *Watani* and ghosts occupy ambiguous liminal zones that are dangerous yet necessary to connect categories ordinarily separated, as shown below:

Ordinary sphere of humans	Medial or liminal sphere	Sphere of the supernatural
living persons	ghosts	God
living kin	*watani*	ghostly kin (*misimu*)
settlement	bush	land of ghosts (*kusimu*)
land	mountainside	sky
life	burials and funerals	supernatural afterlife
path from one's village	crossroads	path from another village

Kaguru behavior toward supernatural beings parallels their ambivalent behavior toward *watani*. Kaguru offer defective goods to ghosts and thus indirectly to God, seeing this as abuse by which propitiated beings are shamed or coerced into helping the living. So too *watani* partners exchange abuse and insults. It also could be said that ghosts abuse the living, not keeping to their own land but repeatedly invading this world to cause difficulties. So too visiting *watani* are persons unpleasantly "out of place," ignoring the ordinary prohibitions against sexual indecency and disregarding rights in property. They make coarse and obscene sexual remarks, accuse their joking partners of crimes and vices, and seize a joking partner's goods without recompense or permission.

The propitiatory rites where *watani* serve may be divided into (a) calendrical rites associated with the clan dominant in an area and similar rites responding to natural disasters involving that region, (b) rites counteracting illness, sterility, and other afflictions within a matrilineage, and (c) rites related to death.

CALENDRICAL RITES

Before the onset of the rains, while Kaguru are clearing and cultivating their land, representatives of local settlements convene at grave sites in the bush to propitiate ancestral ghosts of the matrilineage dominant in their area. A small shelter (*chijumba mulungu*, hut of God) is built. Fires have been extinguished in homes, and people are supposed to remain sexually continent. At the conclusion of these rites, *watani* kindle new fire with firesticks, from which the household hearths in the area are relit. Between extinguishing household fires and their rekindling is a liminal time period renewing a year. During drought, such rites are more elaborate then otherwise, rejuvenating the land, weakened through cultivation but also through quarrels and ill will. In addition to slaying a black sheep, *watani* scatter flour and beer, preferably of poor quality. Even the containers in which these are brought should be damaged.

AFFLICTION WITHIN A KIN GROUP

Sacrifices are performed to assuage the dead disturbed by the misdeeds of the living, or sometimes annoyed for being ignored too long. These rites purify the lineage of moral pollution,[3] which Kaguru imagine in terms of excessive heat and agitation as well as a mixing or tangling of things. This is likened to the kinds of pollution generated by sexuality, the spilling of blood, and defecation. Ritual purification is a kind of cooling (*kuhosa*), loosening, or disentangling (*kulegusa*). While all sexuality is polluting, even though both pleasurable and necessary, male sexuality is somewhat less dangerous than that of women, if only because women are periodically unclean due to menstruation, regardless of whether they have sexual relations or not. Of course, moral pollution extends far beyond sexuality to include all unjust and selfish conduct toward kin, but the sexual image informs these other spheres.

One type of ritual of affliction illustrates how moral and sexual pollution are combined. This involves purification of sexual offenses (though never clan incest, which is tantamount to witchcraft and uncleansable). When Kaguru speak of *watani* cleansing a sexual offense, they refer to a broken pro-

hibition (*muhilo*) against relations between affines. Kaguru forbid sexual relations with a member of a spouse's clan. Such offenses are not uncommon,
and so long as they are undetected the kin of the two culprits face supernatural
danger, such as illness, sterility, or even death, caused by offended ghosts.
Detection may be difficult, since the offenders have little reason to confess,
inasmuch as they themselves are not endangered supernaturally. If they are
found out, the offending couple pay fines and undergo a cleansing (*kuhosa*)
rite (*nhemera*) to remove the taint (*muhasa*, mixture; *kuhasa*, to mix).[4] Offenders are taken to the bush by their *watani*, who have been given a black
sheep by the kin of the offending man. Kaguru say, "Those who spoiled
(*wabanile*) things like that, the man and woman, sit together and then the
watani take the sheep still alive and strike its head against their loins." The
watani kill the sheep and twine its intestines (*lutembu*) around the couple's
loins. Then they smear the two with the feces and undigested contents of the
sheep's stomach (*ufu*, feces, trash). They asperse the offenders' loins with
water mixed with *luhosa* (from *kuhosa*, to cool, to purify) herbs (*Crassocephalum bojeri*). As they do this, the *watani* recite the wrongs done by the
offenders and ask them to "leave their badness" (*kalamba uwihi wakwe*). A
mutani then cuts the twined intestines, separating the two offenders, and says,
"I cut this intestine that you do not again couple. If you couple, may your
intestines be cut out as I have cut this!" Then the *watani* butcher the meat
and take it off to be eaten. Often they cut up the sheepskin to make wristlets
(*mikowa*) to be worn on the left wrists of those matrilineal kin now free
(*digowa*, peaceful) from the supernatural dangers brought on by the offense.
Until these rites are accomplished, the clans which are mixed have been
spoiled, broken up, disturbed (*kubanigwe*).[5]

RITES RELATED TO DEATH

Watani play prominent roles in all acts and rites related to death (*ufa*), which
is even more polluting than sexuality, which it parallels. *Watani* slew suspected witches in the bush. They executed recidivists and those guilty of clan
incest, killing close kin, or sleeping with the wife of a maternal uncle or
sister's son. *Watani* also disposed of lepers; some claim the term *matana*
(leprosy) derives from this association. *Watani* were required to dispose of
inauspicious children (*chigego*, pl. *figego*), usually strangling them so as not
to spill blood.

Watani perform important rites at burials and funerals. To reduce pollution,
burial occurs as soon after death as possible. Some Kaguru joke that in the
past fear of the dead caused persons to be rushed into their graves before they
actually died. *Watani* wash the clothing (*isua*) of the corpse before returning

it to the heirs. They bathe the corpse and wrap it in new, plain cloth (*sanda*), preferably black or white. Formerly skins were used. This shroud parallels the cloth in which an infant is wrapped and carried by its mother.

All members of the deceased's hamlet refrain from work and open pleasures on the day of death. Close kin of the deceased should neither work nor have sexual relations until completion of the mortuary rites, which may last several days or even weeks. Immediate kin remain confined within the house during the first day of mourning (*lukala*). Mourners should not attend to their personal appearance, not cutting or grooming their hair or shaving or anointing their pubic regions. They should cry "*Ifa! Ifa!*" (He's dead! He's dead!) from within the house.

On the day of death the corpse is taken away by *watani*, who dig a grave and bury it. Children are hastily removed from the scene and told that the deceased was devoured by a monster (*dikoko*).[6] The corpse, "the broken up one," is sometimes referred to as the *nhembo* (elephant). The duty of the *watani* is "to tie up the elephant" (*kuhaga inhembo*). For their labors they receive cloth and a few fowl to cool them from the pollution of death.

If the deceased was a pregnant woman, the *watani* must cut the fetus from the womb before burying her. If this is not done, the woman's husband, lover, or, if they cannot be found, her family must later give a pregnant sheep to their *watani*, who slay the animal, remove the fetus, and eat both. The sheep serves as proxy to the corpse, and until the rites are performed the kinswomen of the woman's clan risk sterility or bearing sickly children. When the *watani* have completed a burial, they wash and turn the water-pot they used upside down over the new grave. This marks the head of the grave, where later propitiations should be made. Between the burial and the final mortuary rites the mourners and *watani* hold a wake (*wiku* or *choto*). The male kin and *watani* sit outside the house of the deceased. It is especially important for paternal kinsmen to be there, since they are the proper spokesmen to greet other mourners and explain the circumstances of the death. At night they build a fire (*moto*, hence perhaps the term *choto*) and cluster about it. Meanwhile the women remain indoors wailing and consoling one another. This is the only time, except at male initiation camps, when men willingly spend nights outside their hearths. Paternal kin and *watani* recount the grisly particulars of the death and remark on and criticize the conduct of the kin. In this *watani* are said to be like witches, since they say what no one ordinarily would say.

A wake is followed by a mortuary feast (*mutanga*), formally terminating mourning. Sometimes this is not held for several weeks, depending upon when kin living far away are able to attend and when enough food and beer have been prepared for a crowd. At a ceremony (*ng'husi* or *ng'hungusi*, emergence) held shortly before this feast, the deceased is fully separated from the living and becomes a true ghost. At this time, and no longer than four days after the death, the deceased's immediate kin are brought out (*kulafa*, come out) from their house by *watani* and reintegrated into society. They give the *watani* a black sheep (*ngholo mhitu*), which is slain. The *watani* mix its chyme and water together in a pot and add straw from the thatch near the entry to the deceased's house. Some say they also add *luhosa* herbs. They asperse (*kunyaga*) the house, all objects inside, and the mourners, who have been "tied up" (*wafiligwa*) in mourning within, in order to release them (*kuwahosa*). Then a *mutani* brings maize, an ax, a hoe, and a jar of water inside the house. He presents these goods and tools associated with the occupants' everyday chores, a hoe or ax to a man, a water jar, grindstone, or maize flour to women, and shows them how to use these. A *mutani* then takes the men and women by the hands (*yekuwakola mikono*) and leads them outside. All of this is imagined as a rebirth and is compared to initiation and marriage, where initiates and newlyweds are also treated like newly borns who must learn the social rudiments.[7]

After the rites of separation are completed, *watani* supervise the distribution of inheritance to the deceased's kin. They tell the widow to cease mourning, and in the past oversaw the assignment of this widow to a matrilineal kinsman of the deceased. *Watani* alone dare openly discuss the merits of the widow's various choices among these men and vent the suppressed notion that kinsmen of the deceased might benefit from his death, especially if the widow is young and desirable. They may even tell a widow, "Now choose which of the witches (those who murdered their kinsman to secure a wife) you will take as your husband." Before the heir may take the widow, a *mutani* must purify her from death by slaying a black sheep (*mfiko*).[8] No such complications arise regarding widowers. At the end of these rites, those who were in mourning shave (*kugeta*) and resume normal life.

Other issues of inheritance, notably those involving property held by a deceased man as bridewealth (both in his own right as a father of a woman and as an elder custodian for his matrilineage), are settled as soon as possible after the end of mourning. No such complications arise regarding widows. Lengthy quarrels and other difficulties may prolong settlement of inheritance for many weeks or months after a death. Such affairs are ultimately decided by the deceased's paternal kin but are actively managed in large part by *watani*. (This parallels lineage rites, which are arranged by lineage elders but are actively conducted exclusively by *watani*.)

In one respect *watani* and elder kin are considered similar: like *watani* such kin (not of one's own matri-clan) who stand in the grandparental generation may be treated with considerable sexual freedom, lack of constraint, and openness in expressing criticism.

WATANI AND OTHER CATEGORIES OF PEOPLE

To understand *utani* and the relevant notions of pollution and change which surround the ceremonies just mentioned, one must consider the attributes shared by persons whom Kaguru imagine to resemble *watani*. By grasping the broader principles one can appreciate that these ambivalent yet dependent relations of conflict yet complementarity characterize all of Kaguru social organization.

Utani relations are so evocative because they are pronounced forms of relations characterizing more extensive connections between matrilineal and paternal kin, natal and affinal groups, and alternate generations. *Utani* relations evoke the gamut of ambivalences and ambiguities in Kaguru social relations. It is for this reason that they are so prominent in Kaguru *rites de passage*, where the pivotal character of Kaguru ties is thrown into contending prominence. *Watani* minister the changes in statuses which confirm or alter these relations, evoking the positive and negative aspects of sex, regeneration, and death on which these turn. I devote the remainder of this chapter to examining the ways these attributes of *utani* are reflected beyond ritual joking partners, encompassing the full range of Kaguru interpersonal affairs.

The verb *kutanya* refers to any conduct appropriate between *watani*; it also means "to insult, to abuse, to have sexual relations or to behave indecently before others." If one assumes, as Kaguru do, that sexuality itself involves danger, leading, at least temporarily, to unfitness to fulfill important stabilizing moral acts, then all such behavior evokes notions of conduct transitional between more stable situations or spheres. *Watani*'s services are most important at unusual, liminal situations: dealing with death (transition between the land of the living and that of ghosts), with ghosts (who stand between the living and God), with inauspicious children and witches (creatures partaking of both human and superhuman attributes). Both affinal and certain cognatic categories of relatives also possess certain medial attributes of both friendly and inimical persons. One's affines are aliens or potential enemies who by marriage have been made into a type of kin; yet they remain in many respects opposed to the interests of oneself and one's kin, especially as to rights over children. Paternal and matrilineal kin, in the embodiment of fathers and mothers and their brothers, vie for the control and loyalty of offspring. Certain other kin also have jural rights so sharply opposed to one's own goals and interests that at times one cannot help but entertain inimical attitudes toward them. Kaguru speak of and act toward such persons in a manner close to *watani* relations, and indeed they sometimes specifically compare such persons to *watani* or actually call them *watani*.

Kaguru whose clan lands adjoin also stand as *watani* to one another. When Kaguru speak of *watani*, they often mean such persons. They occasionally refer to other persons as *watani*, but explain that this is an analogy to the *watani* involved in clan and lineage ceremonies. Kaguru sometimes explain *utani* and its relation to sexuality by observing that descendants of those who were married by a clan are now *watani* to them. Those clans whose land bordered one's own were advantageous allies but also one's nearest potential enemies in disputes over boundaries. Many marriages were made with such neighbors through the years. The abusive negative aspects of *utani* relations are said to derive from the negative, aggressive, shameful aspects of sexual relations.[9] Kaguru maintain that one cannot entirely respect those with whom one has shared nakedness and sexuality, even though such ties were formalized through marriage. That a man has slept with your sister is a source of shame or embarrassment to you.

These ambivalent notions about sexuality may appear clearer through considering further examples of both *utani* and related sexual quips. Kaguru explain that they stand in *utani* relation toward uncircumcised tribes (*makonongo*), such as the Nyamwezi and Hehe, because such men, being uncircumcised and therefore unclean (*sika*), need not be treated politely. Sexuality is also closely related to the aggressive aspect of alimentation, as seen by euphemisms for sexual relations such as "to eat," "to devour," "to grind flour," "to pound flour," "to rub firesticks" (to make a cooking fire). These expressions combine constructive and destructive features within one action, as does sexuality itself. Hostile aspects of affinity are also reflected in sometimes referring to a spouse as *chihaja*, one who causes another's death. If a wife quarrels violently with her husband and angrily puts his possessions outside the house (commits *mhajangila*), he cannot return until her kin slay a goat or sheep for him. Were he to do so, he would die. The implication is that a man's possessions are taken out of his house only when he dies, and they become inheritable property. Correspondingly, a husband may break his wife's cooking pot in front of her. This suggests that he desires her death (her pots are broken at a woman's death). She should leave home and not return until a sheep or goat has been slain for her.[10]

If a Kaguru requires the ritual services of a *mutani* and none is available (as when one resides in town), a spouse or affine of either sex may serve, though men are preferred. This further indicates the close parallels between *utani* and affinity. The relation of sexuality and affinity to potential difficulties in social relations may be behind the fact that both affines (*walamu*) and *watani* are sometimes jokingly spoken of as witches. This is said to be because neither knows proper restraints. One sees the nakedness of a spouse, and Kaguru say that this shame extends to a spouse's kin. Similarly, witches are naked when they do their nefarious works at night. This ambiguous aspect of affinity explains the Kaguru custom of sometimes jokingly referring to all affines in one's own generation as *watani*.

One factor behind the conflict and ambiguity surrounding Kaguru ideas of affinity is that for people who reckon descent matrilineally values of domesticity and lineality tend to conflict. In the past many Kaguru men resided with their wives, but prosperous men resided virilocally. Most men residing uxorilocally would have preferred to found their own hamlets and considered residence with wives' kin a result of their own weak economic and political positions. Such men endured long brideservice, hence the terms *mukwe kulima* or *mukwe kumafiga* (cultivating affines or affines at the hearthstones).[11]

There are other categories of persons sometimes called *watani* whose characteristics shed light on how Kaguru view pivotal, ambiguous relations. These are cross-cousins (*wahisi*), father's sisters (*mai sangasi*), and grandfathers (*kuku*), grandmothers (*mama*), and grandchildren (*wajukulu*). Kaguru say that their relations toward all of these resemble relations toward *watani*. Kaguru may marry many persons within these categories of kinship, and these are all persons associated, even before marriage, with a lack of sexual restraint as well as some covert hostility.

There is also a parallel between unrestraint in sexuality and a jeopardizing of material property. Persons whom *watani* may insult sexually are also those whose property they may threaten. *Watani* might come into one's home and walk off with what they fancy. One has only two ways of coping with such threats. One might later retaliate by visiting that *mutani* and behaving in a similar manner, or one might spit upon an object just before the *mutani* seizes it and thus imply a curse on him or her if that object were taken. Most of the aforementioned categories of kin also stand as dangerous contenders toward one's property in cases of conflicting terms of inheritance. They fall into the categories of kin who are opposed due to competing terms of matrilineal and paternal allegiances. In this sense the modes of sexual and material conflict and competition merge.

Kaguru disagree as to whether one should marry ritual *watani*, those of clans whose lands adjoin the region of one's own clan. Some maintain that such marriages should not occur, because they would establish eventual cognatic ties conflicting with ritual joking relations; others contend that these alliances are consistent, because the hostility toward affines and that toward joking relatives are similar. Kaguru express the ambiguous attributes associated with such categories in terms of marriage with *wahisi* (cross-cousins), *mai sangasi* (father's sisters), and grandparents as well. The dangers of such relations lie behind the belief that if one steps over the legs of a seated *muhisi*, a grave act of sexual insult has been committed; the offender is expected to contract ugly sores (*mutulila*, for *kutula*, to erupt).

I lack data on the rate of marriage to classificatory grandparents, but about a quarter of Kaguru marriages are with classificatory cross-cousins. Kaguru insist that in such alliances persons should not marry close kin, those sharing the same grandparents.[12] They say that while such close marriages sometimes occur today, these represent the deterioration of kin ties in contemporary Kaguru society.

These categories of marriage kin involve a wide range of relatives. *Muhisi* refers to anyone of ego's generation who is a child of a woman of one's father's clan or a child of a man of one's own clan. *Mai sangasi* refers to any woman of one's father's clan, though usually a woman of one's father's generation. *Mama* (grandmother) and *kuku* (grandfather) refer to women and men of the second ascending generation of the four clans to which one's four grandparents belong; however, these terms may also be used toward anyone, regardless of generation, who is a member of these clans. The terms are especially favored toward clans other than one's own and one's father's. The reciprocal term for grandparent is grandchild (*mujukulu*, pl. *wajukulu*).

To appreciate the ambiguous attributes which Kaguru assign these kin categories, one should contrast the behavior and terminology considered proper before and after alliances are made. One should also consider the reasons Kaguru give for these marriages, which are often arrangements by which an elder Kaguru achieves dominance over a junior kinsman, the new husband, whom he would not otherwise be able to control so closely.

The most problematical marriage with kin is to a *mai sangasi* (father's sister). Kaguru themselves recognize the structural asymmetry of this; a man once asked me, "You know about customs. Explain why a man may marry his *mai sangasi*, but a woman cannot be married to her *bulai* (mother's brother)." Kaguru say a person should respect his father's female coevals, especially his father's uterine sister. She and certain grandmothers perform important rites separating a newly born child from the land of ghosts, bringing it fully among the living. One makes private sexual jokes with such women and may even marry them, though not a father's uterine sister. Kaguru joke that a *baba sangasi* (one's *mai sangasi*'s husband) would not like one to be alone too much with his wife since he may suspect sexual dallying. One may, however, also marry the child (*muhisi*) of such a woman, and if this is done, one may no longer have an unrestrained relation toward her since she has become a mother-in-law. Some say that any union with kin "throws away a marriage," adding no new kin but altering an existing relation for the worse, considering the stringent prohibitions against sexual familiarity with affines and the strict rules about avoiding parents-in-law. It is therefore abusive to call a *mai sangasi* by the term *mukwe* (senior affine); this spoils the relation because one refers to her children's sexuality in front of her thereby violating the strong prohibition against sexual allusions toward mothers-in-law. This is an indirect reference to the fact that any such marriage will negate the present easygoing relations one probably has with the aunt.

Kaguru say that a person marries enemies, and a *mai sangasi* fits this category. Among Kaguru (and this might be assumed on structural grounds for all matrilineal societies) "father's sister" is a status of ambiguity and hidden animosity. Such women are one of the key protagonists in what Audrey Richards (1950:246) terms "the matrilineal puzzle," the conflicts between bonds of domesticity and lineality within a matrilineal society practicing virilocality. Every Kaguru desires "to have it both ways" structurally: parents desire to transmit wealth and other benefits to their own children, yet desire and need allegiance from their brothers and their sisters' children. As Kaguru put it: (1) Your father would help you more, but his sisters are always telling him to help your cousins (*wahisi*), their own children. Your father's mother is always supporting this (that is to say, your grandmother is also an enemy). (2) Your mother's brother should help his nieces and nephews, but his wife is always telling him to help their own children (your *wahisi*). His mother (your grandmother) will be taking your side in this (that grandparent is an ally). In this sense, sentiments of domesticity conflict with lineal norms, and Kaguru women, especially grandmothers, play powerful roles in creating and maintaining such sentiments, both of a household and of a matrilineage.

I have noted that about a quarter of Kaguru marriages are with classificatory "cross-cousins," though not first cousins. Kaguru provide seemingly contradictory or ambiguous interpretations about motives behind such marriages. All one's coevals who are children of any *bulai* (mother's brother) or any *mai sangasi* (father's sister) are called cross-cousins (*wahisi*, sing. *muhisi*). Although one may refer to them by this term, it is considered impolite to do so. The terms *wahisi* and *watani* are abusive and should not be used toward kin in direct speech unless one intends insult. To suggest solidarity, "cross-cousins" may be addressed by sibling terms. Sometimes a mother's brother's child may be called *muhongu*, a jocular term, implying that one stands in debt. More often one addresses such persons with reference to statuses they will inherit within their matrilineages. Thus, the politest address toward paternal *wahisi* is "father" or "mother"; the rationale for this is that these cross-cousins succeed to authority formerly held by one's father. (Oddly, one never calls such a woman *mai sangasi*.) Kaguru say, "At one's father's death, such persons will attend his funeral" (supervise decisions over inheritance). Such paternal cross-cousins inherit the positions of arbiters and speakers at one's own and one's siblings' funerals, tasks held by one's father's clan but also, as noted earlier, associated with joking relations. Conversely, such persons could call one *mwana* (child). Ironically, but consistent with the preceding interpretation, these polite terms of address still smack of the aggressively negative since they allude to the deaths of senior kin from which junior cross-cousins stand to profit. According to the same principles discussed with reference to father's sister, all cross-cousins, as the children of *bulai* (mother's brothers) and their sisters, are potential enemies in the struggle for property. Such persons justify their individual claims by endorsing the principles which fit their own ends at a particular time and demean competitive claims of their rivals.

All kin with whom one jokes sexually may be referred to, even addressed, as "spouse." This is abusive, for a spouse would never be addressed publicly in this manner, since this calls attention to one's sexual connection with a person with whom a more stable relation is desired, stability being incompatible with open sexuality. Instead, one addresses a spouse by a teknonym or by a name derived from the spouse's father's matri-clan. An affine might be called "wife" or "husband," depending on whether he or she was related through providing a husband or wife to one's kin group, regardless of the gender of the affine addressed. This form of address is considered mocking and contemptuous, and would not be used on formal, polite occasions.

If one marries a cross-cousin (*muhisi*), all joking with members of that person's clan ceases. Kaguru explain this by saying that joking relations are equivalent to sexual relations, and one must never have sexual relations with two living persons of the same clan. There is a tendency to refer to such persons as "spouses"; but they should not be called by any affinal term, since this negates an already compromised kin tie. The respectful "child" and "parent" terms, with their rigorous implicit exclusion of all sexual connotations, tend to be used in such address.

A final category of kin, certain classificatory "grandparents," are often married. Kaguru recognize great informality between alternate generations. Thus sexual instruction is often provided by grandparents, and one makes dirty jokes with them. If they do not fall within the incest prohibitions (members of one's own clan, persons having fathers with the same clan, or a parent to one's biological parent), such persons may be allowed in sexual liaisons and even in marriage. Kaguru emphasize these ties by calling classificatory grandparents and grandchildren "spouses," rationalizing this by noting that a person may have the same name as a grandparent and is therefore generationally equivalent. Kaguru speak of the grandparental generation standing between the living and the dead, in the double sense that grandparents are the elders in charge of organizing ritual propitiation as well as being those most likely to die and rejoin the ghosts. I also noted earlier that grandparents, especially grandmothers, are potential allies or opponents in the machinations among kin to secure inheritance and support from fathers versus matrilineal uncles.

When Kaguru use grandparental terms with reference to prospective sexual partners, generally they refer to any person of their own age, of a father's father's or mother's father's clan, whose genealogical relationship cannot be traced easily. These are the main types of "grandparents" one can marry. All persons within the grandparental category are genealogically too distant to be involved in those direct jural claims which concern kin in the same and adjacent generations, though some are indeed profoundly involved behind the scenes through their influence on one's parents, aunts, and uncles.

Cross-cousin (*wahisi*) marriage is generally viewed with ambivalent sentiments by Kaguru, which is consistent with such marriages being associated with similar feelings toward *utani*. Cross-cousin marriages are means by which elders, a "father" or "mother's brother," seek domination over junior kinsmen while retaining influence over female dependants, daughters, or nieces. Bestowing such a girl under easy terms of bridewealth, the elder expects the new husband to reside nearby and remain subservient. The youth often performs arduous brideservice and is sometimes termed a kind of "slave" to his wife's relatives, albeit these are his kin as well. The extreme form of this, obviously no longer practiced, involved marriage to the daughters of slave women. Prosperous Kaguru elders often sought to draw dependent youths to them by bestowing their daughters by concubine slaves. Since these girls had no proper matrilineal kin, their fathers had a particularly free hand in dominating such a situation.

A cross-cousin marriage is a mixed blessing, depending upon the perspective of the different protagonists involved. It is a marriage associated with poor or weak young men and/or prosperous or powerful elders. In any such arrangement, one category of elders, matrilineal or paternal, benefits at the expense of another. All marriages evince ambivalently viewed compromises in payments, residence, and control. Cross-cousin marriages are a pronounced form evoking especially strong sentiments from Kaguru. The more problematical aspects of marriage and sexual demands are as neatly expressed by cross-cousinhood (*uhisi*) as by joking relations (*utani*), so it seems appropriate that the two terms are sometimes interchanged.

All such marital partners discussed above fit within a broader, somewhat hostile or ambivalently loyal category, a grouping in which attributes of joking relations and these potential affines merge. These occupy a pivotal, problematical moral and social sphere linking and blurring central conceptual distinctions held by Kaguru, ones distinguishing moral and nonmoral people and places, friends and enemies, settlement and outside, us and them. These opposed yet complementary relations reflect an uneasy and profound reality of Kaguru life: all social relations, and even the larger physical world in which society is set, exhibit powerful, unresolvable principles; these may be seen as contending yet also supportive of one another. Meaningful life derives from constantly picking one's way through the minefield of reality composed of both these features, each of which must be given its due.

Ordinary sphere of persons and places	Medial category of persons and places, sometimes useful but sometimes very dangerous	Difficult but powerful persons and places
immediate kin and immediate neighbors	affines	enemies and geographically distant Kaguru

	joking relations
	    cross-cousins.
	    affines
	    grandparents and
	    grandchildren
	    father's sister	

living persons		ancestral ghosts
elderly, proper persons	witches certain uncircumcised peoples	nonhumans or animals
own village	borderlands	alien villages
own lands	crossroads and boundaries	other lands
	mountainsides	land of the ghosts

CONCLUSION

Rituals conducted by joking relations, whether actual *watani* or others compared to them, contain and direct the powers of sexuality (fertility) and death. Ultimately, these forces are joined, since birth leads to death and is bestowed by the dead on the living. Death and birth link the spheres of this world with that of ancestral spirits. Indeed, death is birth for the dead, and birth a kind of dying. Death and birth are two extremes in a series of transformations marking each person's career. Each of these transformations is compared to a death from one status and a birth to another.

Rituals of *utani* socialize the profound forces that propel human existence. Hence, those who are best qualified to undertake them, *watani* (joking relatives), epitomize the same disjunctive and conjunctive qualities that characterize birth and death. Kaguru society is best seen as a way of organizing human affairs so as to survive as cultured beings, and this involves the production and allocation of resources. These are food (the product of land and labor) and offspring (the product of sexual unions). Both land and sexuality sustain or produce life, yet both function properly because of the dead. Securing and maintaining these resources of food and offspring are primarily organized through the rules and restraints of kinship, which are in turn rooted in the sanctions and names of the dead. Kaguru kinship necessarily reflects the same dynamic, powerful forces of conjunction and disjunction that epitomize the broader physical world with which it is meant to cope. The relations between women and men, elders and young, cognates and affines, and matrilineal and paternal kin both complement and conflict.

Each Kaguru's life is an endless struggle to play off these forces to her or his advantage. It is therefore appropriate that the powerful but potentially dangerous forces of sexuality and death are ministered by *watani* (joking relatives) who are drawn from those fellow Kaguru who stand structurally in Kaguru social organization in pivotal, problematical positions that also exemplify this same dynamic tension and force. Therefore such rituals are best conducted by neighbors at one's boundaries or by affines, cross-cousins, father's sisters, and those from alternate generations.

The broadest, deepest features of Kaguru cosmological reality are echoed and affirmed by the character of Kaguru social organization. This is demonstrated in the institution of *utani* (ritual activities of joking relatives). These *watani* take those features of greatest potential danger and power and turn these forces on themselves to maintain the social order as something not opposed to struggle and conflict but rooted in them. This truth holds at the level of social organization and interrelations as well as cosmologically.

In this chapter we saw how rituals are used to maintain or reestablish some form of social and cosmological order, even though this sometimes involves plunging into the realm of mess and disorder as a way to reorchestrate persons and things back into workable harmony with one another. For the most part, these rituals relate to disruptions in social relations, through death, illness, misfortune, or wrongdoing, and serve as much to mend or confirm jeopardized social relations as to remove impurity and danger resulting from such difficulties.

So far, I have considered symbolic imagery as it relates to order, but in the coming chapters I consider more negative and subversive aspects of these same tensions and conflicts. The coming chapter deals with how Kaguru imagine evil, how they picture profoundly antisocial behavior. I press further toward the edges of Kaguru imagination by discussing how people envision what should not be but clearly is, the badness of kin and neighbors. We are also led to consider how Kaguru look inside themselves, if only obliquely, in order to articulate the deep resentments and anger which most sometimes feel at being constrained and repressed by social demands. I admit that I do not think that witches exist, and in that sense for me Kaguru talk of evil persons with supernatural powers is imaginary in the fanciful sense. Yet the emotions and ugly motives that characterize witches are very much part of how Kaguru experience life with others, and in this sense what they seek to picture is powerfully accurate. Misfortune is a constant and perplexing feature of Kaguru experience, and it is a troubling truth that some secretly (or not so secretly) take pleasure in contemplating the troubles of others.

NOTES

1. This is a revised version of 1966a; there I cited some of the African literature on joking relations, which I do not discuss here.

2. Kaguru *utani* is similar to the institution among their matrilineal neighbors, the Ngulu, Lugulu, and Zigula. I conducted fieldwork among the Ngulu and found that my analysis here also holds for that people (cf. McVicar 1941, 1945). Christensen's analysis (1963) of Lugulu joking relations takes no account of McVicar's work (1935, 1945); neither investigator considers the basic notions behind this institution.

3. A basic prohibition, such as that against clan incest, is termed *mwiko*; an important but less basic prohibition which may by cleansed by ritual is called *musilo*.

4. That those who commit such prohibited sexual acts are not supernaturally endangered but that their kin are appears to be a belief not reported elsewhere in East Africa. A comparable ceremony is also performed to allow sexual relations which would ordinarily be forbidden. This permits marriage between two Kaguru whose fathers have the same clan. This prohibition is relaxed through slaughtering a sheep whose carcass is divided longitudinally. This ends respect and trust between the two matrilineages, who now may become affines and therefore potential disputants over bridewealth and children.

5. Kaguru use this same verb, *kubanika* (to break up, spoil), to refer to the death of a person.

6. The monster swallowed the sick one, *yedikoko ,dikolie mutamu*; devouring has strong sexual connotations for Kaguru.

7. The expression *kukola mikono* (to take by the hands) refers to initiation, where young people are led into the world of adulthood. A devouring monster (*dikoko*) is a prominent motif in initiation rites, just as it is in talk to children about death. Similar imagery of daily tasks accompanies the symbolic rebirth of persons after initiation and marriage.

8. This is a form of the common Swahili term *mviko* or *tambiko* (prohibition).

9. My discussion of Ngulu sexuality (1964d) closely parallels that for Kaguru.

10. Compare this to Moreau (1941), who describes a similar practice among the Bondei and Shambala, north of the Kaguru.

11. Hearthstones (*mafiga*) express the essence of a woman's part of a household.

12. In a typical Kaguru area, I conducted a census of all households (115): 12 were formed by marriages with classificatory mother's brother's daughter, 14 with classificatory father's sister's daughter, 1 with classificatory father's sister. None was between persons with a common grandparent.

CHAPTER 9.

Witchcraft and Sorcery

Thou shalt not suffer a witch to live.

Exodus 23.18

They are neither man nor woman—
They are neither brute nor human,
They are Ghouls.

Edgar Alan Poe, *The Bells* I.86

. . . the act of envy has somewhat in it of
witchcraft so there is no other cure of
envy but the cure of witchcraft . . .

Francis Bacon, Of Envy, *Essays*

The idea of a witch is a "complex construction of the imagination" (Needham 1978:33), one exerting a profound effect upon Kaguru. The character of a witch is physically and morally inverted from what the ideal, proper human being should be. Kaguru witches are not truly human at all. Yet they appear in human form, living and interacting with others; otherwise they would not be dangerous.[1]

Kaguru beliefs in witches and witchcraft are attempts to imagine beings morally outside society, even as they are in some sense part of it. Witches are not fully accountable in a world where social beliefs and rules should provide a working order by which people secure their ends and needs in the company of others. Yet they also exemplify what it means to be free of others, to be unconcerned with the tedious confines of neighbors and kin. The problem for Kaguru, as for others, is that their experience frequently runs counter to their assumptions that society should serve them well.

Belief in witchcraft is a mode of imagining evil, judged harmful, bad, and beyond any moral justification. Suffering and misfortune may be due to stupidity and ignorance. They can be credited to punishment from God, to activities of demons, or to malevolence of outsiders. Kaguru have not imagined true evil thus but instead give it familiar human form, a witch. Some suffering may be morally justified, caused by God or by the wrath of ancestral dead. Such misfortune can sometimes be eased by rectifying one's wrongs and by purificatory ceremonies. Such suffering is reasonable and supports the framework of Kaguru moral precepts. Witches, however, cause misfortune that in no way can be credited as deserved.[2] In recent years Kaguru traditional religious beliefs about misfortune have declined, but preoccupation with witches appears undiminished.

While Kaguru insist that they abhor everything about witches, they are fascinated by what witches are like.[3] Popular Kaguru tales center about witches, often characterizing them as hyenas or old women living alone, as wicked wives or as stepmothers. Duerr argues that "we ourselves are to become wild in order not to place ourselves at the mercy of our own wildness, in order to gain thereby an awareness of ourselves as tame, as cultural creatures" (quoted in Zipes 1983:13). Witches bring the wilderness of animals, bush, and night into societal order. Kaguru thereby vicariously approach dangerous edges of human feelings and behavior stemming from resentment and rebellion against constraints which social life imposes upon individuals.

Kaguru deny the humanity of witches, yet witches stand among the cast of characters in many scenarios of conflict. Kaguru imagine witches as what they themselves are not but as what recalcitrant kin and neighbors may be. Witches exist, but their identity is not always clear. They poison social relations so that many ties and obligations sometimes end in betrayal, disappointment, and ill will. Their deeds reveal "the superficiality of social intercourse" (Simmel 1971:138) and embody the individual's need to rebel and express hostility against an invading society that thwarts and curbs appetites and desires (ibid.:75). In all societies people are aware of the indeterminacy of relations which create a gap between one's position and one's disposition toward it (Jackson 1982:27).

THE DEFINITION OF A WITCH

Kaguru have two words for a witch, *muhai* (pl. *wahai*) and *mukindi* (pl. *wakindi*).[4] A *muhai* is anyone, male or female, possessing supernatural powers (*uhai*) used to harm others.[5] *Uhai* refers to substances bearing such power and to this power itself. *Uhai* may poison someone's food or drink. It may be some unaccountable skill; for example, in Ungulu sorcerers dance on tightropes to demonstrate their powers. It may be packets of medicine or formulas for human and crop fertility, preventing adultery, seduction, killing an enemy, or combating the *uhai* of others. Some make *uhai* to sell to others. Such a person is politely spoken of as a doctor (*muganga*, pl. *waganga*), since *muhai* has antisocial connotations. Kaguru say that such a doctor is a kind of witch, for although he uses his powers to help others, one cannot be sure about all his activities. One who buys *uhai* from such a doctor does not know its nature and is therefore not inherently dangerous. Such a buyer can later discard *uhai* without retaining any stigma.

Uhai also refers to stronger, more dangerous power which is deeply evil. A witch may teach another person how to attain such power, but it is truly possessed and revitalized by committing acts horrifying to Kaguru. Such a witch must commit clan incest and/or kill a human being and then devour him. The most common word for incest is *uhai*. These witches are *wakindi* (from *kukinda*, to dance). While *wakindi* can work their powers through ill will, these powers are strengthened when the *wakindi* dances naked in the clearing before a victim's house, thereby defiling that person's public, moral space. Night-dancing witches enjoy the evil they do. They are not like someone buying *uhai* for protection. Pleasure in incest and love of human flesh cannot be renounced, because they are inherent by birth or irreversible choice. Such witches are characterized by ungovernable appetites, unrestrained alimentary and sexual gluttony, expressed through cannibalism and incest. Although Kaguru publicly confess minor witchcraft, almost no one admits *ukindi*. After hearing vivid accounts of night-dancing witches, one wonders whether Kaguru do dance naked at night and commit incest in hope of gaining power. A few insist that they have seen night-dancers and identify the culprits.

Muhai is the word Kaguru usually employ for witch, though it fails to specify the severity of a suspect's offense. In contrast, *mukindi* is not frequently heard. While not all witches dance at night, knowledge of any *uhai* may eventually lead to night-dancing, incest, and murder.

ACTIVITIES OF WITCHES

Many misfortunes are thought probably due to witchcraft: illness (especially pulmonary diseases, leprosy, and dysentery), miscarriages, accidents, sterility, difficult childbirth, poor crops, sickly livestock and poultry, loss of articles, bad luck in hunting, and sometimes even drought. Each gives fresh evidence that witches are active and numerous.

A witch can bewitch anyone, except perhaps a more powerful witch. A witch does this out of revenge, ill will, greed, jealousy, or desire for power. These are all recognizable feelings, but witches possess these to excess. While witchcraft often stems from rancor, its most horrible aspects, incest and necrophagy, exceed the limits of fathomable human desire and for Kaguru are inexplicable. Witches are aware of their own evil acts. Kaguru cannot conceive of witches unconscious of their activities, such as are described for some African societies.[6]

Night-dancing witches are sometimes organized locally, meeting at unfrequented spots, such as mountainsides or ruined villages. Some practice alone; others share their revels and necrophagic feasts. Some prefer eating particular portions of bodies and at such feasts a corpse might be divided according to the rank and predilections of the guests, just as the carcass of an animal is divided at legitimate ceremonies. Such choice cuts are called *chingila*.

Witches travel at night, often accompanied by hyenas and owls (cf. *Proceedings of the Church Missionary Society* 1904–5:88). They sometimes deceive persons into buying an owl bewitched into appearing as a chicken. They also favor ground-hornbills, although these do not travel with them. Owls and ground-hornbills should not be killed, because the slayer will be punished by witches.

Witches prefer night, when they cannot be seen at work. They are not inconvenienced by dark, because they have night vision like hyenas and owls. Witches cover great distances by means of hyena familiars, which they hug by the belly as they race through the sky with fire shooting out the hyena's anus. All witches travel far more easily and rapidly than non-witches. Association of witches with night, speed, and transvection further inverts their characters. Some have familiars, such as lions and snakes, which attack their victims. They sometimes feed these familiars blood stolen from menstruating women or newly circumcised youths. The familiars then attack those whose blood they tasted (cf. *Proceedings of the Church Missionary Society* 1904–5:89). Some witches employ anteaters, which burrow under the walls of houses, enabling a witch to enter. Witches often hide familiars in food bins or lofts where grain is stored, underscoring the association of witches with greed over not sharing food. Only a few Kaguru claim witches take on animal form.

Night-dancing witches travel naked, walking upside down, smeared with white ashes. They resemble newly initiated youths who are ash-smeared. Ashes convey a sense of the peripheral and transitional, concealing social attributes. Witches travel corporeally, not merely in spirit. Although they must be physically present to be effective, they can sometimes make themselves invisible. Some have power to render themselves invisible by day. Witches sometimes possess sticks to beat graves of victims, making the dead rise to follow the witches to where the corpses may be eaten by a coven. Others rely upon hyenas to exhume victims. If a corpse is fresh, it is eaten by witches; if decomposed, by hyenas. Some Kaguru place charmed stakes at the corners of graves to frighten away witches.

The sexual fluids of cats are thought to be used to prepare especially lethal witchcraft. Kaguru believe that if one sees cats having intercourse one will die because witches are then hovering about to collect what is spilled.

Witches have powers to keep those with whom they live from knowing their activities. A witch may turn one's head upside down or reverse one's sleeping position. Then one sleeps soundly though uncomfortably. After a hard night one may suspect a spouse or relative of having been night-dancing.

Witches have innumerable ways of bewitching. They have a stock which forms an ugly, dark mess, as though composed of charcoal and oil. One deadly substance comes from pulverized skulls and teeth. *Kusinga* closes a victim's eyes to theft. *Ishahike* makes a victim say anything. Another causes hunters to stumble, injuring themselves or firing at termite hills or bushes in mistake for game. *Musukule* transforms a victim into a zombie (*isoki*, pl. *masoki*), which then works for the witch. This is done by pricking one's palm, inserting the witchcraft, and then shaking hands with the victim. The zombie's kin remain unaware, for the witch charms a banana stalk to appear as the victim. This stalk languishes, dies, and is buried, while the actual person slaves for the witch. Kaguru claim that atop the mountains entire zombie communities have dances, marriages, and initiations. Sometimes one hears a humanlike cry in the night or passes a stranger on a path at dusk who averts his or her face and gives no greeting. These are zombies, discernible only to their relatives. Witches can instruct a feather or a fly bearing witchcraft to enter a bodily orifice. Witches may secretly defecate or urinate in beer or food or put human flesh in it. Suspicious dregs or taste in food or drink cause vituperation and alarm. Sometimes a witch puts food utensils or food in contact with his or her genitals. Sometimes a witch leaves bewitched food on a path, hoping a victim will foolishly assume it has fallen from a traveler's basket and eat it. He may take an object lying in a victim's shadow or footprint and use that.

Not only do witches convey evil through charged materials, but they bewitch merely through ill will. The witch may even bewitch by pointing (*kulota*) a finger at a victim, his kin, or his possessions. To point to or count another's children or livestock using a finger is the act of a witch. Witches try to serve at circumcisions or birth in order to bewitch a child, which is espscially vulnerable. Pregnant women are prone to being victims of witchcraft and never openly discuss their condition, concealing it from outsiders as long as possible. One must guard against enemies but also against the overly friendly, even when one detects no suspicious action. It is only by close association that a witch finds an opportunity to use his or her powers.

A witch makes potions for seduction. Ordinary love potions (*chipendo*) preserve or increase the love which one already feels, and these can be made by anyone and are not bad. Only a witch makes *ndele*, which forces an unwilling person into violent sexual passion for someone whom he or she would otherwise dislike.

Witches are inverted: nocturnal, ash-white, and traveling upside down without ordinary impediments. They treat kin like like non-kin, having sexual relations with them. They treat humans like animals, killing and eating them. They treat wild animals like people, cooperating to gain and share food. A few say witches have sexual intercourse with animals.[7] A witch's nakedness is a further inversion, since Kaguru are prudish regarding exposure, and public nakedness suggests incest.[8]

HOW TO BECOME A WITCH

The simplest way to become a witch is to purchase *uhai* from a reputed witch. This may harm others but does not convey true power. That is achieved by committing incest and murdering and devouring others. A taste for human flesh, incest, and other horrors are inherited matrilineally. While female witches usually produce other witches, it may happen that a child is born free of taint, though if two witches have incestuous relations, any resultant child is invariably a witch. Here is how witches discover whether their offspring are witches:

> When a child is born, its father must leave the house. The women of the child's clan assist. If they are witches, they open the child's hand and place a packet of witchcraft within and close it into a fist. If the child has cast off the packet the next morning, it rejects the invitation. If it kept it, it is a witch-child, and they put the packets away until the child is old enough to be indoctrinated. When the child becomes a witch, it has sexual intercourse with its teachers, strengthening both its own and their powers. A boy has intercourse with his mother or sister, a girl with her brother or uncle. Since these persons enjoy each other sexually, they never betray one another. Sometimes a person wants witchcraft but cannot afford to buy it and has inherited no power. He or she then tries to gain power by incest.

IDENTIFICATION, ACCUSATION, AND PUNISHMENT

Kaguru describe witches as ugly with dark skin and red eyes. Yet many whom Kaguru conceded to be attractive were suspected. Personal appearances provide little help in identifying witches. Someone with unusual dress or grooming might be a witch. Quarrelsome persons are often witches, but friendly persons might be even more deadly because they are better able to get at others. The worst witches conceal ill will.

Witchcraft suspicions are not determined by a single trait or act. The same behavior may be interpreted as proof of guilt or of innocence, depending upon other experiences:

A boy wanted to send eggs to Yeremiya. He asked Rebeka to take them. She refused, saying, "I do not take food to Yeremiya because he calls me a witch." The boy told Yeremiya. Later the boy wanted to send Yeremiya tomatoes and asked Rebeka. This time she agreed. When she arrived with the food, he rejected it saying, "Before, you refused to bring food because you hate me. Now you bring these tomatoes. Perhaps you poisoned them. I don't want them." Rebeka left, telling Yeremiya, "I am going to court to complain that you are spoiling my name by telling everyone that I am a witch." Yeremiya replied, "I doubt you will do that, but go ahead if you want. If you don't go, I'll know it's because you're a witch and don't want to be recognized. If you do go, I'll tell everyone at court why I said what I did and why you want to make trouble for me. Just think what you want to do." Rebeka did not go to court even though she was very angry.[9] Rebeka and Yeremiya lived in the same village. Yeremiya's wife was staying in town. Yeremiya had hired Rebeka to cook for him while his wife was away. Rebeka wanted both wages and a share in food. When Yeremiya refused, she suggested they sleep together to adjust the price. When he still refused, they became enemies. Rebeka announced in public, "When Yeremiya dies, I shall laugh and be happy."

Some Kaguru have no doubts who is bewitching them. Some are even warned through dreams. Others resort to divination (*maselu* or *malamulo*). One consults diviners secretly, so I had no opportunity to watch, but informants said it involves only the diviner and that a client never helps interpret the signs. The means of divination vary: gazing for patterns in a bowl of water or oil, listening for sounds in a pot, casting beans or sandals on the ground, or watching movements of grass in a bowl of water or how wicker trays fall when balanced on a gourd. The diviner does not name a suspect but provides general clues which cannot fail to involve someone. He may then sell counterwitchcraft (*malegu* or *mhingu*). Sometimes a client brings a suspected substance to determine whether it is witchcraft. A diviner adds salt and water, which should dissolve it to reveal its nature. Kaguru consult diviners living at some distance: they do not want neighbors to know their problems; witches have less influence over distant divination; and greater divinatory powers are credited to outsiders. Renowned non-Kaguru diviners operate on Ukaguru's borders.

In the past, a person sometimes compelled a suspect to visit a diviner. In any case, after a suspect had been accused, she or he was tried by the local community. While diviners might err, Kaguru believe that ordeals at a trial never did. A suspect took an oath and then submitted to some test. He might try to withdraw a stone from a pot of boiling water or sheep fat without being burned. He might agree to a diviner's trying to pierce his earlobe with a twig—if this was painful, he was a witch. Sometimes he drank medicine and was then questioned. If he lied, he was supposed to become sick. Rarely, Kaguru placed medicine "on the head" of a chicken. The bird was given to the suspect, who dropped it on the ground. If the bird died, the suspect was guilty. It was the diviner's words, not just the medicine, that killed. Another way of detecting a witch was to assemble people and then give one medicine (*imausa*, probably datura). That person became crazed and would seize likely witches, who then were put to ordeals. One might also trap a suspect by adding earth from the grave of an alleged victim to the suspect's food or drink. He would have to confess when confronted by a diviner.

A person convicted through an ordeal was *muhai kalakala* (a burned witch), referring to the boiling water by which he was scalded. Today this describes anyone considered an obvious witch, even though not subjected to tests. In the past, anyone convicted of witchcraft was clubbed to death in the bush.[10] Like a leper, recidivist, or one whose fatal illness involved excessive bleeding, a witch was neither buried nor mourned. Close matrilineal kin were suspected and tested as well. If someone accused was found innocent, the accuser paid compensation.

Since it has been impractical and illegal to try witches in this fashion for many years, no one remembers how proceedings were conducted. Kaguru agree that ordeals were the only sure way of coping with witches and that current measures are inadequate. A dead witch's powers are ended, though some say the spirit may encourage children to seek witchcraft from living witches.

Occasionally, illegal witch-finders operate in Ukaguru today. Accusations broke out at Berega in 1961 during a famine. A witch-finder passed around accompanied by a headman, forcing many to drink medicine for a fee. Some confessed and were fined, but no one was injured. The witch-finder was later imprisoned. Another illegal witch-finder, an Ngulu, still operates in a remote part of Ukaguru.

Now that there are no witch trials, and most suspects cannot be made to confront diviners, there is little point in openly accusing someone. If one is drunk, upset at a funeral, or angry in court, this may happen, but indirect signs (*mangali*) are more often used. At night, cinders are thrown on a suspect's doorsill, or his garden is cut down or trampled; in extreme cases his house may be burned. Injured parties are often not eager for notoriety by lodging complaints. The commonest way to deal with a suspect is to move away or make him do so, for a witch needs contact with a victim. One rarely moves far, sometimes rebuilding in sight of the previous dwelling. Kaguru dislike moving far if they have good fields nearby. Moving even a short distance is said to help.

Witches take advantage of crowds where people are drunk, celebrating, and off guard. Where beer, food, and music abound, people mingle who do not know each other well. If a host fears witches, he strews branches of euphorbia (*igole*) or *Ehretia* sp. (*mukilika*) (which have blinding sap) at entryways to ward them off. Sometimes an all-night dance (*magini*) is held to dilute (*kulohola*) witchcraft. Where food and drink are served, a plucky Kaguru may demand that a host sample them before serving.

Sometimes a person who appears successful in opposing a reputed witch gains a reputation as a strong witch himself, for only a witch defeats another:

> Robert became ill after quarreling with a neighbor. Not even founding a new homestead apart from his enemy helped. He moved to Ungulu, renowned for witchcraft,[11] and visited a governmental hospital. When he returned healthy and with purchased counterwitchcraft, he was considered stronger than his adversary.

Many Kaguru learn that they are suspected of witchcraft by others' gossip. Kaguru dislike open conflict and rely on rumor and backbiting. Fear of gossip is one reason Kaguru give for conforming to people's expectations and for concealing what they think.

PERSONS SUSPECTED OF WITCHCRAFT

One may suspect any adult of witchcraft. Persons within a clan are less apt to bewitch each other than to bewitch outsiders. Yet actual cases reveal that those within the clan are sometimes considered the worst witches of all, and accusations within the same matrilineage do occur, especially over sharing goods or inheriting wealth or rights to office. In the past, belief in the inheritance of witchcraft may have inhibited accusation of matrilineal kin since one risked being tested for witchcraft oneself.

Although anyone might be a witch, certain types are suspected more frequently than others: those with prosperous gardens, much livestock, fine clothing, attractive wives, or many lovers; and shopowners, powerful chiefs, headmen and some church leaders; nonconformists such as war veterans returned with new ideas and cash, strong personalities who go their own ways, the highly neurotic; wives not easily controlled by husbands; co-wives envious of one another because some have more children or receive more of their husband's favors than others; persons refusing to meet important obligations toward kin; tribal outsiders settled in Ukaguru. This last category refers especially to matrilineal Bantu, such as the Ngulu and the Zigula, with clans, languages, and customs similar to Kaguru. These peoples often intermarry with Kaguru and settle near or even within Kaguru settlements. They are often traders, brewers, or diviners, with more livestock, cash, and sometimes even better political connections than many Kaguru. They are often educated and hold important posts in the Native Authority, in schools, and in local missions. Kaguru feel ambivalence toward these aliens. Their advantages provoke jealousy and suspicion, but their nominally identical clans, similar culture, and economic advantages encourage acceptance, though they cannot be easily subjected to the sanctions and restraints imposed upon fellow tribesmen. Some of these outsiders are not descendants from immigrants but have themselves arrived recently. Kaguru say, "Why does a person leave home? Did his neighbors call him a witch?" On the other hand, Kaguru admit one may leave for other reasons, including escape from the witchcraft of others.

In contrast, the wealthy Paranilotic, pastoral Baraguyu minority in Ukaguru are never accused of witchcraft (see Beidelman 1960, 1961b). Baraguyu and Kaguru carry on considerable trade but at a risk to both. They are bitter traditional enemies, often conflicting violently; they never intermarry. Yet hatred and violence will not provoke witchcraft if no moral expectations for help and loyalty exist. Similarly, no European can be a witch, for they are too powerful and alien for proper moral expectations from Kaguru.

WITCHCRAFT CASES AND SUSPICIONS

Fears of witchcraft provide some individuals with means to maintain power through the conformity and intimidation which such fears prompt. While few Kaguru leaders claim openly to have witchcraft, many imply this. One paramount chief was notorious for witchcraft insinuations and threats, which he used to seduce others' wives. A current chief is sometimes compared with him because he has taken his sister's son's widow as one of his wives. People say that he would never have dared do this before he became chief since this is traditionally prohibited. Kaguru say he bewitched his nephew.

Suspicions of witchcraft are especially strong in clans with government-sanctioned control of an area. A clan leader is often said to be a witch, perhaps having bewitched his predecessor. He is not, however, the only witch in the clan, only the most successful. Consider the selection of a new subchief:

> The popular choice, Chitemo, refused election by his clan fellows,
> yielding to Isaak, an unpopular and aggressive son of the last
> subchief, who had been fired by the district commissioner. Chitemo
> feared involvement with the old subchief (who favored his son),
> feared the hatred of his rival, and wanted to avoid the intrigue and ill

will such a post involves. These pressures were expressed as fear of witchcraft, and the populace in turn spoke of the superior witchcraft of Chitemo's rival, Isaak.

The Kaguru paramount chief's counsellor provides a further example:

The chief is old and illiterate, his ability questioned by younger Kaguru. He refuses to relinquish any power to his sister's sons, even though one has considerable education. He is influenced by headman Patrik, who is his counsellor and literate. Patrik convinced the chief that if he relinquished any power his nephew would seek witchcraft to secure the rest. Patrik fosters his own reputation as a witch. He held his office before the last war but joined the army, training as a driver and motor mechanic. When Patrik returned, he strove to regain the headmanship. When the headman who replaced Patrik died, Patrik reassumed the post. Kaguru believe Patrik bewitched his replacement. Patrik's ability as a driver and mechanic and his savings from service give him an economic advantage. Kaguru claim that Patrik profits by bewitching passing lorries and then repairing them.

A witchcraft reputation is also used to maintain power:

A Kaguru war veteran who is unique in cultivating land by hired labor on a cash basis encouraged suspicions of witchcraft. When drunk, he boasted that he journeys to the coast and back overnight by sailing through the air on a winnowing-tray. He is aggressively eager to intimidate others into serving him.

My most spectacular encounter with a witch involved an old woman living with her husband and daughter far from other Kaguru. She seemed neurotic and intimidated others. She wore her hair unusually long and unkempt and spoke aggressively even before strangers. Kaguru relate many anecdotes about her, but I confine myself to describing her first visit to the village where I lived. Such an unusual person proves to Kaguru that witches exist:

She and her unmarried daughter visited a kinswoman living in my neighborhood. She asked for me and my clerk. "Where are Tomasi and Yustino? They are my children." She said she had a child that died but returned to her as a lion, which lurks about her house following and protecting her. Her daughter repeated this even when questioned alone. The woman and her daughter stayed until late. Then they set out in the dark, walking home through desolate country, unusual even for Kaguru men unless drunk. The old woman said, "I must go home tonight. I did not bid farewell to my lion child, so if I don't go back, it will come looking for me and frighten you." My neighbors appeared upset.

Courts are used in many disputes, but corruption, lack of cash to initiate cases, and lack of time and sufficient evidence encourage many to rely upon fear of witchcraft for redress:

Ezekial lost his third matrilineal relative within a year. Although he and his kin profess Christianity, they avoid mission medical facilities, sending ailing relatives long distances to diviners. A man in Ezekial's matrilineage was reputed to have stolen from a neighbor. He denied this and refused to provide compensation. Instead of going to court, the complainant is said to have procured witchcraft. He himself implied that he was bewitching members of the offender's matrilineage. While the offender remained healthy and unrepentant, Ezekial and his kin were often ill. Unfortunately, they did not succeed in forcing their relative to confess.

At revival meetings Christian Kaguru confess purchasing witchcraft. Some interpret this not as reform but as advertisement to inspire fearful obedience and to secure customers.

A relative or neighbor who avoids a funeral is considered a witch. If one is not informed of a relative's illness, one is probably suspected of witchcraft. If people with whom one quarreled become ill, one should avoid them to escape accusation of witchcraft. One's presence may denote a desire to bewitch, and one's absence hostility; any course may be interpreted negatively.

Accusations of witchcraft between kin of different clans is likely, given the cross-purposes at which such groups are set. Sometimes bitterness involves kin of both sorts:

Abeli's father died, so he found it difficult to secure wealth for a wife. His mother's brother, Yohanna, gave him his daughter at reduced payment. Shortly after the marriage, the girl was found to be pregnant by another paternal cousin, her secret lover. Abeli gave the girl back to Yohanna and asked for a refund in bridewealth. Yohanna refused, "I only gave you a wife. I am not responsible for who sleeps with her." (Since the adulterous male was of Yohanna's matrilineage, this is not reasonable.) Abeli's father had died, so Abeli considered his uncle Yohanna his protector. Abeli's mother, Yohanna's sister, agreed. Both Abeli and his mother demanded that the bridewealth be

returned, but Yohanna claimed that the adulterer should repay it since
it was he who was the troublemaker. Yohanna's sister angrily left her
brother's settlement though they had previously been close. (Their
parents were dead.) The sister said she would seek witchcraft against
Yohanna and later became famous for exorcising spirit-possessed
women. (She was a Muslim while Yohanna was a Protestant.) When
she died, Yohanna attended the funeral, but there were bitter words
between him and her sons. When Yohanna became ill and died, his
children blamed their cross-cousins. Yohanna's children said that
these cousins were witches like their mother. Though the estranged
brother and sister are now both dead, their children remain enemies.
When Yohanna's son learned that the adulterous cross-cousin who
started the trouble had fallen ill, he would not enter that
neighborhood, so as to avoid accusation of witchcraft.

The village of subchief Isaak illustrates the complex clan relationships
where witchcraft suspicions are grounded, especially when coupled with political power:

The village has two factions whose antagonisms are expressed through
witchcraft. Isaak's dead father was of the local dominant clan while
his mother's clan was dominant in Ungulu. Isaak was chosen to
replace his father because of his aggressive personality and literacy.
He is in a difficult position because he must follow his father's clan
on account of owing them political power. Yet he should not alienate
his own clan since he can rely on them above all other kin. A Kaguru
leader needs support from as many quarters as possible.

    The factions and resultant witchcraft suspicions in Isaak's village
are due to his conflicting loyalties to both groups. One faction is
headed by Isaak, the other by Chisanga, an unmarried elderly woman
of Isaak's own matrilineage. All villagers follow either Chisanga or
Isaak. Isaak has not shown as much preference to Chisanga and her
children as they feel they deserve. Neither Chisanga nor her daughter
Rebeka is married. They brew beer and encourage men to enjoy
drinking, smoking, and other things. They appeal to Isaak as subchief
for preferential judgment when their activities cause litigation. They
are an embarrassment to Isaak, yet he desires their support as clan
members. Chisanga has another daughter, Helena, living in Isaak's
village. She is married to Muluhogo, an aggressive man who does not
care for Isaak. Muluhogo has a second wife living a few hundred
yards away in another hamlet, and Muluhogo divides his allegiance
between the two settlements. Chadibwa, a paternal kinsman of the

subchief, lives on the edge of the hamlet. Previously, he lived within, but he moved when Isaak became subchief. A gentle, amiable man, he dislikes Isaak but keeps his opinions to himself. Chisanga's son, Martini, and his wife and children live in Isaak's village. Two clan sister's sons live in a bachelor hut nearby. Sipriano, a son of Isaak's lineal kinsman, is married to Isaak's sister's daughter. Sipriano comes from another locality but moved to Isaak's village after Isaak took office. He is dependent upon Isaak for securing land rights but also for bridewealth to marry his cross-cousin, Isaak's niece. Another married nephew, Mikaeli, a son of Isaak's sister, also lives in the village. Isaak attracted four nephews to his village because of his influence and wealth as subchief. Other village members are in favor of Chisanga, although Chadibwa and Muluhogo strive to appear neutral.

Kaguru say that only children of the three strongest witches of the village, Isaak, Chisanga, and Rebeka, can be healthy. They claim the other children become ill and die from exposure to the crossfire of witchcraft from these three. Sipriano lost a son, and his wife refused intercourse until he procured counterwitchcraft. Helena's child was ill and she blamed Mikaeli's wife, saying it was revenge for her own child's death due to Helena's sister, Rebeka. Mikaeli and his wife moved to town to live with Mikaeli's mother to escape witchcraft accusation. Chadibwa also lost a child, but I could not discover whom he blamed. Shortly before I left Ukaguru, Isaak's infant son contracted dysentery, and Isaak's adolescent son got leprosy. Tension was high, but all still visited and chatted with one another.

The division was between Isaak's kin whom he supported and those close to Chisanga. Both factions had ambivalent attitudes toward Isaak. He was feared for his political power at court and for his reputation as a witch. He was disliked for his unpleasant personality and failure to grant the demands of his poorer, less useful kin. Yet everyone in the village asked favors when need arose. The poverty and weakness which led them to follow Isaak also made them jealous, resentful, and insecure. The situation was aggravated by two aggressive women who were economically independent and sufficiently distant lineally to be difficult to control.

Here is an example of accusation used to sever kin ties:

Harbeli accused his sister of keeping a cow which was part of his inheritance from a brother. The sister brought two more sisters and her son as supporting witnesses. Despite them, the court favored

Harbeli, probably because the subchief of the court wished Harbeli to
secure cash to pay a debt owed the subchief's sister's son. Senyagwa,
a paternal relative of the litigants, intervened on the women's side,
but believed the subchief had prejudged matters, so he would not
pursue the case. He warned Harbeli to forget about future debts with
him or Harbeli's sisters, to forget they were kin. Senyagwa said
Harbeli was bad because he had never helped his brother when he was
sick. Harbeli was publicly humiliated and accused his sisters of
bewitching their dead brother. He said they did not deserve any
inheritance. Several months later Senyagwa died. Now some of his
relatives say Harbeli was a witch and killed both his brother and
Senyagwa.

Kaguru believe a witch may harm anyone who does not help him or her.

Malanda asked a government lorry to pick him up. Since he refused
to pay, the driver refused. Later the lorry stalled en route. Malanda
secured a free ride in another lorry which passed. He signaled
indicating it was his witchcraft which caused the breakdown.

Securing cooperation is related to Kaguru accusations of Ngulu and a Zigula
as witches. While alien people are often suspected, suspicion can fall on any
stranger long among Kaguru. A suspect must be sufficiently free of social
ties to defy Kaguru sanctions. Even a Kaguru arriving from another locale
about whom little is known is suspect. The most renowned witch I encountered
was a Nyamwezi whose intelligence and boldness inspired respect, who built
up an extensive counterwitchcraft and alleged poison trade. His unusual dress
and fierce bearing encouraged this.

Kaguru consider certain locales more witch-ridden than others. These tend
to be areas with large settlements, not for common defense or cooperation as
in the past but centered around a mission, government, or trade facility. Living
close together without need for cooperation encourages accusations of
witchcraft.

A person succeeds in immoral behavior because of witchcraft, or a person
excuses himself by saying he was bewitched:

Headman Danyeli committed adultery with his brother's wife's
brother's wife. This is not prohibited but shows contempt toward his
brother. The woman claimed she got little sexual satisfaction from her
husband. The cuckold's kin believed both the woman's desire for
Danyeli (who as headman has cash and influence) and the cuckold's
reputed impotence were due to witchcraft.

Kaguru husbands and wives often accuse each other of witchcraft. If a man has many children by a woman, he is less likely to accuse her or her kin, since by matrilineal descent this would mean that he was accusing his children as well.

It appears that most accusations between spouses are by husbands against wives. These relate to fears that these husbands cannot control their wives. While residence is now often virilocal and a husband's rights to his wife's and children's labor perhaps stronger than ever, many Kaguru see wives as subversive. Children belong to one's wife's clan, and a man believes his wife teaches their children to favor her brother rather than him. A woman and her clan want children to augment their clan and care little who the father is. If they have few or none, they become very dissatisfied and may publicly accuse husbands of impotence or sterility. Kaguru songs and proverbs emphasize the sexual voracity of women, implying that one man cannot satisfy a woman. This is unsettling to prosperous old men who have taken young wives. Kaguru say, "You know your mother, but who is your father?" Kaguru men rejoice if a child resembles them. This insecurity is intensified by the fact that brewing beer is almost exclusively in the hands of women. A major source of ready cash, brewing allows wives to be somewhat free of their husbands even though they are supposed to give them such money. Where beer is sold, adultery is frequent. Christianity's condemnation of polygyny and divorce also adds to male insecurity. Since Christian girls cannot divorce men if they tire of them, they bewitch or poison husbands.

Chimwela was returned to her father. This was because she was a witch and therefore the bridewealth should be refunded. (Witchcraft is one of the few grounds by which a man may regain bridewealth when he, not his wife, initiates a divorce.) The woman made beer. Before taking it to a beer club, she illegally sold two shillings worth at home. She hid this money in her bedding. While she was at the club, her husband returned home, lay down, and discovered the coins. He took them but said nothing. At the club, someone asked the woman for change. She went home for the two shillings and discovered them gone but said nothing. Later her children teased her about having money from selling beer. She suspected them of stealing her money and abused them. Her husband overheard and asked why she had not reported her loss earlier, saying she probably earned the money by adultery. She did not reply, so he beat her. Then she tried to hang herself, but neighbors prevented her. Then she tried to pacify her husband, offering him beer. He said, "Why are you serving me beer now? You never let me have any before. You always want to sell it to other men. You probably bewitched it." Instead of drinking some to

show this was untrue, the woman threw the beer to the ground. Her
husband said that proved she was a witch and had poisoned the beer.

Co-wives often accuse each other of witchcraft. This is often out of jealousy
over a husband's affections. Sometimes a co-wife is jealous because she has
no children while another has many. A wife is often unwilling to let her
children take food from a co-wife, or from her husband's sister or her brother's
wife (all of whose children compete as heirs with her own). Since a woman
sometimes causes sickness of her co-wives' children, a woman prefers letting
her children eat with her clan sisters and mother. A childless wife accuses a
co-wife with children of causing her barrenness. The most complex witchcraft
case I observed was rooted in jealousy between two young co-wives and their
reports of each other's infidelities to their jealous, aging husband (Beidelman
1963f:88–90).

Witchcraft accusations are more frequent during personal difficulties.
Witchcraft increases with crop cultivation, when work peaks and neighbors
quarrel over boundaries. This is a time short in food and long in fatigue and
tension. Sick Kaguru see witches hovering at their bedsides, even at the
mission hospital. A drought may lead to a search for a witch.

Witch anecdotes were collected from Kaguru Christians, who consider these
as underscoring both traditional and Christian values:

> A catechist found a dead hare on his meat rack. He knew someone
> was trying to bewitch him, for neither he nor his wife put a hare
> there. Later, he found a smudge in the flour his wife set out to dry.
> The witch wanted him dead because he preached for God and against
> evil. Later, at a revival meeting, a man confessed that he had done
> these things.

> A man purchased *ikago* witchcraft to protect his gardens from theft.
> Later he was saved at a mission revival and dreamed Christ forbade
> using such medicine. He ostentatiously returned it to the man who had
> sold it to him. No one was surprised when this convert and his wife
> died. He had offended a witch, and everyone agreed that such
> medicine must be worth securing.

Suggestions that a relative is a witch resemble intimations by Kaguru that
they themselves are witches:

> Charles is an orphan with no siblings. He depends upon his mother's
> brother for support. He is insecure and speaks about people working
> against him. He insists he has seen his mother's brother walking

upside down, naked. He says this man has witchcraft to combat the local headman, with whom he often quarrels. Charles enjoys telling people that he has the support of a witch. By descent Charles too would probably be a witch if his mother's brother is.

Affluent men are often considered witches. A prosperous cultivator was said to have zombies who worked at night in his fields. Kaguru said that he did not work hard enough to produce so much alone. Shopowners also fit this category, especially if they are sufficiently businesslike to refuse kin credit. A prosperous man may be dangerous to others and to himself. He may have secured wealth by witchcraft, but if this is not shared, other witches envy him. Wealth is concealed, and undue mention of another's property indicates a witch. When I measured Kaguru fields as part of my work, Kaguru asked jokingly if I were a witch. The following shows economic leveling due to fear of witchcraft:

> Ezerkayam worked for Europeans in town. When he left work, his
> employers gave him toys for his son, Solomon. When Ezerkayam
> returned to Ukaguru, Solomon became ill. Ezerkayam feared his
> neighbors had bewitched Solomon out of envy, so he buried the toys.
> If his son had European toys, perhaps he had further wealth
> concealed. Solomon recovered.

SOME MODERN TRENDS

I could not determine whether Kaguru harbor more suspicions of witchcraft now than in the past. Certainly today fewer factors inhibit gossiping and accusation. With no death penalty, Kaguru can even accuse matrilineal kin with little risk. Modern factors have broken down political forces encouraging matrilineal and neighborly cooperation.

One paradox of modern life is that while both government and mission condemn witchcraft, such condemnation supports Kaguru conviction that witches do exist and remain a danger. The church publicizes witchcraft by allowing confessions at revivals. Mission emphasis upon Satan and his works in African custom gives new dimensions to witchcraft fears. Some Christians say witches will be kindling wood to light the fires of hell. The Swahili Bible, which converts study, states: "Thou shalt not suffer a witch (*mtawi, mchawi*) to live" Exodus 22.8); "Regard not them that have familiar spirits, neither seek after wizards (*watawi*) to be defiled by them . . ." (Leviticus 19.31); "A man also or woman that hath a familiar spirit, or that is a wizard (*mtawi*) shall surely be put to death. . ." (Leviticus 20.7). References to witches occur elsewhere.[12] Missionaries condemn witches but do not deny that they exist.

Government regulations make no distinction between a diviner, a seller of charms, a counterwitchcraft doctor, and a night-dancer, merely referring to "witch" (*mchawi*).[13] To Kaguru the Witchcraft Ordinance proves that even Europeans have a confused comprehension of these dangers.

CONCLUSION

Witchcraft is not clearly defined among Kaguru, since it includes a wide range of activities. This is not a case of my being unable to fit Kaguru characterization of their beliefs and practices into my own preconceptions. Despite the fact that Kaguru repeatedly describe witchcraft as bad and antisocial, their behavior itself indicates that it is not judged entirely negatively. This ambivalence reflects how Kaguru think and feel about relations between the individual and society. While nearly every Kaguru unhesitatingly avers that the worst personal misfortunes stem from witches, many dabble with such beliefs and practices, using them to assert personal claims and needs against others. Viewed negatively, witchcraft embodies the power that some have to spurn the claims and rights of others. Witches epitomize selfishness, greed, and contempt for others. Viewed more positively, as a kind of self-defense (presumably feigned and not actually practiced except as sorcery), witchcraft epitomizes the anger, frustration, and aggressiveness by which individuals assert claims against those who either fail to respond to obligations as they should or abuse their proper relations with kin and neighbors. Where witchcraft is viewed as evil, it is inherent to one's being rather then a passing product of contingencies. It is expressed through horrible perversities.

Kaguru imagine witches through a wide range of qualities, from those perhaps secretly coveted, such as power and aggressiveness, to those vigorously denied, such as incest and cannibalism. At the less repellent, more ambivalent level, witchcraft is dark (complex), impenetrable, energetic, the product of extraordinary knowledge and untrammeled abilities. At the worst, it denies proper humanity, reducing humans to the level of wild beasts.

Kaguru fear both witches and accusations of being ones themselves, but the intensity and frequency of their fears and the actions resulting from them vary widely with individuals and the situations in which they meet. Individuals accused of witchcraft often reject social sanctions which their fellows try to apply. Most occupy positions of power and/or security which provide independence. Consequently, they sometimes disregard objections made by others. A few are independent because they are so anomic that they have little to lose by rejecting norms. Yet most Kaguru are afraid of being accused and only rarely find independent conduct worth risking or even possible. Most are secretive and suspicious, dislike depending upon anyone, but are grudgingly aware that their survival requires continual cooperation and approval by kin and neighbors. Through cooperation and affability they maintain security and try to keep free from attacks and accusations. Yet these fears encourage subterfuge, veiling aims and motives against the danger that those on whom one depends are not what they appear. The fearful assume attributes of witches themselves. They nurse suspicions and fears about others, perhaps even exacerbated by their sense of frustration and powerlessness about not voicing and asserting their own demands.

Outstanding and deviant persons do not respond to accusations or threats of witchcraft in so fearful a manner. To them, accusations present little danger and may even be used to advantage. Attributes of independence and power strengthen reputed witches in that they are not expected to conform but can demand conformity from others. These powers reinforce more tangible ones based on economic, political, or personal advantages. Anomic individuals foster such suspicions; they have relatively little to lose, especially now that witchcraft is no longer punished by death. Personal aggressiveness and eccentric individuality may awe others, even though one risks being derided, avoided or, rarely, thought mad.

Even apparently cynical, self-reputed witches are not free from witchcraft fears. In a society with few enduring economic or political pressures necessitating cooperation, witchcraft fear and accusation provide one ideological means by which individuals enforce cooperation from others.

The Kaguru witch recalls what Scheler terms *ressentiment*. This is a "self-poisoning of the mind, . . . a lasting mental attitude, caused by the systematic repression of certain emotions and affects which, as such, are normal components of human nature. . . . The emotions and the affects primarily concerned are revenge, hatred, malice, envy, the impulse to detract, and spite" (1972:45). Ugly as these feelings seem, they are human. Resentment is caused by those seething with emotions being thwarted from expressing them. These fester and are redirected inward. Such negative attributes characterize both the witch and those who accuse others. The victim of witchcraft believes he is entitled to better treatment than he receives, but lacks power to bring this about. Where abuse persists due to differences of age, wealth, and gender, resentment is greatest. Comparing themselves to those they neither equal nor control but with whom they must interact, victims nurse resentment and endow others with mounting animus. Resentment grows from frustration over rational expectations that are denied legitimacy. Prevented self-realization in social discourse, the suspector of witchcraft transmutes his energies into assaulting his world. He or she endows the witch with monstrous egoism and greed invalidating humanity and the social roles and relations associated with it. Witches therefore superficially appear human but lose their rights to be treated so. They are beasts imbued with disorder and a lack of measure antithetical to moral life. Normative beliefs "would be fatal unless in some degree kept

158 Moral Imagination in Kaguru Modes of Thought

at bay'' (Empson 1964:158), and witches vicariously embody this suppressed condemnation of morality, even while themselves being rejected on moral grounds. A witch crystallizes the oppressive aspects of a society, where individuals appear to subvert its purported values and aims to their own ends.

The imaginative picture of a witch is subversive on two counts. It provides a mode through which the frustrated and discontent reject relations that seem more exploitative than supportive. Second, it casts a shadow over the crucial tie between the individual and society. Rights and obligations between Kaguru may be moral and right in a world of no witches, but in one where they exist, society itself embodies the means by which individuals use and abuse others. Humans are not what they seem, and consequently neither is society in practice. I do not argue that Kaguru beliefs in witches and witchcraft result from a total rejection of society. Rather, these provide modes by which subversive questioning may be formulated into appeals, threats, and explanations negotiated in social action. Witchcraft epitomizes the agonistic aspect of social interdependence. Humans are superior to animals because of speech and customs, but words lie as well as bind, and customs allow domination as well as fair exchange.

This chapter has bridged the realms of the readily discernible and the fantastic. The social motives and behaviors described are real and common, even though, to an outsider, some aspects of witch behavior seem imaginary in that they are undemonstrable in our terms. Indeed, even for Kaguru, part of the great danger of witches is that one cannot be absolutely sure who they are and how they operate. Kaguru invariably describe witches as bad, despite implications of some secret empathy toward some of the hostilities and hatred which witches embody. Kaguru concede that witches do exist, even though they themselves recognize that not all that is credited to witchcraft is accepted as such by everyone at all times.

No such blurring between reality and fantasy occurs in tales which all Kaguru agree are mere fiction, that they are ''not important'' but ''merely'' play. Yet the characters and actions of the protagonists in Kaguru stories are portrayed in far more ambiguous or even ambivalent moral light than are witches. In the next two chapters I explore the fully imaginary by relating and discussing tales that Kaguru themselves readily describe as not true. What we should keep in mind here is the direct correlation between the degree of imaginariness and the degree of subversion and antisocial judgments that such imagery entails. Basic rules and motives governing all aspects of social life are cast in a questionable moral light whereby little appears free from doubt and questioning. In these stories, Kaguru imagination goes furthest toward exploring the dangerous significance and possibilities of human feelings, motives, and conduct as bounded, valenced, and masked by social conventions.

NOTES

1. This is an expanded and revised version of 1963f, 1970b, 1971b. Many additional cases and anecdotes of witchcraft are published in 1963f.

2. We cannot prove that witches do not exist, and whether they do has little bearing on the key issues concerning anthropologists (Winch 1964; Needham 1978: 27–28). In the field I gave Kaguru every indication that I believed in witches and purchased antiwitchcraft materials on appropriate occasions.

3. Early missionaries in Ukaguru comment: ". . . [witchcraft] is the bane of the country—it enters into almost everything. All losses, crosses, and disappointments are supposed to be the result of witchcraft. Hence the great demand for charms. . . " (*Church Missionary Gleaner* 1902: 52–53).

4. The Swahili word for a sorcerer or witch, *mchawi*, has little force when used by Kaguru. *Uchawi* appears in Swahili versions of government regulations and missionary tracts.

5. Witches must be adults. Kaguru find it ridiculous to imagine children as witches, although this is reported elsewhere in Africa. A witch must have moral and jural responsibility which he or she rejects. Children lack such qualities or have them to a poor degree.

6. Kaguru believe that someone (called *ifuma*) may unconsciously cause bad luck (*chisu chihele*), but such a one is never a witch nor is the trouble serious.

7. Some Kaguru said witches might have intercourse with animals because they stop at nothing. Kaguru believe that bestiality might be a sign of witchcraft, but not all who engage in bestiality are witches (see Beidelman 1961a). Kaguru insisted that homosexual relations do not occur, though a few had acquired such interests from town. Presumably these too might imply witchcraft.

8. A parent disowns a child by symbolic incest, standing naked before a child, who is then cursed.

9. Presumably she would accuse him of abuse. The case would not have dealt officially with witchcraft since such cases cannot be heard by Kaguru courts.

10. Last describes saving a Kaguru from such a death (1883:519). He describes a Zigula witchcraft trial and punishment which may correspond to Kaguru methods since they claim influence by Zigula (*Church Missionary Intelligencer* 1880:743). A missionary report from Ukaguru lists various ordeals similar to those I have indicated (*Church Missionary Gleaner* 1902:53).

11. Early African mission employees in Ukaguru purchased counterwitchcraft medicine on the coast (*Proceedings of the Church Missionary Society* 1898–99:99).

12. See: Leviticus 20.6; Samuel I 15.23; Kings II 9.22, *Maagano ya Kale* (Old Testament in Swahili 1935).

13. By law, " 'Witchcraft' includes sorcery, enchanting, bewitching, or the purported exercise of any occult power, or the purported possession of any occult knowledge." The Witchcraft Ordinance states: "Any person who commits an offence against this ordinance with intent to cause death, disease, injury, or misfortune to any community, class of persons, person, or animals, or to cause injury to any property shall be liable to imprisonment of either description for any period not exceeding seven years or to a fine not exceeding four thousand shillings, or to both such fine and imprisonment" (*The Laws of Tanganyika* 1947, I:321 to 322).

CHAPTER 10.

Speculations about the Social Order: Stories and Society

> Some have in reading so many tales and stories, as there is nothing they would insinuate, but they can wrap it into a tale, which serveth both to keep themselves more in guard, and to make others carry it with more pleasure.
>
> Francis Bacon, On Cunning, *Essays*

> Necessity makes an honest man a knave.
>
> Daniel Defoe, *Serious Reflections of Robinson Crusoe*

KAGURU FOLKTALES AND SOCIETY

At night during the dry season it is common to find Kaguru gathered about a hearth or assembled under a house's overhanging roof where one or more skilled storytellers recount tales and anecdotes.[1] This is especially likely where a neighborhood has many young people still not old enough to be interested in courting, dances, and drink. While Kaguru themselves say that stories are for children, most adults know these tales and at storytimes one often finds older people showing as much interest and amusement as children. When I asked Kaguru why they told these stories, most said it was to entertain the young and pass time. A few added that some stories helped the young learn about life. Despite frequent remarks that stories are trivial, when I began collecting such tales Kaguru showed considerable interest, making sure that I got them right. Many remarked that they associated such stories with some of their happiest and securest past moments, nights around a fire after a good meal, warm and comfortable and entertained by grandparents or great-aunts and uncles—for the ideal storytellers and their audience consist of those of alternate generations, those least constrained by the ordinary rules involved in domestic and lineal authority.

Kaguru recognize that initiation songs and riddles have hidden meanings, so that for them it makes sense to discuss how they should explain these properly. But few Kaguru accept the idea that there is anything deep to explain in stories. Yet one has only to observe Kaguru involved in storytelling to appreciate how absorbing and pleasurable they find such tales. However disinclined Kaguru are to explain their stories, these serve expressive purposes, even though only vaguely realized by Kaguru themselves. The significance of these stories lies in their supposed irrelevance, in their fantastic qualities. It is through such tales that Kaguru safely yet imaginatively explore possibilities about their social world by stressing some discrepancies with reality. As Simmel states: "For whoever stands outside his boundary in some sense knows that he stands within it, that is, knows it as boundary" (1971:355). Simmel himself says that such a stance is imaginative art and, as such, is liberating.[2] These tales describe society, but it is a society somehow haywire, resembling, yet wildly different from, reality.

Everyday life and ritual occasions confirm and sustain pervasive moral concepts. In contrast, the imaginative and fantastic places and times of oral literature, what Bakhtin terms the "folkloristic chronotope" (1981:84, 146–151, 159) or Frye the "topocosm" (1963:64), provide means by which these same concepts are probed and questioned, even to the point of seeming subversion. Kaguru stories are packed with action, but they do not represent how Kaguru actually live. Rather, they unfold some of the logical and also contradictory permutations that Kaguru beliefs and values may take when developed to extremes, due either to the confrontation of opposing principles or to the failure of those principles to contain and withstand the individual interests and passions of contending people.

Kaguru stories represent a scrutiny of social order through the long end of the telescope, as it were. This fantastic distancing is a way of both understanding and yet containing through deceptive trivialization. It may even be that one of the outcomes of such stories is that they imply the fictive quality of all social life, the fact that its moral worth is existentially based. If this is so, and I believe that it is, then Kaguru claims as to the unimportance of stories actually reflect their reluctance to approach subversion except in a roundabout way. As Empson notes, "accepted official beliefs may be things that would be fatal unless in some degree kept at bay" (1964:158), and the fantastic, grotesque, and mocking quality of many tales does that, though only if it is not given undue prominence.

Jackson notes that folktales "are not 'charters' for social action. They are explorations into the problems of right conduct" (1982:31), that these narratives make and remake the world in a manner resembling the constructs of ritual (ibid.:3). Imaginative moral inquiry is at the heart of many Kaguru stories. Indeed, the more fantastic and bizarre they may at first appear, the more likely they contain hidden and disturbing speculation.[3] What Kaguru tales do, above all else, is undertake moral inquiry and speculation. If these also amuse and divert, so much the better.

In the course of my fieldwork I collected many forms of Kaguru oral literature, including 178 folktales. These are published and therefore available for further consideration by those curious to see how well my present arguments fit a broad sample. In this and the following chapter I consider some basic features characterizing these stories as imaginative speculation about Kaguru morality and society. I cannot cover all aspects of such diverse material in two chapters, but I believe that what I provide is representative of the kinds of dilemmas or problems which Kaguru stories confront. In this chapter I present tales with human protagonists. I postpone considering animal stories until the next chapter since those raise further, more complex analytical issues better faced after I have first set more basic interpretive matters straight.

Rather than continue discussion of Kaguru oral literature in this abstract vein, I present six texts, commenting and developing arguments as I progress from story to story.

The Evil at the Foot of the Fig Tree: Sharing and Community

Long ago there was a great famine in the land. Then the chief of the land told his people, "I dislike my country. People should leave and none should remain here. What else is there to do? I am not pleased to see people dying of famine. Find somewhere for you and your children to go to escape the famine. When things become better and the rains are falling nicely, those who want to come back, let them return. But if a man does not want to return, it does not matter."

When the people heard this, they saw that these words of the chief were the only course left to follow. Now among these there was one elder along with his children and his sons-in-law (*walima*). He called his children and their husbands to come and then he told them, "I want one child to come with me to look for a land which has a small valley good for cultivating vegetables. If I told everyone to go together, we would not know where to go since the children would not be able to wander about."

One of his sons-in-law said to him, "Father-in-law (*imukwe*), I am ready to go. Let us prepare food for the journey."

The women cooked *sunga*-vegetables[4] which were collected to eat during the famine. They cooked enough vegetables to be used for six days. The next day the elder left with his son-in-law and their vegetables wrapped up in parcels. They walked for seven days and still had not seen any well watered place for cultivation. Then the vegetable provisions were finished. On the eighth day they reached a small valley which had many fig trees (*makuyu*) and which was very well watered. The elder told his son-in-law, "Sir, climb that fig tree to see if this valley will be large enough for everyone."

The son-in-law climbed the fig tree and when he reached the top, he looked down on every side. Down below, the elder was opening a concealed parcel in which some *sunga*-vegetables were wrapped, which he then ate. The son-in-law was looking down in that direction in order to tell his father-in-law what he had seen and he saw his father-in-law eating the vegetables by himself. When the elder had finished eating, he called to his son-in-law, "What does the valley look like to you? Is it large enough and is it good?"

The elder asked his son-in-law, "What if the fig tree spoils the rest of the valley? Should we continue searching further?"

The son-in-law said, "Sir, we can improve things by the time that the harvest is ready. It is only at the base of this tree that there is something bad. All the rest of the valley is good."[5]

So he came down and then they returned back. All those days they had been traveling they had no provisions and ate only wild fruit. When they reached home, they explained that they had found a valley which was well-watered with streams through its length and which was large enough for the entire settlement. So they all went. Since the way was known, it did not take them many days to reach there. Then each person divided off his own garden and hoed it and planted it. In a short time vegetables were up which they ate until the gardens in which they had planted maize were ripe. Then the famine was over.

The course which a famine takes is not understood by people, so when it has ended, people say, "Bad deeds and suffering are forgotten when a famine is ended." The people harvested their crops, filled their storehouses, and made beer. They forgot all about the famine which was past.

One day beer was made in the house of the son-in-law. When the people were drinking, the elder remembered the words of his son-in-law about how the foot of the fig tree was bad. So he said, "Now then, how was it bad? Haven't we harvested these crops there?"

Then the son-in-law replied to him saying, "Sir, when I climbed the top of that fig tree, I was astonished to see how a famine can make a person's mind foolish. You know very well that we were two and that our food was nearly finished. We had kept only a little with which to carry on. But you took and ate that food by yourself. Then when you asked me what the valley was like, I answered speaking not about the valley but about you, the elder of the village from which we had come and the man who was the leader on our journey. When I

came to the valley and saw the trees in it, I saw the fig tree. I
climbed it because it was the biggest of the trees, and in doing so I
had a way of saying to you what I found out about you through
climbing that tree.''

When he had said these things, those who were there said that the
elder had done a selfish thing. But bad deeds done during a famine
should not be kept track of later, so they drank beer and danced together happily again. They built a good village and many people
stayed there comfortably and there was no famine for many years.

This tale is mainly concerned with the vexing fact that those with authority
and power do not as individuals always measure up to the moral demands of
their positions. As Jackson observes for similar West African texts, there is
a gap between "birth and worth, position and disposition" (1982:27). The
only way for such abuse to be contained is through "practical morality based
on mutuality" (ibid.:30). One approach to this difficulty, and that seemingly
advocated by Jackson, is through developing sympathetic awareness of others.
Some would argue that morality generally derives from just such imaginative
sensitivity (cf. Scheler 1954:247). This is the approach taken here as well as
in the story that follows. This works, however, only as long as there is a
communal sense that respect and affection are worth keeping and cultivating.
Then corrective punishment follows from a sense of shame, a recognition that
other members of a group would not care for someone with such mean qualities. As we shall see, other Kaguru tales imagine mutuality in a harsher vein,
implying that abuse of power is best punished not by withdrawal of affection
and respect, but by withdrawal of cooperation and help or by a counterof-
fensive of hostile acts.

I subtitled this text as one dealing with disruption within a settlement,
whereas the next story, while similar in theme, is characterized as dealing
with a disruption between affines. Yet both stories deal with affinal relations.
My reasons for making this contrast lie in the texts, relating to a notion
mentioned earlier, Bakhtin's term *chronotope*. All narrative has some sense
of time and place, however odd or restrictive, even if it is, as in these folktales,
kept deliberately vague. What is omitted is as significant as what appears,
and in this case it is important that the only group is a settlement and the
only protagonists are an elder and his son-in-law. To get a good sense of this
tale, we must focus on these features. The group is presented as a solidary
settlement. It moves under the duress of famine, but that movement underscores the group's unity because it is a search for a site where the settlement
will find sufficient lands to remain together. Furthermore, any Kaguru recognizes the problem implied by the choice of characters. The son-in-law
(affine who cultivates) has married into the group, probably because he could

not secure sufficient bridewealth to take a wife to his own settlement. Whatever the reason, he is a lone outsider obliged to work off brideservice. Yet he is also an asset, providing labor and defense and fathering children. He is obliged to the elder (group) for securing his wife, but he has a right to support and protection in return. He was a stranger, but he is now a member of the community, although vulnerable as a junior affine. He is, as it were, "kin on probation." In the past a wise elder would have sought to give everyone in the settlement just due, even affines, since the larger his village became, the safer and more productive it would be, and as a result his own name and influence would be promoted. Thus, the selfish elder of the story is not only mean, but shortsighted.

Finally, the theme of famine represents an important kind of time; it is a crisis, but not an unusual one. Traditionally, resources were always in some sense scarce. They were less plentiful before than after harvests; they were felt wanting by young men seeking bridewealth and by anyone involved in litigation or propitiation of the dead. Lean times occur every three or four years in Kaguruland, with a really hard famine at least every decade; true famine is thus likely to confront any mature person several times in her or his lifetime. Famine, then, is no extraordinary theme; rather, it is a shorthand expression for a vast and continued range of needs and difficulties which any group experiences, not only because of the vagaries of climate but because of the varying fortunes and developmental life cycles of people.

I opened this chapter with a "nice" story in the sense that it portrays people as frail but not truly bad. The tale ends implying the elder may have learned a lesson. This was possible because a disadvantaged person dared speak out and a privileged person agreed to listen, and because the damages done were not irremediable. That is very far from Kaguru reality.

The Son-in-law and His Father-in-law: Sharing and Affinity

Long ago there was a certain boy and he went to a faraway land to marry. When he married, he stayed there a year, but his food was porridge and meat for he was not eating any vegetables. His in-laws were eating vegetables such as peas, but he himself had told them that he never ate peas and that he had been accustomed to eating meat and milk at his home, but all that was just lies for at his place there were no cows nor milk and he was likewise eating peas.

The name of that boy was Chilongola and one day he set out on a journey to pay his respects to his sisters in a certain country near where he was staying with his in-laws, and when he reached his sisters, food was prepared and its relish was peas which were nicely cooked and which he then ate. He spent all day there and when he saw that the sun was about to set, he started to return to his place.

On the way returning he felt his stomach upset and so he relieved himself in the bush, and when he had relieved himself, his shit was peas which he had eaten there where he had spent the day. Then when he had finished, he started to walk, but his shit of peas became animated and followed him. He tried to run off but the shit followed him.

He walked and the shit did the same until he arrived with it at the house of his in-laws and then his in-laws swept the shit away with a broom, but as they did so they recognized that it was the shit of their son-in-law. Then they didn't say anything and that shit did not stir again and was thrown into the bush. The boy felt great shame that his shit had been seen by his in-laws and still greater shame that the shit was from peas which he had said he never ate.

Here affinity and residence are further examined, though in terms of only one main character, another youth working off his brideservice in a distant settlement. Unlike the first story, this contrasts two moral spaces that should be more alike than they are. It is implied here that the boy should become more like a kinsman to his affines if he wants a proper marriage. The moral seems simple enough on the surface, but for Kaguru ambiguities arise. The theme of alimentation is explicit, but that of sexuality is only implied, though the two are closely linked for Kaguru. While the actions in both this and the previous story stem from greed, in the first, actual bodily processes were not mentioned. Here, not only does alimentation dominate the tale, but its more negative aspect, defecation, prevails. This calls attention to the ambiguous nature of these relations. Sexual relations, while necessary, are unclean, and it is the providers of women who are sexually compromised by the relations. Sexual relations are profoundly intimate, but conjure up associations of hostility, domination, and pollution. While eating is often compared to copulation, commensality and feeding bear no such ambiguous load but rather suggest trust, reliance, and support. If alimentation involves any shame, it is only in two senses expressed here: greed and defecation. For the distrustful affines, the youth's alimentation assumes negative tones. If the youth were more sociable, he would change his ways and eat with his affines in the way he does with his natal kin. Yet Kaguru know that this cannot be: affines become like kin but, because one copulates with them, they are never "complete kin";[6] that is why they may not be entirely trusted. Because of this sexual connection there is said always to be some shame in the relations between affines, and this, in turn, inhibits truly candid expressions of what one thinks and wants.

While this tale is about dishonesty and greed, its overtones imply that the situation between affines can never be entirely resolved. This is especially clear from the theme of excrement itself. It should never be seen by others, yet here it is ever present and confronts others as the basest side of the youth's appetitive nature. So too his sexuality confronts his affines. The youth is expected to present a socially constrained self to affines (quasi kin), yet since their link is his sexuality, this cannot easily be. The youth's bodily appetites both bind and separate him from the two groups, his copulating affines and his commensal kin.

The Man and Wife and the People Who Could Not Shit: Eluding Affinity

Long ago there was a man who had a wife and two children. They stayed there in that land of theirs and then both the father and wife died and the children were left alone. One of those children was a boy and one a girl. Those children had many problems getting their food, and it was a very hard task. The boy was trapping guinea fowl in the forest, and when he killed them, he would eat them there alone, hidden from his sister.

That girl was in deep trouble because of hunger, so she was eating fruits nearby their settlement where they were staying. One day that boy went again to the forest to hunt and trap and as he wandered here and there he found himself at a village there in the forest. The sun was setting, so he entered that village. That village had large herds of cattle, but the owners of the village were not there and the village was left empty. That boy went into the houses and ate the porridge along with the milk that had been left by the owners. Then when he was full, he left and went home.

Then when he arrived home he told his sister, and so the next day they both went, and when they arrived there, they still did not find any people. All the people had gone to the gardens or were off herding. So they went into the houses and ate all the porridge along with the milk which the owners of the village had left. Then they were tired and the sun was setting, but they were unable to walk on account of being so full. So they hid in one of the houses.[7]

In the evening when the owners returned, they found that all their porridge and milk had been eaten, so they began to prepare more food. Now the children were told to fetch firewood to put on the fire for cooking and that firewood was in that house where those two were hiding. As the children were gathering the firewood, they heard people laughing, so they said, "Now then who's there?"

Then those two children told them, "It's we who ate your food."

Then the others answered them, "Now why are you hiding?" So they brought them out from there where they were and then those two children told them, "Show us where the latrine is because now our insides are full and we want to shit." But the others answered them, "What is that?" Then those two said, "Now don't you know what it is to shit?" So then those children shat in the bush in the way that they were accustomed.

At dawn the next day the owners of the village told those children, "Show us how to shit." Then the youth showed them. Then they said, "Yes, we don't know about that. By what were you punctured?" Then those children told them, "We were pierced by rods of metal." So those people told them, "There are rods of metal here. Now pierce us as well." So that boy told them, "You'll sleep until evening." Then they said, "But we wouldn't mind that if we'd then be able to shit at a latrine."

Then the villagers gave those children iron rods and then they put them into a fire and let them there until they got red hot. When they were ready to take them, the two children told them, "Now the irons are hot. People should approach and we'll start our work, but let's start with the village elder." So the people came near.

The village elder was the first to be pierced by the iron rods. The boy took the iron and then he pierced the village elder in the buttocks and then the elder fell down there. Then the boy said, "Cover him with cloth so that he recovers. Let him sleep." Then the boy pierced all the men and women and children and so they all died. When the boy saw that he had killed them all, he told his sister, "Let us pick up the people and throw them into the bush."[8] So they carried off the corpses of the people until they were done.

When they were done, both he and his sister stayed there in that village for many days and they were rich. Now one day two strangers, a man and wife, came and those two were relatives of the ones the children had killed. Then they asked those children, "You, children, where are the owners of the village?" Now those strangers told those children, "Prepare food for us to eat."

The girl prepared food quickly while that boy ran into the bush and struck down a woodrat and then he mixed its gall with milk and gave it to the visitors and they ate it. When both finished eating, they died. Then that boy and his sister continued to stay in the village along with their riches happily for many years.

This is a tale about the pleasures of incest. It is a story about profound subversion. These meanings are ones I doubt that Kaguru would ever freely acknowledge. The story has two spaces of reference, one that is momentary but significant and one that dominates the plot. The story begins with an ordinary village where a brother and sister and their parents live; the parents die, and the brother and sister leave the village for the wilderness. All of the rest of the tale takes place in the fantastic, upside-down world of that wilderness. There in this sphere of disorder the siblings try to build a new life. The first thing the storyteller gets clear is that after the two siblings are cut free from normal, moral society, they have abnormal and hostile relations, consistent with potential sexuality. The brother repeatedly cheats his sister about food. He does not share. Yet this is not here a source of approbation; instead, it is presented as a mere trait of character. The couple do not share food, and so the immediate implication is that they are not true kin and therefore they may have sexual relations. The couple are implicitly incestuous and therefore witches, but this is presented in favorable terms—not easy, to be sure, but perhaps acceptable given that the people whose village they enter are clearly not fully human.

Gone from conventional society, the sibling couple steal food and hide (presumably in a food loft) in a village of strangers, behavior also suggesting witchcraft. When the strange owners appear, they turn out to be people who cannot defecate, who cannot give up what they receive. Not only are these people incomplete physiologically, but they are metaphorically unacceptable affines in that they take but do not yield. The siblings do defecate; yet clearly it is a troubled defecation in that their diet has come from acts of betrayal and deception in the bush. Now the alien village has plenty, and if the siblings employ subterfuge, it need no longer be toward one another as before, but toward strangers. These strangers do not defecate and so are quite innocent about the negative, corporeal nature of property. The siblings claim that they will normalize them by giving them anuses, but in reality they annihilate them. They then later also destroy these people's kin by using poison (witchcraft or sorcery), turning on them in quite an opposite way from being the naively hospitable strangers they have just slain. The siblings are clearly witches yet are presented as clever, not as bad people: the story presents a forbidden relationship as a solution to "the matrilineal puzzle" in that these siblings now constitute a new social world. Outsiders are denigrated and excluded, and society is reduced to a brother and sister of one clan. Given their newly found wealth, the previously untrusting and suspicious siblings of the wilderness again stand together to found a new, albeit perverse, world.

The Men Who Married Man-Eaters: Affinity and Danger[9]

There was a hunter who took a wife who bore him a son. When the child was grown, he became a herdboy. His father told him, "My

son, take care of our sheep but don't enter the forest. You look after
them there in the pasture."

The boy obeyed his father's words. But then one day the boy said
to himself, "Sometimes parents are only frightened for nothing. I'm
going to look into the forest to see if there is good grass there." Then
he went toward the forest forbidden by his father. When he reached
the forest, he put his herd within while he himself remained outside.
Later everything was quiet. He could not see or hear where the sheep
were. They had all gone away. He started searching for them. He
looked all day in vain and then he began to shout. Suddenly two hunters appeared and so he yelled and cried all the harder. "Oh! Oh! Oh!
Today I am going to be beaten by my father." The two hunters whom
he saw were chasing a bushbuck. When they saw the boy, they asked
him, "Young man, why are you crying and throwing yourself down
on the ground? Why did you do that when your father told you not to
take sheep into the forest? Go home! It is nightfall."

Then the hunters continued chasing their bushbuck. Further ahead
they killed it and then they skinned it. When they had removed one
leg, the bushbuck stood up alive and ran off. The bushbuck's standing
up and running off astonished the hunters. They asked one another in
surprise, "What strange thing is this? Now let us follow to see how
this strange thing ends."

The hunters followed their bushbuck and further on they found it
and slew it again. They skinned it and when they had removed a leg,
the same thing happened as before. It stood up alive and ran off. One
of the hunters asked the other, "Should we leave this matter alone?"
The other told him, "Let us see how it turns out."

Then they followed chasing the bushbuck. Further ahead they
reached a village. There in the village were two young girls. When
they saw the girls, the hunters decided that they would like to marry
them. Then they asked one another if they should speak for them in
marriage. One said to the other, "Comrade, if we marry these
women, we won't return home. For how can we leave our offspring
behind with the owners of the village?" His comrade replied, "You
are speaking like that because you're changing your mind, but mine is
made up to marry them." His comrade then agreed and kept his
doubts to himself.

The hunters married the girls and then stayed with them for three
days. On the fourth night while they were sleeping together the
women turned into wild beasts. They became beasts with tails waving
in the air and they tried to eat the hunters. Then one of the hunters,
the one who had doubted the plan to marry, waked and saw the

strange sight of humans having become wild beasts (*makala*). Then he
coughed in order to see what the beasts would do when they knew
that they were being watched. When he coughed, they turned back
into humans and lay on their beds and slept. The hunter was unable to
sleep that night. At dawn he told his comrade, "Comrade, these
women are turning into wild beasts. Last night I saw these women
turned into wild beasts."

Then his comrade said, "Now don't tell bad lies. How could such
beautiful girls turn into wild beasts? You only want some excuse to
leave them."

Then his comrade replied, "Now this evening get a long cord and
tie it to your toe. Then at night when you find that I'm pulling it, you
wake up and you'll learn that they have turned into wild beasts. Then
you can see for yourself."

So that evening they acted according to the plan that they had made
that morning. True enough the women changed into wild beasts. The
one fellow pulled the cord on his comrade's toe. He was waked up
and saw for himself that the women had really changed into wild
beasts with tails waving in the air. Then he coughed and the wild
beasts changed back into humans again and slept in their beds.

At dawn the men spent the day working on a chicken coop
(*itundu*).[10] Then when it was finished, they both got inside it along
with their bows and arrows and then they sang this song:

> Magude, ring, ring the bell!
> Magude, ring, ring the bell!
> Ring, ring, ring the bell! Send us home!
> Ring the bell! Ring, ring the bell today!

Then when they sang like that, the chicken coop flew into the air and
took them to their home. And that is the end of the strange affair of
the bushbuck which was flayed that time.

This is the most subtly constructed story I collected. Its theme is a male
aspect of the "matrilineal puzzle," how men are given away to strangers in
marriage yet retain their primary interest in the fate of their sisters' children
and not their own.[11] Men's place of orientation is possibly threefold, depending on the kinds of marriages they and their kin have made: to the
settlements from which they came, to settlements where they now reside after
marriage, and to the settlements (people) where their sisters live after marriage. The story well illustrates Lévi-Strauss's observations that "repetition
has its function to make the structure of the myth apparent" (1958:65). The
same plot is presented three times, each with added intensity and significance

for Kaguru in that the symbols employed involve increasing power. In the tale we therefore gain a threefold spectrum of Kaguru notions about power and affinity. The final version of the plot represents an insoluble problem: because of the prohibitions against incest, men must marry alien women whom they cannot trust. In some cases, especially where they are poor and lack large quantities of bridewealth, they must actually suffer the disadvantage of living with these alien and untrustworthy affines. Furthermore, men must depend not on their own sexuality but on that of their sisters, who sleep with someone else to produce heirs (sister's children). Not only, then, do men sometimes face marriage into a strange group, but their own sexuality is deflected to the advantages of outsiders, and the sexuality about which they are most concerned jurally, their sisters', is out of their immediate control. This story is about men and their marriages, but it implies that men's insecurities about their sisters feed the anxiety they feel about their own relations with their wives.

When I first encountered this story, I was deeply perplexed that Kaguru find it cohesive. To me the story fell into three unconnected episodes. Later, as I learned more about Kaguru speech and thought, I realized that these three episodes represent three aspects of one process.

The key to understanding how these three seemingly separate stories are connected lies in the Kaguru metaphors for sexual domination by men over women: herding, hunting, and marrying. None of these is what it first seems, and it is clear that in fact men do not dominate women, at least in the ways they imagine that they should. Or, if men do dominate women, it is a risky enterprise fraught with anxiety to men attempting to pull it off.

The story opens with a youth herding livestock who disobeys instructions for keeping these out of the wilderness where they would be lost. Here it is important to know that Kaguru often describe male leaders of matrilineages as herdsmen or as rams controlling a flock of sheep. The first scenario portrays a male unable to control the women in his care. The forest, the wilderness, represents an alien disorder confronting all men seeking wives outside their own ordered world. The second version of the scenario emphasizes the motif of hunting. Now to hunt and to slay are both common Kaguru metaphors for sexual gratification by men. (Remember the boy's father, domestically successful, is a hunter.) Hunting expresses domination of the wilderness and for Kaguru, and many other East African peoples, is associated with especially successful, manly leaders. Even women sometimes voice these themes, though they view these supposedly negative aspects in a rather positive and amused way. In the tale the quarry cannot be slain; it resurrects itself repeatedly. This drives the hunters on. This relates to men's fear of being unable to bestow sexual fulfillment to women. Sex is considered a crucial weapon for men to control wives who, they fear, keep thinking of how to use their children to relate back to their brothers, who, alas, cannot copulate with them.

The third version of this scenario is the most overt in its message. Men marry those who are strangers and allow their sexuality to induce them to leave their natal villages and kin to reside with strangers. They even, temporarily, resign themselves to allowing their sexuality to work for strangers by fathering children, who they will find difficult to take back to their own kin. Marriage becomes a kind of betrayal of their sociable humanity. At night the men go to bed with these women, who then appear as beasts. In a strange place, as night settles, forming a frontier between conformity and deviancy, the women become man-eaters (*makala*) or witches, with tails (*mkila*, tail, but also a euphemism for penis) waving in the dark. Discovering the true, bestial nature of their wives, the youths flee by means of an *itundu* (chicken coop, but also bridewealth), returning to their kin. The storyteller makes it clear that they take their bows and arrows (sexual vitality) with them.

The tale lays out a central dilemma of Kaguru society: how can one retain the essential loyalties of both men and women in a matrilineage if one allows either to depart to settle elsewhere with a spouse? Furthermore, while people seek marriage and say this is good, after women bear children it may be to their advantage to promote ties with their brothers at the cost of those toward their own husbands. For Kaguru men, but not women, ties to their children run against those to their matrilineage; ties to their wives run against those to their sisters, but that parallels the situation for women, whose ties to their husbands conflict with those toward their brothers. Matrilineal relations pose problems, but these are here presented as tougher on men than on women. The story offers no solution; none exists, and Kaguru know that.

The Beast Which Finished the People of the Land: Succession and Domination

Long ago there was a certain land and a man-eater (*ikala*) entered the land. That man-eater had finished off people by catching them and eating them and continued like that for many days swallowing whole villages and all the people in them. One day as it was swallowing villages a woman escaped by having been fetching firewood. When she returned, she found the beast had swallowed her village and that it was the last village in the land. When the woman saw that, she ran far away and found a cave in the rocks and stayed there many days and that was her home. Now that woman was the only one left in the land and she was pregnant. When she stayed there in the cave, she ate food from fruit in the bush.

Later that woman produced a son. That child grew and then was of the age to be called a boy, but every day his mother was telling him how all the people in the land had been eaten by the beast. Every day the boy was feeling very sad. His mother told him, "Your father, your mother's brother, all were swallowed by the beast." When the boy was told that he felt angry.

One day the boy made a bow and arrow for himself. And when he had finished, he said goodbye to his mother and went into the bush to fight with the beast. When he had gone far like that, he climbed a tree and then called the beast to come and fight with him. The beast came, and when the beast came, the boy ran off because he found that it was very large. He returned home and told his mother. On the next day, his mother prevented him from going again to the bush.

Then that boy made himself a chicken coop (*itundu*). One day he told his mother to bake breadcakes. The following day the boy put the breadcakes inside the chicken coop and then went again to the bush and called the beast. "Beast, beast, come! I have brought you sweet things to eat." The beast came, and then he told it to open its jaws, and then when it had opened its jaws he dropped in two breadcakes, and when it had eaten them it found them sweet and it told him, "You, now you are my comrade. Fetch me these again tomorrow."

Dawn of the second day he called it again and then their friendship continued. One day that boy took six stones and then fetched much firewood and made a fire and put those six stones in it. Those got red from taking on heat. The boy took his chicken coop and put all the stones in it and then he went to the bush. When he got there he called, "My comrade! My comrade! I have come! Come eat the breadcake." The beast had run and when it reached there, it had opened its jaws as it was accustomed to do every day, and then the boy dropped in all the stones which were hot, and when it had swallowed them, it burned up and died.

That boy returned home and told his mother that he had killed the beast. The mother was very pleased to hear that. She went along with her child, and when they got there his mother saw the beast was truly dead. Then that boy's mother told him to make a cut on the beast's stomach. That boy took his knife and then he cut. When he cut there, out came many houses which had been swallowed by the beast.

One of those houses was that of the boy's mother's brother. Then when those houses were out, the boy's mother's brother called to him and told him, "Why have you cut me in the eye? Now pay compensation," for that scratch which he had made cut him in the eye as he was looking out from the monster's wound. So then that boy paid his uncle that day.

That boy had a metal chain necklace and he made a game of swallowing it. Then he would open his mouth and the chain would come up from below again. That mother's brother who had fined him was pleased by his nephew's game and so he asked for the chain so that he might play with it.

His nephew gave it to him, and he swallowed it. Later his nephew asked for his chain, but his uncle was not able to bring the chain up from his stomach. When he had failed, his nephew kept telling him, "Now, uncle, give me back my chain." His uncle told him that he would pay him anything that would please him, but the boy himself refused and wanted only to be given back his chain by his uncle.

Later that case perplexed everyone, and so it was decided that the uncle's stomach should be torn open for his nephew's chain and indeed he was torn open. When he was torn open, he died. That chain was taken out after he had died, and then he was buried in a grave.

Do not do something bad to a person because he has done something bad to you, especially if he has done that without intending to. Besides, forgive him who forgives you, but not the one who does not forgive you.

This complex story is mainly concerned with the ambiguities of matrilineal succession and its relation to notions of reciprocity. Since Kaguru are matrilineal, traditionally the primary form of succession is from mother's brother to sister's son. Kaguru express this in two ways, by equivalence or replacement and by reciprocity. Both of these function somewhat ambiguously through time in that a junior is generally assumed to be subordinate to a senior and therefore in his debt. Yet it is recognized that if a senior is to maintain his influence, he must provide his subordinate with bridewealth to marry. This increases his nephew's indebtedness and decreases his dependence since this broadens the youth's own ties. Bridewealth represents an ambivalent good from the perspectives of both protagonists. Assuming that such a particular matrilineal relationship worked, the nephew would replace his mother's brother at death, not only in authority over lineage resources in people and things, but inheriting widows as well. Yet while the uncle lives, the two men are circumspect in sexual matters. Kaguru play on this reciprocity and equivalence by sometimes reversing terms in address. For example, an elder seeking favors from a nephew may call him mother's brother and be called nephew in return. Given the high degree of ambivalence attached to such relations, it is important that they be held together by the common affectual loyalties embodied by women. A nephew is most likely to obey his uncle while his maternal grandmother lives, the old woman bolstering the sibling loyalties between the youth's mother and her brother, the uncle. It is therefore significant in this tale that at the outset the youth is unimpeded by such ties, residing with only his mother. Impeding relatives appear only after he is a mature and able adult rather than at the onset of his career as in real life. Indeed, these relatives appear due to the youth's endeavors rather than vice versa. If this story is about succession and reciprocity, it is about these processes going awry.

The story proceeds as a complicated series of dialectical exchanges between the youth and the threatening outside world, as a corresponding series of debts and dependencies between the youth and his elder. The outside, representing the wilderness, dangerous outsiders (affines), and death itself, is characterized as a man-eating monster (*ikala* or *dikoko*), a kind of animated maw devouring wealth and the ordered social world. In Kaguru stories and rituals devouring monsters or man-eaters often personify these dangerous outside forces.

The first significant exchange involves the youth's conquest of these threatening forces by slaying the monster. As a sign that he is ready (sexually mature) to attack the monster, the youth leaves the primal maternal cave and fashions a bow and arrows (cf. the previous story). The youth destroys the monster through a fantastic set of gifts, which suggest the exchanges characterizing payment of bridewealth. The reference to bridewealth is clear in that the monster is appeased and ultimately slain through goods given in a chicken coop (*itundu*, bridewealth; cf. the previous story). The first payment is in food that is the exclusive domain of women, cooked flour. The second and lethal payments are heated stones, recalling the hearthstones embodying the female center of a household. In short, the gifts to the monster combine both what is given and what is received through the payment of bridewealth, thus representing a conflation of the normal reciprocal order, but also the essence of Kaguru matriliny. Ordinarily bridewealth (resources, food) is given in exchange for an alien woman whose marriage allows a man to secure a hearth (household). In short, this extraordinary youth triumphs over the usual constraints of marital exchange, employing both what he gives and what he receives in order to advance himself. The monster dies giving birth to the youth's predecessors, who now stand in debt to the youth, who would ordinarily be in their debt instead. The youth has inverted the normal order of succession and death and consequently disturbed the ordinary sequence of hierarchical reciprocity.

After his rebirth from death, the mother's brother tries to reassert his own authority by claiming a debt against the youth to whom he owes so much. He claims his eye was injured when he was delivered from the monster's maw. This seems to have a sexual connotation; Kaguru themselves occasionally refer to the aperture of the penis as an eye that does not see; and, indeed, a mother's brother succeeds to his uncle's wives upon the uncle's demise, his loss of sexual life. The storyteller implies that the mother's brother is wrong in asserting these claims, his unanticipated return to life presumably involving a debt that the mere injury of an eye can hardly negate.

The story then relates a second sequence of exchanges. The youth has a metal chain (a valued form of bridewealth payment) that he can devour and then disgorge at will. This echoes his earlier fantastic ability to surmount the usual limitations of bridewealth payments. The youth has now himself become a kind of maw and indeed by this time he is a kind of sociable monster. The uncle demands that he too be allowed access to these tricks but is unable to disgorge the chain when he swallows it. The youth demands the return of his gift and persuades the community to allow him to kill his mother's brother so that the mother's brother yields (gives birth to) the chain and dies. The story concludes with some pious remarks about the dangers of people not being properly cognizant of their reciprocal obligations.

The tale is extremely complex and difficult to grasp, but there is no question about the general themes aroused in an audience. The proper succession between a nephew and uncle are examined and played with. The sexual ambience is present but only discreetly indicated, as is proper in such relations. The highly ambiguous and ambivalently regarded problems of death, obligations, and succession are scrutinized through a grotesque and fantastic lens, and then capped with conventional platitudes absurdly out of proportion to the wild, violent and fantastic demands and acts that went before.

Mukejuwa: Women and Domestic Order[12]

Once there was a man who had married two women. Each woman had one child, and each of these children was like the other. One day the man went on a trip. The elder wife did not like her co-wife nor that woman's child. One day she told her comrade, her co-wife, "Let's go for firewood." Her comrade agreed, so they set out with their ropes and axes. They reached the forest and found a dry tree and started to cut it down. Whack! Whack! When the tree was about to fall, the woman told her comrade, "Stand there." Then her comrade stood there where the tree would fall. The tree sounded, Crunch! Crunch! Bang! and fell on her comrade who died. The woman cut some branches and covered the corpse.[13] Then she took a few sticks for firewood and went home.

When she reached home, those children asked, "Where is our mother?" She replied, "I left her behind cutting firewood." Then the child of the dead woman waited until the sun set. When they were

eating together that night, they did not give any food to the child of
the dead woman.[14] The night passed and in the morning the woman
told that child to climb up onto the rooftop storeroom to fetch some
melon seeds. Meanwhile, down below she dug a very deep pit. When
the child had finished collecting the melon seeds, she said, "Elder
mother, help me down." The woman replied saying, "Swing by your
arms from the roof and I shall catch you." The child said, "I'll fall."
But the woman said, "No, swing like that and I'll catch you. Hurry
up! I want to cook those melon seeds to put in a vegetable sauce." So
that child jumped down thinking that she would be caught, but she
was not and she fell into the pit. Then the woman took a stone and
closed up the pit.

When her child returned, she asked her mother, "Where is my
comrade?" The woman replied, "I don't know. I haven't seen her
since she went out."

When the child heard this, she cried and cried, saying, "My comrade, where has she gone?" The name of her comrade was Mukejuwa
and she too was named Mukejuwa. Five days passed, and on the sixth
day she heard her comrade crying in the pit. Her mother had gone to
the garden to hoe. Outside the child listened while inside the pit the
other Mukejuwa sang. The girl outside asked, "Who is calling me?"
The other answered saying, "I am in the pit." "Now what are you
doing there?" "Your mother told me to climb onto the rooftop store
to fetch melon seeds. She told me, 'Swing by your arms and I'll catch
you.' Then I let go but she didn't catch me and I fell into the pit."

Her comrade took a very long log. Then when the mother went
again to the garden to hoe, she took the log and put it into the pit.
Then she told her comrade, "Hold on to this log. Remember I am
outside." The one inside agreed and then the one outside made a
heave-ho. And she was thrown out of the pit. Now the side of the
girl's ribs was rotting and had maggots in it. Then the girl took her to
their unmarried girls' hut and hid her there. Every day she washed her
with water and anointed her with oil.

While the mother was at the garden she heard her child laughing,
"Hee! Hee!" She asked her, "What are you laughing at, my child?"
She replied saying, "A man has just passed by with one leg."[15]

On the second day the woman again went to hoe. The child removed some of the maggots and cooked them nicely and added melon
seeds to make them very delicious. The woman was asked to return
home and when she reached there she found that her child had made
just enough food for her, the mother, alone. Then the woman stayed
to eat the food. Her child said to herself, "You are eating the mag-

gots of Mukejuwa.'' Then the woman said, "What did you say?'' The girl replied, "I am sorry for you because you are tired from hoeing.''

Every day the girl did the same thing until her comrade's ribs had recovered. On that day her father returned from his work bringing a great many cloths. When the child saw her father, she ran after him and told him, "Father, mother killed my younger mother when they went out for firewood. Then when she returned, she dug a pit and told my sister to climb up to the rooftop store to fetch some melon seeds. When my sister was ready to get down, she deceived her so she fell into the pit, which was covered up by a stone. She stayed there five days, but on the sixth I heard a person crying and I took her out. Now she is in the unmarried girls' hut.''

That day he beat the drum and summoned the people. Then he covered the mistreated child with many cloths. When the people came, he told them each to take a cloth. Each person was uncovering the child more and more until only one cloth was left. Then that woman was told to take her cloth. When she took it, she uncovered the child and so she put the cloth back. But the people told her, "Uncover her! Who is that?'' She said, "Mukejuwa.'' Then the father of the girl told all that had happened. Then they asked the man what should be done. He replied, "I want the woman killed.'' They replied, "Yes! Kill her!'' So he took a gun and bang! She was finished. Then they ululated with joy. That was the end of that!

This story is about the conflicts between women within one man's household. Such conflict here repeatedly expresses a male point of view; the women act in ways that harm one another but that ultimately play to the man's advantage. The first theme to appear is conflict between co-wives, an obvious difficulty in any polygynous society. What seem odd are the relationships between the two half-sisters. These two girls have the same name (not possible except for a *welekwa* name) and exhibit deep loyalty, even though they are not of the same mother (matrilineage) but of one paternal household. Ordinarily, such girls would be unfriendly, or at the least suspicious of one another, each animated by the interests conjured up by her respective mother whose lineal interests divide the offspring despite a father's efforts. Here the two half-sisters conspire together, even to the death of one of their mothers. It is the kind of situation that might please any Kaguru man and appall any Kaguru mother. Motifs of witchcraft are also prominent. While it is obvious that any murderer risks the label of witch, in this case the daughters plot to confirm this. The evil mother is repeatedly fed the maggots which have fed off the

girl, so unknowingly she becomes a cannibal and thus a witch. She is duped
into being literally what she is metaphorically.

The two girls' conduct is the central problem of this tale. They conspire
to make the woman a witch. They speak to her in an elaborate form of
dissimulation, again parodying her own witchlike behavior. Finally, they
assume the duties that ordinarily would be a mother's. The persecuted girl is
treated like a newborn babe or adolescent initiate, being washed, oiled, and
fed in the girls' hut (*ibweti*) reserved for initiated, unmarried women. Finally,
this newly nurtured girl is covered in cloths (cloth, carrying-cloth) which
signify a womb, from which she is publicly delivered as the witch is correspondingly disclosed. The girls take on their own birth and initiation and
thereby deny the generative powers of their mothers, both of whom are dead
by the tale's end. That two girls would end up tied to their father and unconnected to either of their mothers (or apparently their mothers' kin) seems
every Kaguru father's pipedream, but it is a fantasy unsustained by Kaguru
reality.

CONCLUSION

The aim of such folkloric speculation is not to overthrow beliefs. Kaguru do
not reject their social world, for until recently they saw no alternatives available. Yet they are aware that the rules and purported aims of their system
contain ambiguities and unresolvable contradictions. Rules sometimes seem
unworkable or even provide means by which people may be exploited and
harmed, contrary to the general wisdom's more banal moral exhortations. It
may be that recital of these difficulties has some cathartic function, but I do
not find that a helpful explanation. I am more persuaded that Kaguru gain
both pleasure and profit through speculation and analysis of their way of life.
The rewards are manifold. Most obviously, it is playful and amusing to fantasize about life's affairs gone haywire. Second, Kaguru are not entirely unlike
anthropologists and sociologists in that they recognize that their beliefs and
rules form a system meriting thoughtful contemplation both as a complex
construct of interworking parts and as a set of directives that often fail to
provide what they promise. Finally, Kaguru are aware of the contradictory
or preposterous sides of their or any code of living. Thus they relish opportunities both to ponder and to jibe at its claims. If the system is, ultimately,
at some levels not entirely workable, what system is? If it works at all, this
is probably as much because of its very ambiguities and contradictions. What
less than contradiction could encompass the myriad difficulties of actual
experience?

Kaguru stories form a communal inheritance, but they are recited, elaborated, and invented by individuals. And they surely mean somewhat different

things to different listeners and tellers at different times. Yet these different experiences rebound and resonate upon one another. Men and women need to fathom each other's views and aims, and the old could well profit by bitterly recalling their own elders. These stories (and these here are but a small sample) illuminate the problems everyone faces in charting a course through life according to Kaguru custom. Each person will find her or his own answers, some wiser than others. Such stories, quite as much as formal rituals, encourage the young to take measure of the various social scenarios which they must play, for better or worse. The theme running through most of these tales concerns survival, "making it," in a complex and frustrating world. If ceremonies and rituals underscore a faith in a coherent and normative social universe, then these stories underscore the ambition, passion, and quest for security which animate individuals. These are sources of danger and destruction for individuals and groups, but they are also means to guile and strength enabling persons to prevail by imaginatively diverting rules and beliefs to their own ends.

NOTES

1. The chapter represents revised versions of portions of 1963i, 1964a, 1965a, 1967d, 1971c, 1971e, 1972a, 1972c, 1979. A more detailed exposition of the social context of Kaguru storytelling, my position on the study of African oral literature, and a full bibliography of Kaguru texts are available elsewhere (1979). The interpretations which I present for these tales are debatable. No one can be sure what these stories really mean. I believe that my interpretations are valid even if not exhaustive. Support for my arguments does not rest on points raised only in this chapter but on the larger set of interpretations repeated throughout all the chapters of this volume.

2. This idea is repeated almost exactly by Hans Peter Duerr, cited in Zipes (1983:13).

3. Hallpike is wrong to claim that preliterate peoples are poor at hypothetical thought (1979:422–423). He argues in terms of their perceptions of the physical world and not their moral and social worlds, but that very restriction in perspective is the most serious limitation of his impressive study (cf. Beidelman 1981c).

4. This is a yellow-flowered, decumbent plant gathered for food primarily during famine.

5. It is difficult to determine whether the tree here holds some deeper significance. The tree bears strong association with the upright post in a house, which is explicitly compared to the male head of a household. Here the tallest tree in a valley (associated with a matrilineage) is related to the elder of a matrilineage, and its uprightness is contrasted unfavorably with his own. Trees are also somehow associated with perpetuity. Kaguru believe that persons should not plant trees but should let them seed naturally. Were a person to plant a tree, he would risk his own longevity, the fact that the tree outlives the man somehow leading to the man's premature demise. Fol-

lowing this sense, one might argue that a tree evokes the upright, rooted continuity that an elder should encourage.

6. I use the terms *copulate* and *copulating* rarely in this book. These hardly convey the full sense of how Kaguru think of affinal relations. In these passages I originally wanted to use the words *fuck* and *fucking* but refrained since these suggested deliberate outrageousness. We speak of fucking as a sexual act but also can say, "he fucked over me" or "that person is really fucked up." Such English usage parallels an important sense of how Kaguru think of copulation.

7. A proper person would not hide inside another's house nor take food unasked. Despite the apparent reasonableness of these acts, given a famine, this behavior conveys a sense of menace, of possible witchcraft. If someone were to hide inside a Kaguru house, it would probably be in the food-storage areas (cf. my discussion of witchcraft in the preceding chapter).

8. They do not bury them as one would proper persons, but treat them like witches, lepers, or other awful creatures.

9. For a similar story, cf. Werner 1933:196–197. I am, of course, aware that many of these stories appear elsewhere. I have no folklorist concern about the diffusion of themes; what interests me is what Kaguru make of themes in terms of their beliefs, values, and experiences.

10. *Itundu*, a portable chicken coop. The term also means bridewealth. The relation of chicken coop to bridewealth is this: in the past initial payment of bridewealth consisted of two fowls brought in a portable coop. Today such a payment may still be made, but it is a small part of bridewealth, all of which is now termed *itundu*.

11. The usual version of this (Audrey Richards 1950) focuses on the role of women as problematical, but men are equally so. Indeed, it is ironic that the originator of this phrase, Richards, presents this from an essentially male perspective, despite being herself among the first great women anthropologists.

12. This is the second and shorter of two versions recorded (Beidelman 1963i). The name Mukejuwa means "Sun's wife," implying great beauty.

13. The woman is left unburied, always a shocking thing.

14. Not sharing food with kin always implies possible witchcraft.

15. Repeatedly, the deceitful woman will be addressed in a way that negates the value of speech. She is thus treated as a witch, who is also a perverter of language. Later food itself, a basic means for communication, is also debased.

CHAPTER 11.

Humans and Animals: Stories and Subversion

And so down to the fables which
beyond the laughter and the tears
serve for our instruction. Through
the dialectic which they express, they
become essential factors in the social
equilibrium. Under the forms of the
Lion, the Elephant, the Hyena, the
Crocodile, the Hare and the Old Woman,
we read plainly with our ears of our
social structure and our passions,
the good as well as the bad.

Léopold Senghor, *L'esprit de
la civilisation ou les lois
de la culture négro-africaine*

All animals are equal, but some animals
are more equal than others.

George Orwell, *Animal Farm*

This chapter continues my examination of how Kaguru explore the moral ambiguities of social life through the imagined world of stories.[1] Whereas in the preceding chapter I presented tales inhabited by people, however strange, I here enter a world of Kaguru animals, of beings even further removed from everyday reality yet clearly still governed by Kaguru aims and experience. Here, similar themes of loyalty and deceit, generosity and greed, kinship and individual ambition, are scrutinized. Yet the emphasis now is even more ambiguous, even more ambivalent, than in the preceding chapter. Now the stories squarely confront a central concern in Kaguru life, the complex and deceptive, even dangerous means by which we may distinguish authority from power, rightful domination and control from illegitimate exploitation; rightful, self-defensive protest from unwarranted disloyalty, and self-protective concealment from deceit. How, too, do we discern tact and discretion from guile and hypocrisy, the quest for security and esteem from greed and envy, and single-minded dedication and forebearance from egoistic ruthlessness? In bad situations, what are those put upon to do but combat such abuse by similar means? Kaguru recognize this as so, but then wonder how they may discern what course of conduct is both right and sensible, not only moral but self-sustaining. Indeed, can and should the person be at odds with the group? No clear and final answers exist to such probing questions. It is not even clear whether the congeries of groups comprising Kaguru society is all of a piece.

Such questions are forever negotiable in the ebb and flow of social actions and the changing conditions that animate our feelings and motives. The use of the word *subversion* in the chapter title therefore has a double implication. This chapter (and the tales in it) is concerned not only with the acceptance or rejection of authority and power, but also with persons' wholehearted acceptance or wily manipulation (selective acceptance and rejection) of norms and customs themselves, as they view these as both sustaining yet impeding the course of their affairs.

Kaguru beliefs often emphasize maintaining boundaries and order, yet some powerful Kaguru notions involve bridging categories, as manifest in ritual and social custom. Through ancestral propitiation, marriage, joking relations, and other ceremonies, the living are linked with the dead, cognates with affines, men with women, kin with outsiders, and old with young. When these same bridging principles are translated into outstanding social beings, into leaders and elders, differences in moral estimation troublesomely appear. To be sure, Kaguru adults recite rules of proper behavior to children (and to enquiring anthropologists), yet at other times these same Kaguru express admiration and envy toward successful men, the "sharp operators" who adroitly play hard and fast with norms. Such figures are familiar; if they are outstanding, it is because it is so difficult to master and embody characteristics, feelings, motives, and roles that cannot always all be embodied by the same person or fulfilled in every situation. Leaders represent the surmounting of basic dilemmas springing from Kaguru attempts to weld normative beliefs to successful social action. The two stories selected for consideration in this chapter emphasize these efforts.

Many Kaguru stories involve questions over elders' authority and knowledge, and the relations of these to power. While authority implies moral assent from the ruled, power and knowledge imply something morally problematical since these sometimes involve coercion, misuse of authority, or exclusion from information essential for right decisions. The very nature of age involves moral ambiguity; one gains wisdom and descendants as one rises toward the apex of a lineage, yet this also leads to social distance between those who ruled and those beneath them. Suspicions of sorcery and witchcraft may be inevitable reflections of such social distances within segments of aging lineages. Such tensions and ambiguities are reflected in Kaguru elders sometimes being portrayed as deceitful figures. In such tales Kaguru exercise and challenge their ability to discern proper from wrong aspects of social roles. Anomalous characters and situations stimulate Kaguru moral imagination to approach existential dilemmas involving choice in conduct and ends. To a great extent this is true of all Kaguru tales, and to consider dilemmas is to consider affectual, moral commitment. Nothing less would drive Kaguru to embrace the embodiments of their confusions and conflicts in stories, ritual, and the manipulated etiquette of everyday life.

These tales involve imagination, since they picture characters and events in the mind's eye in a manner resembling, but significantly different and removed from, reality. Kaguru storytellers present extremely simplified groups and situations. For example, two protagonists, such as an uncle and a nephew, struggle for power, but other kin and neighbors may not figure in the plot. Or two such characters struggle over allegiances toward only one common relative, or a pair contend over only one set of issues. In reality, problems such as settlement of bridewealth or determination of residence would not be made without reference to numerous past and future factors. Characters are presented larger than life, as exceedingly greedy, crafty, wily, patient, generous, or gullible, whereas few such clear-cut and enduring stereotypes are found in real affairs. Instead of considering situations and persons as inextricably linked to a totality of phenomena over a long period, a storyteller presents a chronotopically limited case. The full complexity of overlapping group affiliations, the long history of past relations, the moral vagaries and ambiguities of personal ties, are simplified or ignored. No more than one or two principles or problems are explored within a limited story-world. Stories avoid the complexities of possibilities in these problems, but do illuminate implications and difficulties posed if one tries to succeed where conflicting loyalties perplex people, and where yesterday's enemies may be tomorrow's allies. Their simplicity gives stories their power, just as simplicity in sociological models reduces yet explains social reality. These tales are strange but not in the sense that they transcend ordinary situations. They are odd because characteristics, roles, feelings, and motives cannot all be fulfilled and judged by one person in one situation. Instead, each situation is juggled and compartmentalized so that duplicity and inconsistency do not sustain survival, as they may in reality. In stories, messy and insoluble problems are defined and resolved. Unambiguous moral judgments and sustained resolutions exist in stories, but are imaginary for real life.

It is also imaginary to find animals portrayed as Kaguru villagers. Elsewhere (1971c) I try to explain this in terms of creating social distance for contemplating acts and ideas that otherwise might appear as intolerably disturbing, such as matricide and fratricide, and theft and cannibalism between kin and neighbors. Theriomorphism establishes distance from the real social world so that it may be played with reflectively. It also allows the reverse, a charging of the social world with powerful impulses not usually granted full countenance, the driving vitality of individuals striving to achieve their pleasures and ends in the face of social and cultural constraints (cf. Leach 1962, 1972).

To understand how Kaguru use animal characters to imagine moral confrontations and difficulties, I consider one pair of such characters in detail, hyena and hare. I first outline the basic attributes assigned to each and relate two stories featuring these animals. I then discuss the plots of these stories in terms of the issues I raised regarding the problems of moral ambiguity and its relation to authority, power, and social interaction.

HARES AND HYENAS

Kaguru themselves remark that hyenas and hares have similar traits, both being clever and tricky, though the hare's cunning works because he is truly clever whereas the hyena's does not, since he is so shortsighted and greedy that his cleverness ultimately amounts to stupidity. Kaguru stories often pit hyenas against hares, almost always to the hyena's disadvantage. This coupling not merely contrasts the clever with the stupid, but, more important, points out different moral implications of cunning and self-interest.[2]

Like many other African peoples, Kaguru have strong notions about hyenas (*mafisi*, sing. *fisi*) based on the moral attributes which they metaphorically associate with certain physical qualities and acts.[3] Hyenas have perhaps the most powerful jaws and teeth in the animal kingdom, easily devouring bones and even metal. They eat carrion, however badly decomposed, but also hunt down live animals. They have dirty, unkempt looks due to frequenting mud-wallows. Their coats are coarse and mottled, which contributes to their negative image, since Kaguru associate smooth texture with refinement and find mottled or broken surfaces repulsive.[4] Hyenas have a clumsy, lurching gait. Their grotesque and somewhat humanoid calls have been described by many besides Kaguru as demonic. In Kaguru stories the hyena's speeches are uttered in a grotesque voice, often with mispronounced words. We have seen that Kaguru characterize themselves as people who speak properly in contrast to outsiders, who either mispronounce words or, if they do speak Chikaguru well, are said to dissemble. The hyena's speech doubly affronts civility, distorting through both brutishness and deception, something to be expected from strangers outside and from witches within. Although hyenas sometimes feed by day, they are especially active after dark, when their laughter and whooping punctuate the night. Hyenas exude an exceedingly unpleasant odor, which Kaguru attribute to hyenas' disgusting diet, although actually this is due to a glandular secretion.

Kaguru believe hyenas dig up the graves of the dead (unless these dead are witches) and that witches employ hyena familiars. Witches are active at night, like hyenas, and sometimes travel at great speed through the sky upside down, hugging the bellies of their hyena familiars, which propel themselves with fire that shoots out from their anuses. Hyenas are believed to be her-maphroditic, a common belief in Africa and elsewhere; this belief is related to the fact that hyenas have unusually well-developed secondary genital char-acteristics (cf. Anonymous 1971a, Shortridge 1934:165). Hyenas are witches of the animal world, by alimentation, nocturnality, voice, and sexuality.

Kaguru mention hyenas with a blend of disgust, fear, and derision. They are loathesome but funny. Only a creature whose appetite has no bounds would eat bones and decaying flesh. Kaguru maintain that hyenas are so perversely stupid that they even prefer bones to good meat. Their eating habits are voraciously bestial (*chikalakala*, from *makala*, man-eaters). Their diet of bones accounts for the frequent whiteness of hyena dung, another odd trait. Hyenas are thought to go to any lengths to secure food to satisfy their greed, but they are too stupid, clumsy, and unheeding of order or limits to be as dangerous as they otherwise might be. Their very greed eventually gives them away. Because of their disgusting habits, hyenas are prohibited as food, but then Kaguru avoid eating all carnivores.

Hyenas are usually referred to with the prefix *di-*, which implies largeness: for example, *difisi*, with the connotation of grossness. In contrast, the hare is often referred to as *chibuga*, small one, the prefix *ch-* being a diminutive signifying affectionate regard.

The hare (*sungula*, sing. and pl.), while also mainly nocturnal like the hyena, is a vegetarian and a desired item of food.[5] Hares are thought to be the cleverest wild animal, their agility and speed matched by nimble thinking and guile. The hare is described as smooth-talking. In actuality, hares appear rather quiet, a trait which Kaguru sometimes associate with wisdom. While Kaguru value eloquence, they associate voluble speech and garrulity with fatuous silliness or indiscretion, qualities more consistent with hyenas' sounds. For Kaguru, hares have *ubala* (cleverness), *usungu* (knowledge), *mboto* (good fortune), or *ugosi* (wisdom, respect), all qualities admired in leaders and elders, such men being spoken of as *wagosi* (sing. *mugosi*). Hares' physical and mental (and moral) dexterity allows them to reach their goals, for they employ words, people, things, and deeds with proper regard for their real worth and order. This contrasts with hyenas' gauche fumbling and bumbling toward their goals. Hyenas' main asset is size (*ukulu*), the most superficial metaphorical qualification of elders (*wakulu*). The very qualities that make hares skillful also make them moral; the ones that make hyenas clumsy make them selfishly bad and ultimately ineffectual. Unlike some characters in Ka-guru tales, hyenas never acknowledge their faults. When exposed, if not killed, they either leave in a huff or remain in a sulky silence. This can be self-destructive, as when a hyena will refuse to eat at all rather than share with others. In contrast, hares are masters at cutting their losses no matter what happens. Yet for all these pervasive contrasts, some trace of moral ambiguity remains between the pair.

Even where not pitted against hyenas, hares are usually portrayed as the cleverest of creatures, always coming out on top.[6] While I know of no story or anecdote that portrays hyenas as good, truly clever, or skillful, and while most accounts of hares are highly favorable, a few do reveal even hares as bad or dangerous, indeed, resembling witches.[7] In some, where the hare is merely brashly overconfident, he is outsmarted and the story concludes by mockingly noting that such was the outcome of the hare's cleverness (*ubala*).[8] It is consistent with this that the feces of both animals are thought to have the same magical properties for stanching the flow of blood in some wounds.

The First Tale of Hare and His Uncle Hyena

One day Hyena had to make a journey and went to tell Genet. He said, "Sister's child, accompany me on my journey."

Genet agreed. Then Hyena told his wife, "Prepare some banana-bread for me. I must make a journey." So she cooked the bread and Hyena wrapped it up. Then he gave it to Genet, and they set out on their journey. On the journey Hyena instructed Genet, telling him, "My sister's child, we shall be strangers in the land where we are going, and we must follow the customs of the people there." Genet agreed, saying, "That's right, mother's brother." Hyena continued, saying, "There are many things which must be done on this journey. Take care of that food, for it is our life. Ahead there is a pond, and I shall go there because in that pond there is a wild creature which is possessed by a spirit of the dead and this creature must be dealt with. If you hear it calling for bread,[9] take the bread and throw some of it, for if you don't throw it some, we shall be killed. That creature is a spirit and that is what travelers have to do for it if they wish to pass."

Genet agreed to all of this. Hyena went ahead until he reached the pond. Then he went to hide where he couldn't be seen and then called, "Bread! Bread! Bread! Bread! Genet took some bread and threw it to where Hyena was. In that way Hyena was able to avoid sharing food with Genet. When Hyena had finished eating, he came out, and they went on. Young Genet asked, "Mother's brother, when shall we eat?" Since Hyena was full, he said, "Where we are going is very far. We shouldn't eat until we are really very hungry." So Genet spent the day hungry and slept that night without eating. The next day when they were on their way, Hyena entered a stream and hid there. Then he called out, "Bread! Bread! Bread!" Then Genet took some bread and threw it into the reeds where Hyena was hiding. Hyena ate the bread, and when he had finished, he returned to the path and asked, "Now did you give that spirit some bread?" and Genet said he had.

They went on traveling like that, with Genet carrying the load of food but not eating any of it. When they returned home, Genet had become very thin. His comrades asked him, "How did you get so thin?" He replied, "Now listen, you people! On the trip there were spirits at every stream. Mother's brother entered the reeds to propitiate the spirits so that we might pass, but when he entered the reeds, the spirits would call out for food, and I would give them some. I gave them all the bread until it was finished, so that we didn't eat."

In a few days, before a week had gone by, Hyena called Genet and told him, "Sister's child, accompany me on my journey. I want to take another trip." But Genet refused. So Hyena went to Civet and said, "Sir, will you accompany me on my journey?" Civet said, "Let's go! I agree." The next day they set out on the trip. Civet took the load of food. On the way Civet was instructed by Hyena, who said, "My sister's child, on this journey which I am taking there are many places where we must pass through streams. When I reach a stream, I go to worship so that we may pass through it safely and if, while I am there worshiping, you hear a spirit calling, 'Bread! Bread! Bread!' take some bread and throw it to that spirit to make it stop begging." Then all that had happened to Genet happened to Civet as well, so that when he and Hyena returned home, Civet's ribs were sticking out because of his hunger. Then everyone knew that Hyena was not a good person with whom to travel.

When Hare heard the others condemning that elder, Hyena, he told them, "Say, you're speaking harshly about an elder. I'll travel with Mother's brother myself, and I shall see whether these things are true, whether you became thin from hunger or whether it was only due to your own foolishness."

A month passed and then Hyena started looking for youths to go with him on another journey. But each one he met did not want to go and refused. They all told him, "Now if all these youths have refused, why don't you ask Hare? Would he refuse as well?"

Hyena said, "Sure enough! I had forgotten him!" So Hyena went to Hare and told him, "You've got feet and I've got a journey. Will you accompany me?"

Hare replied, "Where?"

Uncle Hyena replied, "To the old lady who is your grandmother."

Hare replied, "I agree, but I must get some food before we go."

Hyena replied, "I have kept food ready. Just say when you want to go."

Hare said, "Since food is ready, let's go tomorrow."

So in the morning when it was light, they set out. Hyena took a big bag for his medicine and his packet of food which he had tied together. Then he said, "Mother's brother,[10] this is your load which you should carry. In it is medicine and food."

Hare said, "That's simple! I'll carry it." So they set out on their journey. On their way Hyena realized that the one who was traveling with him this time was cleverer than his previous companions. Then Hyena told Hare, "Mother's brother, I, your comrade, have been sick these days. My teeth and stomach trouble me. Look carefully, and I shall show you the trees from which the medicines are made. Then if I become sick and need them, you come back and dig some roots for me."

Hare said, "I agree! How can I refuse? My job is to help you out in difficulties."

Hyena then went on to say, "Mother's brother, now we are passing along our route by means of worship, because there are many spirits on the way. When I reach a place with a spirit, I enter to worship alone in the bush. Then the spirit of the place comes out and sings, asking, 'Bread! Bread! Bread! Bread!' Then take some bread and throw it into the bush so that the spirit can eat. If you don't do that, we won't be able to continue."

Not long after, Hyena began to call, "Bread! Bread!", but Hare said to himself, "This elder is a liar. This spirit begging for bread is there where the elder is himself."[11] So Hare took a stone and threw it to where the sound "bread" was coming from. Soon after, Hyena reappeared, saying, "You, my sister's child, you threw a stone instead of bread. Don't you know that that was a bad thing to have done?"

Hare replied, "Well, never mind, let's pass on and find a place to eat."

Then Hyena told Hare to look at a tree saying, "This is the tree I need when I am sick." When Hyena had showed him this, Hare secretly dug up some of the roots for medicine. That evening when they had stopped for the night and got into their shelter, Hyena said to Hare, "I am sick! Go dig some of my medicine which I pointed out to you." Then Hare said, "Here, take the medicine! I have come with some."

When Hyena heard that, he knew that Hare had guessed his trick for getting food for himself, so he said to Hare, "You want to eat, so go on and eat! I'll let you eat." So Hare agreed and took the bread he was carrying, but Hyena slept hungry. The next day Hyena told Hare, "My stomach aches! Just go dig some medicine." But Hare just put his paws into the bag and drew out some more medicine. When Hyena saw the medicine from the bag, he said, "You, Hare, you have to eat by yourself. Go on and eat! I know that bread is what is making you so clever."

Since Hyena did not want to give food to Hare, he kept finding errands for Hare to be going on so that he might eat behind Hare's back. Or else Hyena would go into the bush and pretend to worship so that when he called, "Bread!" bread would be thrown to him. But Hare did not give Hyena a chance to prevent him, Hare, from eating. They traveled along like that until Hyena had become very thin. When Hare returned home, he boasted to his friends, saying, "I am your comrade. I have beaten him. Don't you see how thin he is?"

Hyena remembered how he had previously returned home with those companions who had been made to be as thin as he now was himself. So Hyena kept quiet and said nothing. When anyone asked him why he was thin, he said that he had been sick.

The Second Tale of Hare and His Uncle Hyena

Once there was a great famine in the land. Hare and his mother's brother, Hyena, got together in order to discuss how they could manage until the famine ended at the coming harvest. When they met, Hare said to his mother's brother, Hyena, "Uncle, this is a great famine. What do you think we should do until things get better? Let us sell our mothers.[12] If we keep them, there will be too many of us to get enough to eat."

Hyena said, "I think it is better if we kill our mothers. Then we can peddle their flesh to get wealth for buying food for our households."

Hare grudgingly agreed to this suggestion. He said to Hyena, "This is good advice. When shall we kill them? My mother is far away. Shall we start with yours?" So they went to Hyena's place, and when they got there, they caught the old woman, the mother of Hyena. Here and there she rushed, crying in vain until she was stabbed. The flayed meat was put in a basket, and the two started off to peddle the meat until it was sold. Then Hare began to feel upset and could not

bear to kill his mother on account of the famine. So he lay low for
many days. The time for Hare to kill his mother came, and he was
very upset. For this reason he hit upon the idea of going hunting, and
by good fortune he killed a bushbuck in a trap. He was able to flay
this in a hurry and took it to Hyena's.[13] He said, "Uncle, are you
there?"

Hyena replied, "I am here, sir. Why?"

Hare said, "The old woman is ready. The meat is here."

Hyena answered, "Hee! Hee! Hee! That is what you've been
putting off doing. Now our famine is ended."

They passed around with their meat until they had none left, but the
famine continued in the land. They didn't have anything to eat. Every
evening Hare went off to the place where he had hidden his mother so
that Hyena should not know that she was still alive. That was where
Hare was eating. But Hyena was really hit by hunger. To whom could
he go to eat? He didn't have any mother left.

One day Hyena asked, "You, mother's brother, where are you
eating? Why aren't you getting thin the way I am?"[14]

Hare said, "I have no place to eat. I am like this no matter how
bad a famine there may be."

Many more days passed and Hyena became unconscious. After a
few more days he died. Then Hare went to the cave where he had
hidden his mother. He called out, "Old woman, Hyena is no more.
He is dead. You are free!" Then Hare stayed peacefully with his
mother for many happy years.

ABOUT THE TWO TALES

Hyena's aggression is expressed in greedy consumption of conventional food
and in murderous cannibalism. Kaguru associate proper allocation of food
with ordered sociability. Control of food is a sign of dominance: at its most
convivial with those in power generously apportioning it; in terms of
dominance by age and sex, with large portions going to men and elders, and
with men mastering hunting for meat (the prestigious part of the diet) as a
mark of their abilities. Abuse of these powers is reflected by greed and, at
its very worst, by turning others, even kin, into food themselves, as in
cannibalistic witchcraft. Indeed, allocation of food is the prevailing theme of
Kaguru stories. In the two tales presented here, hyenas hold authority because
of their age (and size); they are *wakulu* (elders, large). In both tales they
pervert their responsibilities and privileges by abusing their juniors, small in
age and size. Their defeat by mistreated underlings also hinges on food,
involving interference with their abilities to eat, through "stoning" their teeth,

through digestive medicines, or through destruction of their mothers, who cook and secure meals.

In these and other stories the greatest abuses occur on journeys or during famines. The treks serve two purposes. They allow a contrast between the supposedly ordered social life of settlements and the appetitively chaotic wilderness. They also express moral movement, in which apparent moral attributes are tested, proved unreliable, and ultimately reversed. The elder is neither wise nor just; the young are clever and, being betrayed, have no further grounds to reciprocate fairly or honestly. Famines resemble journeys, for they too drive Kaguru out of their settlements to seek food, thereby jeopardizing ordinary social life.

Hyena's powerful teeth manifest voracious disorder. His dissimulation about his own appetite, and about his digestive and masticatory prowess, and his projection of hunger onto the spirits of the dead discredit him. The elder directly abuses both his authority (having access to the spirits of the dead) and his supposed knowledge (familiarity with medicines). In other stories, hyenas are associated with voracious, sharp-toothed cannibalistic women, such as grandmothers, alien wives, or jealous co-wives.[15] In two other tales, hyenas are menacing affines. In one of these a witch-hyena employs zombie laborers (which he repeatedly devours and regurgitates) to perform his agricultural brideservice. He is exposed and slain by stones (alimentarily) by his wife's brother, who then enjoys the bounty of food with his widowed sister (quasi incest) (Beidelman 1976:72–75). In another, he competes with a chameleon (weak, contemptible). Chameleon and Hyena have married sisters and dwell with their affines, doing brideservice as cultivators. Exposed and defeated through his greedy appetite and unproductive cultivation, Hyena is shown up by the supposedly weaker Chameleon, who eats in an orderly manner but produces food bountifully. Hyena is driven off and the smaller competitor takes over both sisters; thus, Chameleon dominates the alien settlement (ibid.:75–79).

For Kaguru, teeth are a physiological embodiment of appetites, in both their positive and their negative senses. Obviously, the hyena's formidable teeth epitomize its witchlike greed, and we have seen how dangerous women, such as those married in alien settlements and old, widowed ones free from male control, are sometimes portrayed as man-eaters, as sharp-toothed cannibals. The *vagina dentata* expresses such fear of female power. In contrast, proper Kaguru should have their teeth constrained, by having two lower incisors removed and the upper ones chipped. This is no longer practiced but vividly reflects the ambiguous nature of orectic impulses. The genitals are cut, and so is the mouth.

In the first tale just recounted, Hyena tells Hare that they are making their journey in order to visit Hare's grandmother. This passing allusion to this woman forms a brief but powerful link to the second tale, where Hyena and Hare make a pact to kill their respective mothers to sell them for food. Hyena does kill his, Hare's grandmother. Yet Hare only pretends, so that his own mother survives to nourish him in secret. The imagery of matricide is clear, and linking it with food subtly associates it with incest, so that it embodies the ultimate attributes of witchcraft.[16] Yet, as we shall see, Hare's fortunate ability to elude this same horror stems from less awful but far more prevalent attributes of antisocial behavior which also appear rather witchlike. Hare lies to Hyena and avoids sharing food with him. The storyteller implicitly justifies this because Hyena is in truth a perpetrator of matricide.[17] Yet the ambiguous and ultimately antagonistic relations between this uncle and nephew rest as much on the ties to their mothers as on any inherent attributes. Their structural positions within a matrilineage predispose them to tensions and possible conflict. Such potential problems always exist; in a few tales the full potential of this danger is fully realized.

In manifold ways, many Kaguru stories explore the difficulties of relations within a matrilineage. None does so more forcefully or disturbingly than the second story presented here. To appreciate what is at issue I provide a diagram of the relations in this second story, noting that this covers the key relations for the first as well (since Genet and Civet, as Hare's younger brothers, function merely as foils to Hare's and Hyena's attributes):

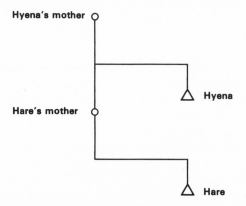

Each character represents an entire category of persons, reduced, as in an anthropological kinship diagram, to one entry. Thus Hare stands for all of the sons of all of Hyena's sisters; Hyena stands for all of his sisters' brothers or all of his mother's sons, *mutatis mutandis*. Hyena is Hare's *bulai* or *kolo* (mother's brother) and Hare, as *mwihwa* (sister's child), owes him obedience and respect. Hare's disobedience rests upon the assumption that Hyena, because he behaves selfishly, does not merit such authority. If such authority is severely abused, a nephew may refuse to obey and even to recognize his kinship obligations at all. The most radical form of such rejection would be to dehumanize the uncle by redefining him as a witch.

Authority and cohesion within a matrilineage depend upon reciprocal aid and support between men and their sisters' sons. These men, in turn, are obliged to protect the mothers, sisters, and sisters' daughters who link them to one another. In their junior years, sisters' sons depend upon their mothers' brothers for economic and political aid and have few resources of their own. As these young men mature and establish their own households, they should repay the benefits they received from their elders. The power of leaders and the continuity of the lineage depend on this. Relations of authority within a matrilineage almost exclusively involve men of the same or of proximate generations.

Now let us consider Hyena's mother and her daughter, Hare's mother (Hyena's sister). These women are viewed lineally as intermediaries, which relates to their exclusion from formal authority. Kaguru describe women as having strong feelings concerning different kin, but ideally not striving for power in the ways that men do. Instead, women should be concerned with the solidarity of the matrilineage and with maintaining goodwill and cooperation between those whom they link.

Kaguru women sometimes mediate disputes. Although women possess no formal authority, men may appeal to them as moral arbiters. Women's security and influence greatly derive from these affectual, intermediary positions between men. I give three examples: (a) A man fails to secure the cooperation he seeks from his sister's son, so he appeals to his sister to urge her son to obey him. If she is reluctant, her brother appeals to their mother to persuade his sister in this. (b) A youth requires aid for bridewealth or some fine. He asks his mother to persuade her brother to help. If her brother refuses, she may appeal to their mother to make him do so. (c) Several men may disagree as to how to divide goods they inherited or secured from bridewealth. If they are siblings by one mother, they may leave the wealth with her or with one of their sisters. It is then available to all when they need it, but none has exclusive control.

Kaguru women, through their dual roles as mothers and sisters, link men together. This works so long as women respond equally to the demands of both these roles, that is, to the needs of their children and to the needs of their brothers. Yet it is clear that in severe disputes a woman may be forced to choose between two men, such as her son and her brother or her mother's brother. Then Kaguru invariably assign primacy to the mother and child relationship, and, if forced, a woman will ultimately support her children over her brothers or uncles in any dispute.

Within a Kaguru matrilineage there is always potential conflict between the male chain of authority and the obligations and sentiments of males toward females. Both are vital to the Kaguru system. In the first tale the chain between men is disrupted; in the second, Hyena gives priority to his own claims instead of following the chain of male authority and ignores the obligations toward women. He draws Hare into his wicked plans and thus tries to set males against females within their matrilineage. Hyena exploits females in a way harmful both to them individually and to the lineage as well.

For Kaguru, the most difficult and disturbing question about the second tale is why Hare agrees to the death of his maternal grandmother. It is partly because her respect and protection are essentially Hyena's responsibility, and the plot hinges on Hyena's abnegation of this bond. Even though Hare tacitly goes along with this, it is in his role as a junior following an elder, albeit an evil one. Hare can lay responsibility for Hyena's mother's death upon Hyena, but Hare could not do so for his own mother since obligations to one's mother outweigh all others, even those to her brother.

Yet it could be argued that Hare has another, more sinister motive for acceding to this plot. In a sense Hare may even secretly or subconciously desire his maternal grandmother's death (earlier we saw the ambivalent relations between alternate generations). So long as this old woman lives, there are strong affectual sanctions for solidarity between all her lineal descendants, and Hyena remains in relatively secure power. Upon her death the process of lineage segmentation may commence and Hare may hope to assume some power himself even while Hyena lives.

Supposing that Hyena's mother has several daughters besides Hare's mother;[17] the descendants of these females would form potential lineage segments united under a living ancestress, Hyena's mother. Hyena holds jural authority over these and uses the mediative influence of his mother and sisters to wield power. When his mother dies, there is no longer a living link between these groups. Hyena may appeal to the woman as an ancestral spirit, but this is hardly as effective as appeals to her in real life would be. Hyena would remain titular head, but his difficulties in maintaining authority have grown. Males in each segment always try to exert their own interests. Each mother sees herself as eventually occupying an apical position analogous to Hyena's mother's and may encourage her son's efforts toward autonomy. Hare thus gains by Hyena's crime, and in this way he is truly craftier than Hyena.

Kaguru themselves reject this deeper structural interpretation. Hyena is a witch, and Hare is clever but not a witch. Yet Kaguru insist that no one would wish a maternal grandmother dead. My account of the values underlying Kaguru matrilineages is consistent with Kaguru protestations, yet it is also true that matrilineal segments are much more likely to split up only after the senior woman linking them together is dead. Kaguru themselves acknowledge this, but refuse to admit that anyone would seek such a death, however beneficial. The difficulty here is not a reflection of a conflict between how I and Kaguru interpret the workings of their society. Rather it is that Kaguru express feared motives through oral literature (cf. Sapir 1963:566).

In all cases that I encountered where Kaguru siblings severed relations by disowning one another through accusations of witchcraft or repudiative insult, the mother uniting them had died. Siblings do not automatically break relations when their mother dies, but there is more likelihood than before that quarrels may become irreconcilable. After the murder of his grandmother, Hare ignores his responsibilities toward Hyena. Hyena asks him why he is still fat and not starving, trying to cajole him by addressing him as mother's brother rather than nephew. Yet Hare lets Hyena die a witch's death, heartless. As Kaguru say, you may have many mother's brothers and even sisters, but only one mother, and her well-being is utterly one with your own.

CONCLUSION

Hypothetical constructs, such as the preceding stories, expand and liberate, if only temporarily, our sense of choice, as they also intensify and enlarge the import and drama of the social characters making these choices. These tales do not produce some vague and formless antistructure, to cite Turner's unfortunate term, but draw attention to the tensions and interdependence between the individual and his role as a social person, to the conflicting demands and interests that contrasting social roles involve, and to the incongruity inherent in the relations between language, thought, and motivation. One way to characterize this is to contrast the ideal and orderly with the real, which is disorderly, ephemeral, and ambiguous. Social ideals are formulated as to what should be, but actual social life is lived within myriad, protean situations. We cannot fully grasp a unitary, normative vision of society in our daily affairs. We can palliate and subdue what we do experience to the extent that we are less vexed and distracted by contradiction. What does not jibe with our norms, what seems disturbingly real or numbingly familiar may be subjected to the constraints of ratiocination and rhetoric, or the animation of wit and imagination as Kaguru do in ritual, etiquette, and oral literature. On the one hand, what may disturb is diffused, and, on the other hand, what is dull may be brightened. In these tales, Kaguru speculate about the nature of their morality and experience, striking connections between their contemplated view of the normative and their more immediate apprehension of reality.

The appraisal of conduct depends upon the perspective from which actions are regarded, not only in terms of the concepts of a society but also from the changing perspectives of the various protagonists. What may represent disorder and conflict for a lineage may represent order for a household; what represents a right for one in authority may represent oppression to one who is subservient. These seeming contradictions are part of any system; rather than being indications that that system is undergoing radical change or breakdown, these are signs of life. Indeed, only a rather removed observer, an anthropologist or perhaps a Kaguru storyteller, is even likely to be keenly aware that these are contradictions. The meaning of beliefs and values cannot be separated from the diverse complexity of social life from actions and feelings, and these inhere in particular and disparate moments which are fairly well defined but not enduring, at least from the perspective of any protagonist.

Part of the significance of some norms is that they are not automatically or readily attainable or even clearly defined in application. They are ever-present, negotiable means by which Kaguru take stock of others and themselves. If Kaguru imagination fleetingly attempts to make broader analyses in oral literature and ritual, it is only with direct reference to their myriad active world. Imagination allows Kaguru to stand both inside and outside society at once—outside, in that they manipulate and select a few ideational and social elements and no more; inside, in that these elements remain embedded in the totality of lived, culturally filtered experience. To paraphrase Wittgenstein, our symbolic expressions get their meanings from the rest of our proceedings (cf. Wittgenstein 1969:30), for "to imagine a language means to imagine a form of life" (1963:8).

From this and preceding chapters, we see that Kaguru define their civility and humanity not only in terms of constraint in diet, but also in terms of restraint and control in sexuality and language. These form the three primary modes through which people find means both to sociate between one another and to subjugate individual to group demands, to unite and to betray. These stories show how these same modes provide means in both ideas and deeds by which individuals may surmount the constrictions and contradictions of their culture so as to survive and thrive. Kaguru are, in a sense, seemingly used by their society and culture, but, in turn, use these as well to sustain and propel their own selves.

NOTES

1. This chapter represents revised versions of portions of 1961c, 1963a, 1967b, 1971c, 1972a, 1974c, 1974d, 1975a, 1979, 1980a.

2. Besides the two tales related here, 1961c, 1963a, I collected others which contrast hyenas and hares, 1963j:138–139; 1975b:570–571; 1976:53–55, 55–57, and the longest most complex of all, 1976:57–71.

It is curious that early Judeo-Christian beliefs also associate hares and hyenas as animals best exemplifying sexual depravity, mainly homosexuality (Boswell 1980:137–143, 305, 317, 356–358; Ley 1968:51).

3. For a survey of the habits and traits of hyenas, actual and purported, see: Anonymous 1971b; Dorst and Dandelot 1969:129–130, 134; Guggisberg 1968:58; Jeannin 1951:210–211; Kambe 1971; Maberly 1960:130; Spinnage 1962:82–84; the most detailed and authoritative survey is by Kruuk (1972).

4. We find this not only regarding hyenas, but in an extreme form among lepers, who are treated like witches. In a more benign form, Kaguru stories sometimes portray a scabious youth (Chauhele) as a wily, heroic underdog in ways resembling hares, see: Beidelman 1964a:33–35; 1973b:90–92; 1976:86–87; 1978b:108–110.

5. For surveys of some of the attitudes toward hares around the world, see Evans and Thomson 1972; Boyle 1972.

6. Beidelman 1965a:24–26; 1974d:247–248; 1976:50–53, 79; 1978b:84–85.

7. Beidelman 1962b:227–228; 1967e:170; 1975b:567–568.

8. Beidelman 1976:77, 80.

9. Hyena constantly mispronounces the word *bread*, a fact that not only reflects his brutish nature but which eventually leads to his exposure.

10. As I noted earlier, a mother's brother may call his nephew "sister's child" when asking a favor from him, reminding the junior of the reciprocal nature of their relation.

11. Hare recognizes Hyena's voice because it is ugly and leads Hyena to mispronounce the word *bread*. Hare's predecessors were not so observant.

12. In the past, Kaguru sometimes pawned kin in order to secure wealth (food) or pay heavy fines. These were usually younger kin, especially women. These were usually pawned locally so that they could be more easily redeemed with better times. One would never pawn mothers of children, least of all one's own mother.

13. It may be that this incident is more symbolically meaningful than it first appears. Given Kaguru hunting imagery, Hare's hunting an animal from outside (exogamy) contrasts with Hyena's slaying an animal within the settlement (incest). This is, after all, the crucial way that Hare avoids being a witch like Hyena. Exogamic marriage to strangers is difficult and dangerous, like hunting, but it is also a sign of proper masculinity and cleverness. It leads to expanded social ties. Incest, however, is thought to lead to nothing but sterility and death.

14. Among Kaguru, mother's brother (*bulai* or *kolo*) and sister's child (*mwihwa*) are terms that sometimes may be reversed; see note 10.

15. Beidelman 1966b:76–77; 1971e:19–20; 1973b:90–93, 93–96; 1976:79.

16. In the longest version of this story, Hare not only saves his mother while Hyena kills his, but Hyena tastes his mother's blood. In that same story Hyena dupes a woman into tasting her slain daughter's flesh, surely a variation on this theme of conflict of interests between clanswomen of successive generations (Beidelman 1976:57–71). For other stories which present hyenas as especially witchlike, see Beidelman 1976:72–75, 84–89.

17. In another version (Beidelman 1976:57–71) it is Hare who introduces the idea of matricide. The use of dangerous speech to trick others who are inherently bad makes sense to Kaguru. Matricide may have been Hare's idea in that story, just as pawning their mothers was his idea in this, but only Hyena is so evil as to enact such notions.

18. In the story no such sisters appear, nor are we told that Hare has any. Yet so long as Hare's mother lives, she may bear offspring so that for Hare perhaps his mother's greatest value is her power to provide him with sisters.

CHAPTER 12.

Conclusion

Knowledge advances by steps, and not by leaps.

Thomas MacCaulay, *Essays*

Presenting a conclusion to any work is a daunting prospect. As a compromise between taciturnity and effusion I will comment briefly on three interconnected issues. First, I suggest the ways in which this work diverges from the prevailing trends currently characterizing anthropological analyses of alien systems of thought. Second, I suggest which aspects of Kaguru life appear especially significant for understanding the characteristic ways Kaguru imagine themselves and their society. I particularly stress those aspects that may account for or facilitate the ambivalent, even subversive quality of some of their imagining. Finally, I indicate what further questions we might want to ask in order to clarify and broaden our understanding of the Kaguru themselves. I view these second two aims as more important than the first since the focus of this work is ethnographic. This is not because I am unconcerned with theory but because I believe that theory is best advanced through ethnographic analysis rather than through more abstract pronouncements unanchored by particular data.

The preceding chapters explored the relation between imagination and morality. To be sure, both are features of all societies and therefore necessarily figure to some degree in all anthropological reports about beliefs and values. I emphasize these aspects here in order to draw attention to ambiguities and tensions between the individual and his or her society and culture. Durkheimean anthropology long ago stressed the central, powerful, yet perplexing relations between individuals and their society, which seems to have an existence and significance of its own, beyond that of the people who compose it. Indeed, for Durkheim individuals have no true meaning outside that of being social persons constructed from the cultural lumber of their society. True, thousands of Kaguru form one society and possess a culture of shared beliefs, values, practices, and artifacts, yet these vary so sharply between persons with different social roles (not to mention individual peculiarities) that assertion of such common cultural features raises as many questions as it may answer. Kaguru individuals assume a great many different roles and statuses, willingly or not, through space and over time. Many of these personhoods stand in conflict with one another. These different social fates, these varying masks which individuals wear, determine what people may do and how they may appear. Yet these never fully account for what individuals are or how they behave. The analogy between roles and masks reveals a deeper, more ambivalent side to social life. The term *person* derives from *persona*, a player's mask (Mauss 1979b:78–82). Social roles conceal and protect inner individuals from external scrutiny while at the same time legitimating individuals' demands and needs to outside gaze by providing generally acknowledged grounds for person's wants. Yet these same masks possess their wearers as much as they are taken up and worn by these actors themselves. Social masks adhere to individuals, infuse their personalities, but also impede them, especially as their individual wants and qualities exceed or fall short of these external, determining labels. A mask (*persona*) may embody a designated role within a social drama, but how this is enacted depends on the perception and skill of the individual player who is cast for the part.

For me, Simmel's view of this relation between the individual and society is more persuasive and congenial than is Durkheim's, since the moral and analytical weight of Simmel's concern rests upon the individual rather than society. For him, culture and society are best considered in terms of how individuals make use of them as much as how they are constructed through them. For him these artifacts, ideas, and values provide the individual with means for expression, realization, and legitimation, much as for Durkheim. Yet they also provide means by which individuals both conceal themselves from others and, tragically, at times lose themselves to the demands of others. In this latter sense, culture may thwart and burden people as much as it may benefit them. Each Kaguru struggles to shape a meaningful and expressive world. This ceaseless struggle stems from a pathetic tension between the individual and others, and the culturally defined objects which they employ. Social and psychic experiences are manifest in a series of dualistic tensions between public and private expression, conformity and individuality, compliance and subversion, and harmony and discord (cf. Levine 1971:xxxv-xxxvii).

The notions of imagination and morality, not to mention that of play (illusion: literally, in play), lie at the heart of these complex correspondences and discrepancies between society and individuals. While a cultural system of beliefs and values is the product of many years of imaginative labor by countless people, it must be constantly renewed and enriched. This must be done not only to replicate the system from generation to generation but also to reinforce and reiterate these features through the changing situations in which they are lived out. It is therefore no wonder that this cosmology is harnessed to the emotions and elementary sensations encountered in everyday affairs, as well as to the climactic occasions of high social drama such as births, initiations, marriages, and deaths. For this system to work requires ceaseless imaginative effort by individuals; otherwise, the metaphorical vivacity of these images becomes atrophied and ineffective. Such repetition is probably more powerfully and persuasively experienced in the myriad cues and habits of quotidian life than in less frequent though more dramatic ceremonies. It is precisely in the ways that Kaguru must constantly rethink, retell, and refeel these notions through imagination that they retain their force. Furthermore, and equally important, such beliefs and feelings require constant refocusing, endless reformulation around different modes and emphases, since they cannot hold uniformly for all social situations or for many shifting roles. Each social encounter, each constellation of interacting persons, draws out new efforts to construct (deconstruct and reconstruct) the background and resultant behavior appropriate to it. This, too, constitutes considerable labor for the imagination as I earlier described it. This work then varies in tone and effort and is reflected upon, whereas the steady base from which these beliefs and values are framed is the unquestioned stuff of everyday experience.

Moral judgments are relevant to particular social situations and to their protagonists. Reframing judgments in these terms figures as the most complex and difficult sector for such imaginative work. At social encounters individuals meet one another as social persons, as assemblages of roles and expectations, but they also confront one another as agonistic, individual beings seeking fulfillment and security both within and outside the culture which they inhabit. To be sure, in a sense one might claim that these beings can know little or nothing outside the matrix of their own culture, but the very particularity of such individuals, their unique perspectives and experiences, precludes any hope of total concinnity between their different aims and views, despite their shared culture. Thus, even while sharing a culture, each Kaguru dwells within a particular experiential chamber that must necessarily be different from that of others. Kaguru society may constitute a cultural world, but, to use Simmel's terms, individual Kaguru construct their own worlds within that world. This should not be seen as contradictory, for, after all, it is the variegated nature of culture, epitomized in divisions of roles and labor, that contributes to its cohesion. Culture coheres precisely because of its profound internal differences and even because of its inconsistencies. Those individuals who compose it and enact it can make sense out of it only through strenuous imaginative effort which allows them to appreciate and transcend these seemingly limiting differences and contradictions, if only in part, within their minds.

While all sectors of social life are arenas for playing out Kaguru visions of the self, areas of everyday activities, of leisure and play, of alimentation

and work, the spheres of everyday sociability and conjugality, allow a degree
and latitude for individual embroidery by which Kaguru can score points not
so readily manipulated in the formal occasions of high drama in rites of passage
and crises, where such meanings are more formally negotiated. In contrast,
quotidian affairs are fields of more subversive sociability. In one of the few
studies of quotidian affairs in African societies, Karp observes of the Teso
of East Africa that these people find their social relations unrewarding and
that disappointments and frustrations are given form and expression through
beer-drinking, which provides a "means of imagining the antinomies of their
experience of self, society, and other" (1980:114).

Imagination is an art by which individuals struggle to transform their social
baggage into gear that suits urgent situational needs in terms of meanings and
moral judgments. The cultural material for such constructions is ever-present,
but how it is employed varies widely with occasions. Some use it more adroitly
than others. From such a perspective Kaguru may be said to share culture,
but what this fully means in terms of beliefs, values, and actions constantly
alters as Kaguru work to put cultural resources to individual profit. Throughout
this study I have emphasized the constant reformulation and construction of
beliefs and values by Kaguru individuals as they seek advantages. This approach differs from many recent anthropological writings, which tend either
to present beliefs as means for securing social solidarity (minimizing the
individual and the possibility of his or her domination through deploying
strategies), or to present beliefs as a kind of nonrational, culturally relativistic
narcotic propelling people into enacting a drama or social script or text that
sometimes has few real, individual advantages to them. Too little current
anthropology stresses beliefs as means for self-justification and rationalization
of individuals' varying dilemmas within the society they inhabit, much less
as veils for concealing deeper, more subversive feelings and ideas. One must
go back twenty-five years to find a first-rate study showing how rituals and
beliefs are employed to manipulate power and authority within a community
(Middleton 1960). Even earlier, Middleton (1954) took up the relation between
symbols and imagination, long preceding Turner; it is hoped he will one day
continue some of the arguments he so imaginatively raised then.

Kaguru repeatedly question many aspects of their way of life. This is not
usually in terms of seeking or suggesting alternate rules or customs, although
Kaguru sometimes even wonder about that. Rather, this is in terms of spec-
ulating about how rules and customs, the formal framework of social life,
may be worked and managed to fill individual wants and ambitions while
curbing demands and inroads by others. For Kaguru, society does not correspond to Durkheim's positivistic, authoritarian model. It is not simply an
enriching mechanism enabling humans to realize their fuller, better selves.
Instead, it resembles a combination of a maze and a tool which individuals

must solve or use for their own ends. Potentially it is as much a source of danger and disadvantage as it is of protection and gratification. Kaguru never ask why society exists, but they constantly do ask how it can be used rather than use them, or, to be more precise, how they can employ rules and values to use others and avoid others using them. They recognize that the rules and customs that compose society cannot be judged outside the immediate context of social interaction, and, within that context, speculation and self-justification remove much of the social mystique.

Any emphasis upon the primacy of the individual over society leads to considering the ways in which individuals envision society. If an individual has any imaginative ability, she or he is sure to construct other versions of existence besides those actually experienced. Every story and tale, even every genealogy, reflects some such reconstruction. To imagine another kind of world is always a judgment about this one. Kaguru are not social anthropologists, but many do think long and hard about their society and certain of its features that vex them. They compare themselves with some of the different ethnic groups that neighbor them, and in their minds' eyes they compare their own experiences to situations and conditions outside their ordinary experience, particularly in the fantasy of their oral literature. These critical speculations about themselves and their world are imaginative achievements. I hope that some portions of this study, especially the later chapters, show that such critical speculation is not the monopoly of anthropologists. These efforts by Kaguru are never consciously directed toward reforming or altering their social system. They are instead directed toward bending it toward their varying and changing individual uses.

In this concluding chapter I also consider some of the implications that this study may have toward understanding Kaguru society and culture. In doing so, I also raise issues related to kindred Tanzanian peoples as well as to Bantu language speakers in general. Some of these points regarding the relations between symbols and social structure have implications even beyond African cultures. To start with the most general, in the introductory section I observe that in some ways Kaguru are typical of Bantu peoples over much of Africa. Their notions about ancestral propitiation, about the nature of age, gender, time, and good and evil closely resemble those for many other peoples over a wide part of East and Central Africa and even beyond. With caution we may employ our insights into Kaguru thought to suggest possible lines of enquiry when approaching material from these other societies. Yet Kaguru are, in another sense, unrepresentative of Africa in that they are matrilineal. In being so, Kaguru typify many of their immediate neighbors and even some peoples to the south, in Tanzania, Zambia, Malawi, and elsewhere, yet matriliny hardly prevails in Africa. I draw attention to this point because it remains problematical to what degree the shape and tone of Kaguru culture and society are related to the particular form of their descent.

In a series of provocative publications (see 1976, 1977) Weiner observes that men and women are caught in different modes of time and space and that women as well as men exert important influences within different and exclusive spheres of experience. She argues that, at least for the society which she studied (Trobrianders), women's power and importance lodge in their enduring embodiment of matriliny and the associated rights to land and office. In contrast, men's powers, while important, are less enduring and pervasive in nature. Her arguments are convincing for her own Trobriand material. We must ask ourselves, however, to what extent her arguments extend to other matrilineal societies. That men and women exert power and influence in different sectors of social life is clear and has been stated often enough recently. What is provocative in Weiner's argument is that these differences and advantages are seen as embedded within the social structure itself and, more particularly, that these may be related to some forms of matriliny. What are debatable are the full implications and potential for such determinants within matriliny. Although coming up with no clear answers, I earlier posed similar questions by contrasting neighboring matrilineal and patrilineal people within the Kaguru area itself (1980b). At present, it remains unclear to what extent matriliny necessarily leads to conferring such advantages on women, though this seems to be so in some societies, certainly the Trobriands. Unfortunately, it is not difficult to conjure up situations in patrilineal societies, as well, that confer considerable structural advantages to women, and that area, too, has been poorly analyzed for the most part.

I do not believe that matriliny is inherently any more problematical or conflict-ridden than any other form of social organization, or even that it necessarily undermines the influence of men. Of course, in the past some anthropological fuss was made about the potential for conflict and ambiguity in "the matrilineal puzzle," but some of this bother was clearly ethnocentric. Patriliny and cognatic kinship also each holds its particular perplexities for those who live such a system.

Clearly Kaguru matriliny is strikingly associated with imagery of the earth, sustenance, and cultivation, as is femininity. Yet Kaguru imagery of gender as well as of the elements and combinations which constitute social structure is far too complex and ambiguous to be reduced to any neatly polar set of symbols. It is clear that certain aspects of Kaguru imagery correspond to those of many other African societies, and some appear to be probably universal. Kaguru employ features of night and day, direction, the body, alimentation, work and instrumentality, and many of the senses, especially color, light and dark, appetite, and tactility, but this merely demonstrates that they resemble the rest of humankind. How these motifs are ordered, associated or judged could hardly be predicted, except to a very limited extent in terms of what has already been reported for many of their neighbors. That space, the body, sensations, the appetites, and some of the fundamental acts of livelihood convey richer meaning and feeling to beliefs and values hardly allows an argument for natural symbols. At the least this would be difficult to maintain in terms of predicting which symbols will be emphasized, how these are associated with one another, or what valences they receive. That the physical world, our bodies, and our senses provide metaphorical and analogic means for ideas and values is a valuable insight, but it hardly represents any breakthrough in analytical perception. What is surprising is how much attention has been paid by many social anthropologists (admittedly myself included, in earlier essays) into sorting such elements into patterns of seemingly constant structural relations with corresponding values. I use the adjective *surprising*, though on further consideration I realize that this activity on the part of social anthropologists does reflect one powerful aspect of our thought, our quest for order and system. I do not mean to argue that system and order are not significant. I do suggest that overemphasizing this orderly aspect may blind us to other, equally powerful sides to symbolization. Hence, my arguments which follow are intended to supplement, not oppose, this orderly and fixed view of imagery.

Metaphorical, analogical, and metonymical imageries evoke deep and powerful ambiguities and contradictions which provide sources of power as well as confusion and weakness in our feelings and thinking. Even though protagonists must have some rough, constant model in their minds' eyes in order to gauge their behavior, explicitness and finality do not always constitute assets for conducting social relations and making moral judgments. For people to play out strategies of interaction, cues and signs of success and failure must be both negotiable and at times even dubious. First of all, the choice of which aspects of beliefs or values are to be emphasized and which downplayed indicates the power and authority of certain protagonists over others. It is through domination that one gains rights to make such definitions, and it is also through display of such symbols that one's position is recognized and confirmed. These symbols have the power to convey a sense of winning or losing. Second, while protagonists may strive for advantageous use and interpretation of ambiguous and complex symbols, at other times they think it worthwhile to continue to interact only because these definitions remain unstable, unresolved, or open to mutually accommodating interpretations rather than settled in one direction. Social life oscillates between both such strategies, between forcing home a decisive resolution, and keeping everyone still vying in hope of winning. In either case it is the negotiability and not the fixity of these symbols' imports that allows society to work.

It is in this sense just noted that Kaguru symbolic imagery necessarily remains ambiguous, at times even seemingly contradictory. This is especially so regarding the attributes of men and women and old and young, though this potential to oscillate or compound valences extends through all key symbols, for example, modes of eating, copulation, interplay between settlements and the bush, and the complex characters of fire and water. No patterns of relations are set. Instead, each congeries of people and situations poses a field for negotiation and struggle over which symbolic qualities come to center stage and which remain in the background or even in the wings.

At first consideration much of the preceding interpretation resembles Turner's views regarding the polysemic, polyvalent character of symbols. Turner's analyses of African symbolic systems and rituals reanimated popular ethnographic interest in these topics after decades of relative neglect, except for the intellectual descendants of Durkheim and Mauss, including those outside France influenced by Hocart and Evans-Pritchard. All these writers showed how the conceptions and symbolic imagery of preliterate peoples had subtle and complex dimensions which merit more effort toward moral and philosophical reexamination than they tended to receive. Every few decades researchers must be reminded of these insights from the past, for at the time of Turner's first publications such anthropological analyses were far from common.

If Turner's early publications encouraged popularization of more sensitive and imaginative ethnographic readings of symbols and ritual, his work also eventually led to constrictions. The ultimate purpose of such symbolic systems was increasingly seen as sustaining society by enriching persons' understandings and feelings about it and its relation to the cosmos. Such an interpretation appears to be a combination of selected bits of Durkheim and Marx, welded together with humanistic, theological solder. This is a useful, even poetic and seductive way of looking at some aspects of society, beliefs, and values, but it is insufficient. I want to acknowledge my debt to Turner's initial work, yet go on to point out that such analyses led to an impass of reduplication and reification in his own later works as well as in those of his followers, who increasingly saw their problem as one of merely decoding a complex but somewhat static moral and semantic system. They certainly failed to enlarge our appreciation of the difficult, even subversive and morally uneasy relations between individuals and their roles as persons in a society with culture.

To review my earlier descriptions of Kaguru imagery in terms of the ambiguity and negotiability of symbols, I now briefly recapitulate several features of Kaguru imagery about masculinity and femininity. While touching on only a few aspects of gender, these observations may be readily extended to other symbolic sectors. I choose gender for this exercise to facilitate a return to some of the questions which I earlier raised in this conclusion. Those problems involve possible connections between choices and emphases in using symbols and the nature of society itself. In the case of the Kaguru, this refers to their matriliny and the inhibiting character which their meager and unreliable resources and unstable political conditions may have imposed upon the range and variability of their imagery.

For the sets of symbols to be reviewed I have selected fire and water, and supposed male activity and female passivity in sexual relations, including not only copulation but some related aspects of parenthood and sensuality.

First, I briefly consider fire. It is associated with protective warmth against the outside world and with nourishment through cooking and brewing, all quintessential to the hearth and thus to the home, settlement, and society. The hearth also marks off each household from any other; it is not shared. It consequently constrains and isolates as well as shelters and joins. The stable hearth produces ashes which constitute the waste-heaps associated with marginality, transitions, and ultimately even witchcraft. Yet even these seemingly negative qualities at times also convey a sense of freedom or abandon or even secretly desired powers. Fire is also destructive, hurtful, and difficult to control, yet its fearful character drives off wild beasts and its destructivity consumes polluting or outworn things. All these contrasting and complex qualities may be evoked through fire and the hearth that holds it.

In contrast, water is associated with rain and fertility yet also with destructive floods arising from too much of a good thing. Water cools fire and therefore can represent subjection of disorder. Fluid and confined water represents a potent, seemingly random range of possibilities. It runs unending in its course and can be drawn along channels and therefore led and constrained, or it can wash out banks and ruin all. Its power accounts for both continuity and destruction. If we were to proceed to consider blood, the complex properties of fire and water would combine to complement, contrast, and negate one another in even more complex ways as Kaguru draw images of matriliny, female fertility, menstruation, and death.

Without belaboring these points, it is clear that fire and water not only each encompasses a wide range of attributes but that each attribute may be judged and interpreted in contradictory or ambiguous senses, depending upon whose view prevails. Uncontrollability is a negative phrasing for being full of potential. Stability is a positive phrasing for what has no more possibilities. Similarly, any other attribute may be judged in opposite ways. Consequently, interpretive situations constitute alternate and competing ranges of choice that allow different moral and meaningful judgments to be conceived and imposed in different contexts and by different protagonists, sometimes even at the same time.

Even more complex are some of the contrasts in imagery which Kaguru make between male and female sexuality in terms of activity and passivity as they associate these with various supposed inherent psychophysiological and moral qualities. Men marry women and copulate upon them, never the reverse, conjugation taking on tones of both physical and moral domination, especially in male eyes. Such activities presuppose a vulnerable exposure of the performing male to the critical scrutiny of the "passive" female partner, who must be satisfied sensually and, more important, made pregnant. In this, male activity is far from being entirely advantageous. The onus of sensual performance is essentially on the male rather than the female, whereas the female bears the burden and often moral onus of producing a child. One could say that a man's sexuality is manifestly demonstrated through his prowess at copulation but that the female's sexuality is more opaque, something yielded or withheld in terms of a fertility beyond the understanding or control of men. Indeed, women need not even be married or faithful to produce children for themselves and their lineage. Men give one another access to women through exchange of payments and services, actively sought and negotiated arrangements which they control. Yet the only truly valuable gift in this exchange is offspring who confirm the union. Securing offspring is viewed as beyond the control of men: offspring are bestowed by women, and by the dead working through them. Women's seeming passivity (and this is mainly a man's view) is rooted in the impenetrable power of their own fertility, which is so indissolubly theirs that no active negotiations between men can alter women's claims to these offspring. Yet if women's capacity to produce children links mothers and children fast, the barrenness of a union is attributed usually to a wife rather than to her husband and represents a far greater calamity to her than to him.

Kaguru images of males actively dealing with women reflect males' jural rights, which derive from their assertive, public negotiations. In contrast, women's rights do appear passive and covert, since these endure beyond any adjudication. In this sense, women's supposed passivity stands for a power beyond question or alteration and therefore in many ways far more potent in its claims and durations than men's. The activity of men is expressed in contractual obligations through works and actions. The passivity of women is beyond either payments or words and is expressed in imagery of blood and nurturance, in biological equivalence, in emotions and feelings. Men's biological ties of bone define the separateness of beings, not their continuing, contiguous, fluid bonds as does maternal blood. If such emotional and physiological attributes are the stuff of passivity, then it is a ferociously powerful sort. Toward offspring, men's claims need to be asserted and may be adjusted, while women's claims simply endure.

It is due to this cast of thinking that Kaguru like to think of men's sexuality as more malleable and controlled than women's, as more responsive to rules and inculcation. Women, in contrast, cannot be really altered through initiation and must be guarded and controlled by men to retain them within men's jural compass. But is it a sign of weakness and true passivity that women's natures are ultimately too deep for modification? Is this not because women's true powers, as mothers of children (heirs for their husbands and their brothers), are their central and pivotal significance, lying beyond men's abilities to promote or fully constrain no matter how they seek to negotiate?

If women are passive, they are also portrayed as more unruly, more appetitive, and more asocial. What they receive from men (seed which they transform into children) is incorporated into women's full being for all their lives and only lent to men as jural custodians. That Kaguru, especially men, repeatedly stress the social orderliness, the jural and physical domination of men, signals men's efforts to counteract the enormous strength and resilience of women as the source of children and the very deepest affectual bonds cementing these offspring to the group. If Kaguru men emphasize their own sexual activity, their performance and virility, it is as a counterplay in imagery against the overwhelming and incontrovertible monopoly which women hold both as sources of recruitment into matrilineal groups and as founts of affect and loyalty between the group and successive generations.

I have reviewed only two sets of sexual attributes, and those briefly since the preceding chapters already indicate how complex and myriad any motif may be as it pervades the different reaches of Kaguru life. What should be clear is that these attributes, couched in a wide range of symbolic associations, may be pulled in manifold directions with contending moral implications. The closer and more intensely any particular attribute or motif is examined, the more ambiguous it may appear. There is little about these symbols that allows a secure interpretive anchor, even though they function to impart sensory conceptuality and credibility to existential notions and values. The overwhelming impression is of considerable flux, of incessant refocusing and realigning of meanings and values. Yet the organizing principle of matriliny with its associated dynamic tensions draws much of this together into what appears to be a central concern of all Kaguru, the concern for working out domination and loyalty in a world of contending women and men, and of elders and young.

As I try to characterize Kaguru society and culture in broad terms, the central features which strike me as most significant in forming Kaguru life are of three orders:

First, the material culture is meager, so that relatively few objects and things are available to sustain the ideological and affectual freight of the culture. Each of these —tools, weapons, the house, and, above all, the human body itself— sustains enormous and complex symbolic weight. Furthermore, none of these, not even tools, weapons, or ornaments, seems to figure as any sustaining thread running through numerous generations to bind Kaguru into enduring groups. The two elements in Kaguru imagery which come nearest to this function are names and land, the former seemingly precise and particular yet ultimately sustaining and connective because of names' replicative generality and utter malleability; the latter not only because land is the ultimate source of all life but because, while unchanging in its substantiality, it is in fact subject to relabeling and redivision in ways even more readily than are groups of sentient beings.

Second, the unstable and unpromising ecological and economic conditions prevailing in this area, along with changing, complex interethnic political factors, have all discouraged any centralized or hierarchical system. Instead, Kaguru society has a predisposition toward encouraging autonomous behavior, atomism, egalitarianism, and short-term planning and commitment, all processes furthering individualism and subversion. Why, then, do Kaguru stay together? What is the glue of their society? This adhesiveness derives from two complementary sources, one socioeconomic and the other psychophysiological. First, Kaguru must cooperate, however grudgingly, because their limited environment, limited technology, and undependable climate make earning a living difficult and precarious, not possible for a family alone, much less an individual. Furthermore, the Kaguru's neighbors, because of their own difficult environment, have raided the Kaguru for generations, and this necessitated that they hold together for defense. Second, Kaguru see themselves as one people with a common language, common beliefs, and common values. They share a rhythm and mode of everyday life that conveys experiences transcending mere differences of clan, lineage, or even age and gender. To be sure, this ultimately must be fathomed as an existential given, but of a deeper and more enduring character than formal tenets about kinship, ritual, or other customs. Paucity of resources and an unstable economic and political environment seem unlikely to encourage any high degree of symbolic elaboration in ritual or associated imagery. They do encourage considerable subversion and conflict, subversion toward accepting beliefs and customs in any unqualified way, conflict in that few if any can sustain their socially defined aims and duties given the limited resources at their disposal.

Third, most powerful and pervasive modes of expression concerning Kaguru culture center around food and sex. Indeed, these two vital appetites are often equated in Kaguru imagery. While these two themes undoubtedly permeate all human thought, for Kaguru the particular patterns and tones of these expressions may be modified by the demands and limitations of matriliny. They also are deeply influenced by notions connected to age, though in this they do not seem to differ from patterns found in other forms of social organization.

We have seen in the preceding chapters that certain contrasting and competing forms of expressivity and imagery have been repeatedly and vividly associated by Kaguru with masculine and feminine qualities and that these in turn have been worked deeply into the dynamics of matrilineally oriented social interaction. I believe that the basic modes of these expressions are clear enough from the earlier chapters. What is now required before presenting any firmer or broader claims is an even more sustained account and analysis of Kaguru sexual imagery and the values and beliefs inculcated at initiation of the two genders into adult sexual status. That is the burden of the volume on Kaguru rites of passage which will follow this present study.

POSTSCRIPT

The preceding paragraph would end this book with a promise, a pledge to strengthen my analysis by providing an account of Kaguru sexual symbolism, a topic central to what has been considered here. That is how I first intended to close this study. Yet that would be unfair in that I have said little explicitly about my own imagination as an anthropologist, a crucial aspect of this study, as I suggested in my introductory chapter. At the risk of appearing confessional, I believe I owe the reader a brief account of what cast of imagination informs this work. While my views may be readily inferred from this and other writings, I have never previously spelled them out.

I picture the relations between individuals in society in an essentially tragic manner. One friend has termed this view pessimistic, but I prefer the term tragic. I believe that the failures and frustrations that haunt all our efforts to achieve our goals and ideals need not lead to mere dejection, for the ways we confront such adversity constitute what is admirable in human character. These failures can inform us of our being by disclosing both our capabilities and our limits. Yet, as the chorus observes in *Antigone*, the only way we may understand the full dimensions of our nature is to exceed them and thereby confront some kind of failure, or worse.

It is the nature of social life that we cannot achieve our ideals through our social productions. The scenarios we first construct cannot be fully enacted as we planned and hoped. These plots never end as we devise them, nor are we always cast in the parts we seek to play. This is due to an autonomy or recalcitrancy in others and in things, and to the impossibility of fully comprehending either the experiences or the thoughts of others or the full effects of time and situation upon ourselves. This view is best expressed sociologically in the works of Georg Simmel and, even more, in those of Max Weber (see Beidelman 1982). Yet it would be misleading for me to claim that my views derive entirely from Simmel's or Weber's works. To argue so would belie much that I have just written about the sources of beliefs and values to which we adhere. The scholarly writings of others may serve as intellectual midwives to our feelings and experiences, but they cannot in themselves provide such a vision. They can only illuminate and sustain it. As in the case of the Kaguru, what we picture in our minds' eyes is drawn from our own experiences. It is these that inform and color our imaginative visions of the world and our places in it.

What then are the sources of the ways I imagine the social world? These are the sum of my experiences, and four facets of that totality of experience stand out and embody the full range of imaginative forms that I catalogue in the opening of this study.

The first source of my vision of society stems from my childhood and youth in a small town in the midwest, not Winesburg, Ohio, to be sure, but with all the limitations and distrust of nonconformity and questioning characteristic of a parochial environment. Yet this was countered (some might say exacerbated) by a family environment of great freedom, permitting individualism sure to set one adrift from the conventional moorings of unquestioned, quotidian reality.

Second, I endured a rite of passage every bit as important and dramatic for me as ritual initiation is for Kaguru adolescents. This was not, as for many Westerners, my experiences at university but those in the infantry in the American South and in Korea, where I first encountered violence, brutality, and mindless misuse of human and material resources on a scale I had not known. This initiation into a larger, harder world made future experiences I had during fieldwork in Africa seem milder and more coherent. The impact of these shocking experiences was heightened by the fact that they were encountered in the name of defending a foreign government which curtailed free speech and whose police brutalized its population.

The third source of my vision of society was also an initiation, but of an even more pivotal sort—my fieldwork. At first recall it elicits visions of arriving in Kenya during the Mau-mau emergency, which in turn conjured up anew my earlier experiences in the army. Yet the true impact of fieldwork lies in my years with the Kaguru and later with the Ngulu and Baraguyu of Tanzania. Fieldwork is or should be the central experience of an anthropologist's life. It confronts one with a world disturbingly unlike one's own. In that engulfing confrontation lies both a challenge and a solace to past and future experiences in one's own home world. Such differences underscore the essentially existential nature of all cultures and societies, one's own included, thereby freeing one from some of the interior (intellectual and affectual) subjection that one's own society compels. There are then other ways to live. Yet these new social worlds are also difficult, with their own forms of conflict, frustration, and repression. Fieldwork may free us from some of our particular preconceptions and values about the inherent necessity of some beliefs or customs, yet it also reveals that all social life entails loss of liberty, even though social life, in some form, is essential for realizing our full being.

Fieldwork, like all education, disconcerts and provides no final answers to the dilemmas of living with others. After the experiences of fieldwork, it is never again possible to see one's own society in the same way, to believe faithfully quite as before.

A fourth important molder of my imagery of social life awaited my return from my second fieldtrip to take up an appointment at a prestigious east coast university. There I soon learned that the priorities of university life were not necessarily to learn or to teach, and that matters of power, personality, and expediency often far outweigh any quest for scholarly attainment or under-standing. The "community of scholars" is not better nor worse than any other; what one finds at a university depends upon one's own character and upon chance. Full belief in the scholarly postures so often assumed at a university is a dangerous delusion. A university and the academic disciplines that compose it claim more than they themselves are or can be, yet they do offer us a prospect for coming to terms with ourselves and our world, even as they provide further techniques for mischief.

Viewing these four key sources of my own moral imagination, I consider my years of fieldwork and its analysis as the central factor determining my image of society, culture, and myself. This is due both to the nature of doing fieldwork and to the nature of anthropology itself. It is also probably due to the fact that Kaguru oral literature and tradition clearly manifest a view of individuals and society that I found intensely sympathetic.

During fieldwork I was uniquely aware of the contradictory facts that I depended profoundly upon others yet was also freer than ever before to think and act as I chose. To be sure, that freedom was due to the rootlessness and ultimate irrelevance that characterized me in the long-term view of the Africans with whom I was living. In this sense, then, fieldwork is culturally subversive. It temporarily detaches one from one's own way of thinking and doing, yet it never entirely connects to an alternate one. It fosters one's imagination about both. The better one empathizes, the better one does ethnography, yet full absorption and empathy within another world would inhibit social insight. For these reasons, one could argue that anthropology (or comparative sociology or history) is a tragic discipline in that it goes far to isolate and alienate its practitioners from full conviction in their own mode of thinking and doing. Furthermore, anthropology as a discipline is a peculiar hodgepodge, manifesting shreds and patches of sociology, psychology, history, philosophy, linguistics, and comparative criticism of art and literature. This bridging of disciplines touching many but probably mastering none, makes anthropologists valuable synthesizers or sometimes jesters in the court of academe, outside and yet inside the more normative disciplines.

These factors cannot fail to have important repercussions for the individual who takes anthropology seriously (see my discussion in 1970c). That an anthropologist doing fieldwork can manage, however imperfectly, to move from one society and culture to another, and that he or she can make this intelligible at all to those at home, can be judged a testimony to a common humanity and reason, and to the powers of imagination. Yet for me this equally suggests how ambiguously and at times precariously each of us is actually tied to the people and institutions immediately around us at any time. Evans-Pritchard is reported to have said that the comparative method is all there is in anthropology, and that that is hopeless. One could well extend and paraphrase this to apply to the relation between individuals and the societies they inhabit. To imagine at all is to do a kind of anthropology and to wonder (in the Sophoclean sense of *deinen*) about the difficult relation between ourselves and the groups and world in which we live.

Bibliography

Of making many books there is no end; and much
study is a weariness of the flesh.

Ecclesiastes 12.12

Anonymous
  1971a   Mating a Zoo Hyena Proves No Easy Job. *New York Times* (2 July): 28.
  1971b   Hyènees tachetées et chacals; famille: Les hyènidés. *La Faune* 14:265–273, 279.
Aristotle
  1961   *Aristotle's Poetics*. Edited by Francis Ferguson. New York: Hill and Wang.

Bachelard, Gaston
  1964   *The Psychoanalysis of Fire* (*La Psychoanalyse du feu*, 1938). Boston: Beacon Press.
  1969   *The Poetics of Space* (*La Poetique de l'espace*, 1958). Boston: Beacon Press.
Bakhtin, M. M.
  1981   *The Dialogic Imagination* (*Voprosy literatury i estetiki*, 1975). Edited by Michael Holquist. Austin: University of Texas Press.
Barley, Nigel
  1983   *Symbolic Structures*. Cambridge: Cambridge University Press.
Barthes, Roland
  1968   *Elements of Semiology* (*Éléments de sémiology*, 1964). New York: Hill and Wang.
Beidelman, T. O.
  1960   The Baraguyu, *Tanganyika Notes and Records* 55:245–278.
  1961a   Kaguru Justice and the Concept of Legal Fictions. *Journal of African Law* 5:5–20.
  1961b   Beer Drinking and Cattle Theft in Ukaguru: Intertribal Relations in a Tanganyika Chiefdom. *American Anthropologist* 63:534–549.
  1961c   Hyena and Rabbit: a Kaguru Representation of Matrilineal Relations. *Africa* 31:61–74.
  1961d   A Note on the Kamba of Kilosa District. *Tanganyika Notes and Records* 57:181–194.
  1961e   Right and Left Hand among the Kaguru: a Note on Symbolic Classification. *Africa* 31:280–287.
  1962a   A History of Ukaguru, Kilosa District: 1859–1916. *Tanganyika Notes and Records* 58 & 59:11–39.
  1962b   Three Kaguru Tales, *Afrika und Übersee* 46:218–229.
  1963a   Further Adventures of Hyena and Rabbit: the Folktale as a Sociological Model. *Africa* 33:54–69.
  1963b   The Blood Covenant and the Concept of Blood in Ukaguru. *Africa* 33:321–342.
  1963c   Five Kaguru Tales. *Anthropos* 58:737–772.
  1963d   Kaguru Time Reckoning: an Aspect of the Cosmology of an East African People. *Southwestern Journal of Anthropology* 19:9–20.

1963e   Kaguru Omens: an East African People's Concepts of the Unusual, Unnatural and Supernormal. *Anthropological Quarterly* 36:43–59.

1963f   Witchcraft in Ukaguru. *In Witchcraft and Sorcery in East Africa*, edited by J. Middelton and E. H. Winter, pp. 57–98. London: Routledge and Kegan Paul.

1963g   A Kaguru Version of the Sons of Noah: a Study in the Inculcation of the Idea of Racial Superiority. *Cahiers d'études africaines* 12:474–490.

1963h   Some Kaguru Riddles. *Man* 63:158–160.

1963i   Mukejuwa: Two Versions of a Kaguru Tale. *Baessler-Archiv* 11:301–326.

1963j   Four Kaguru Tales. *Tanganyika Notes and Records* 61:135–146.

1964a   Ten Kaguru Texts: Tales of an East African Bantu People. *Journal of African Languages* 3:1–38.

1964b   Three Tales of the Living and the Dead: the Ideology of Kaguru Ancestral Propitiation. *Journal of the Royal Anthropological Institute* 94:109–137.

1964c   Intertribal Insult and Opprobrium in an East African Chiefdom (Ukaguru). *Anthropological Quarterly* 37:33–52.

1964d   Pig (*Guluwe*): an Essay on Ngulu Sexual Symbolism and Ceremony. *Southwestern Journal of Anthropology* 20:17–41.

1965a   Six Kaguru Tales. *Zeitschrift für Ethnologie* 90:17–41.

1965b   Notes on Boys Initiation among the Ngulu. *Man* 65:143–147.

1966a   *Utani*: Some Kaguru Notions of Death, Sexuality and Affinity. *Southwestern Journal of Anthropology* 22:354–380.

1966b   Further Kaguru Tales. *Journal of African Languages* 5:74–102.

1967a   *The Matrilineal Peoples of Eastern Tanzania*. London: The International African Institute.

1967b   Kaguru Folklore and the Concept of Reciprocity. *Zeitschrift für Ethnologie* 92:74–88.

1967c   The Hehe of Ukaguru. *Afrika und Übersee* 50:304–314.

1967d   Eleven Kaguru Texts. *African Studies* 26:3–36.

1967e   More Kaguru Texts. *Baessler-Archiv* 15:169–182.

1968   A Case of Kaguru Oral History. *Baessler-Archiv* 16:357–371.

1969   Addenda and Corrigenda to the Bibliography of the Matrilineal Peoples of Eastern Tanzania. *Africa* 39:186–188.

1970a   Myth, Legend and Oral History. *Anthropos* 65:74–97.

1970b   Towards More Open Theoretical Interpretation of Witchcraft. In *Witchcraft Confessions and Accusations*, edited by Mary Douglas, pp.351–356. ASA Monograph 9. London: Tavistock.

1970c   Some Sociological Implications of Culture. In *Theoretical Sociology*, edited by J. C. McKinney and E. A. Tiryakian, pp.500–527. New York: Appleton-Century-Crofts.

1971a   *The Kaguru: A Matrilineal People of East Africa*. New York: Holt, Rinehart and Winston; reprinted 1983, Prospect Heights, Ill; Waveland Press.

1971b   Some Kaguru Notions about Incest and Other Sexual Prohibitions. In *Rethinking Kinship and Marriage*, edited by Rodney Needham, pp.181–201. ASA Monograph 11. London: Tavistock.

1971c   Foreword to *Kpele Lala*, by Marion Kilson, pp. xi–xxi. Cambridge, Mass.: Harvard University Press.

1971d   Kaguru Descent Groups. *Anthropos* 66:373–396.

1971e   Nine Kaguru Tales. *Zeitschrift für Ethnologie* 96:16–31.

1972a   Approaches to the Study of African Oral Literature. *Africa* 42:150–157.

1972b   The Kaguru House. *Anthropos* 67:690–707.
1972c   The Filth of Incest. *Cahiers d'études africaines* 12:164–173.
1973a   Kaguru Symbolic Classification. In *Right and Left*, edited by Rodney Need-
         ham, pp.128–166. Chicago: University of Chicago Press.
1973b   Three Kaguru Texts. *Zeitschrift für Ethnologie* 98:90–101.
1974a   Kaguru Names and Naming. *Journal of Anthropological Research* 30:281–
         292.
1974b   Further Addenda to the Bibliography of the Matrilineal Peoples of Eastern
         Tanzania. *Africa* 44:297–299.
1974c   The Bird Motif in Kaguru Folklore. *Anthropos* 69:162–190.
1974d   Kaguru Texts: the Ambiguity of Hare in Kaguru Folklore. *Baessler-Archiv*
         22:247–263.
1975a   Ambiguous Animals: Two Theriomorphic Metaphors in Kaguru Folklore.
         Africa 45:183–200.
1975b   Kaguru Oral Literature: Part 1. Texts. *Anthropos* 70:537–574.
1976   Kaguru Oral Literature: Part 2. Texts. *Anthropos* 71:46–89.
1978a   Chiefship in Ukaguru. *The International Journal of African Historical Stud-
         ies* 11:227–246.
1978b   Kaguru Oral Literature: Part 4. Texts, *Anthropos* 73:69–112.
1979   Kaguru Oral Literature: Part 5. Discussion. *Anthropos* 74:497–529.
1980a   The Moral Imagination of the Kaguru: Some Thoughts on Tricksters, Trans-
         lation and Comparative Analysis. *American Ethnologist* 7:27–42.
1980b   Women and Men in Two East African Societies. In *Explorations in African
         Systems of Thought*, edited by Ivan Karp and Charles Bird, pp.143–164.
         Bloomington: Indiana University Press.
1981a   Third Addendum to the Bibliography of the Matrilineal Peoples of Eastern
         Tanzania. *Anthropos* 76:864–865.
1981b   The Nuer Concept of *Thek* and the Meaning of Sin. *History of Religions*
         21:126–155.
1981c   Review of Hallpike: *The Foundations of Primitive Thought*. *American Eth-
         nologist* 4:812–813.
1981d   Review of Grohs: Kisazi. *Africa* 51:880–881.
1982   Review of Turner: *For Weber*. *American Ethnologist* 9:586–588.
1983   Moaning about Meaning, Review of Parkin (ed.): *Semantic Anthropology*.
         Times Literary Supplement (July 8): 735.
Bohannan, Paul
1968   Extra-Processual Events in Tiv Political Institutions. *American Anthro-
         pologist* 60:1-12.
Boswell, John
1980   *Christianity, Social Tolerance and Homosexuality*. Chicago: University of
         Chicago Press.
Boyle, John
1972   The Hare in Myth and Reality, a Review Article. *Folklore* 84:313–326.
Brain, James
1972   Ancestors as Elders in Africa—Further Thoughts. *Africa* 43:122–133.
Brooke, Clarke
1967   Types of Food Shortages in Tanzania. *The Geographic Review* 57:333–
         357.
Burke, Kenneth
1957   *The Philosophy of Literary Form* (1941). New York: Vintage Books.

1962   *A Grammar of Motives* (1945) *and a Rhetoric of Motives* (1950). New
        York: Meridian Press.
1970   *The Rhetoric of Religion.* Berkeley: University of California Press.
Burkert, Walter
1979   *Structure and History in Greek Mythology and Ritual.* Berkeley: University
        of California Press.

Busse, J.
1936–7 Kaguru-Texte. *Zeitschrift für Eingenborenen-Sprachen* 27:61–75.

Christensen, J. B.
1963   Utani: Joking, Sexual License and Social Obligations among the Luguru.
        American Anthropologist 65:1314–1327.
Church Missionary Society (London)
        Church Missionary Gleaner.
        Church Missionary Intelligencer.
        Proceedings of the Church Missionary Society.
Coleridge, Samuel T.
1977   *The Portable Coleridge*, ed. I. A. Richards, Harmondsworth: Penguin.
Collingwood, R. G.
1958   *The Principles of Art* (1938), New York: Oxford University Press.
1961   *The Idea of History* (1946). New York: Oxford University Press.
Culler, Jonathan
1983   *Barthes.* London: Fontana.
Doke, Clement
1956   The Points of the Compass in Bantu Languages. *The Bible Translator*
        7:104–113.
Dorst, J. and P. Dandelot
1969   Hyenas. In *A Fieldguide to the Larger Mammals of Africa*, pp. 129–130.
        Boston: Houghton Mifflin.
Dumont, Louis
1954   *Une Sous-caste de l'Inde du sud.* Paris: Mouton.
Durkheim, Émile
1934   *The Elementary Forms of the Religious Life* (*Les Formes élémentaires de
        la vie religiéuse*, 1912). London: Allen and Unwin.

Elias, Norbert
1978   *The Civilizing Process, The History of Manners* (*Über den Prozess der
        Zivilisation*, 1939). New York: Urizen.
Empson, William
1955   *Seven Types of Ambiguity* (1930). New York: Meridian Books.
1964   *The Structure of Complex Words.* London: Chatto and Windus.
Evans, George and David Thomson
1972   *The Leaping Hare.* London: Faber.
Evans-Pritchard, E. E.
1939   Nuer Time-reckoning, *Africa* 12:189–216.
Firth, Raymond
1973   *Symbols, Public and Private.* London: Allen and Unwin.
Fortes, Meyer
1961   Pietas in Ancestor Worship, *Journal of the Royal Anthropological Institute*
        91:166–191.

220   *Bibliography*

Frye, Northrop
  1963   *Fables of Identity*, New York: Harvest Books.

Grohs, Elisabeth
  1980   *Kisazi, Reiferiten des Mädchen bei den Zigua und Ngulu Ost-Tanzania*.
          Berlin: Reimer.
Guggisberg, C. A. W.
  1968   *Game Animals of Eastern Africa*. Nairobi: Patwa.

Hallpike, C. R.
  1979   *The Foundations of Primitive Thought*. Oxford: Clarendon Press.
Huizinga, Johan
  1950   *Homo Ludens* (1938). Boston: Beacon Press.
Hyman, Stanley E.
  1947   *The Armed Vision, a Study in the Methods of Modern Literary Criticism*.
          New York: Vintage Books.

Jackson, Michael
  1982   *Allegories of the Wilderness*. Bloomington: Indiana University Press.
  1983a   Knowledge of the Body. *Man* (n.s.) 18:327–345.
  1983b   Thinking through the Body. *Social Analysis* 14:127–149.
James, William
  1948   *Psychology* (1890), Cleveland: Fine Editions Press.
Jeannin, Albert
  1951   *La Faune africaine*. Paris: Payot.
Johnson, Frederick (director)
  1939   *A Standard Swahili-English Dictionary*. London: Oxford University Press.

Kambe, A. K.
  1971   Hyaena Mythology. *Uganda Journal* 35:209–210.
Karp, Ivan
  1980   Beer Drinking and Social Experience in an African Society. In *Explorations
          in African Systems of Thought*, pp. 83–119. edited by Ivan Karp and Charles
          Bird, Bloomington: Indiana University Press.
King, S. J.
  1921   The Power behind the Sickness. *Awake!* 31:76–77.
Kopytoff, Igor
  1971   Ancestors as Elders in Africa. *Africa* 41:129–142.
Kruuk, Hans
  1972   *The Spotted Hyena*. Chicago: University of Chicago Press.

Lakoff, George and Mark Johnson
  1980   *Metaphors We Live By*. Chicago: University of Chicago Press.
Last, J. T.
  1878   Letters. *Church Missionary Intelligencer* 3 (n.s.): 645–646.
  1881   The Usagara Mission: Mamboia. *Church Misionary Intelligencer* 6
          (n.s.):554–561.
  1883   A Visit to the Wa-itumba Iron-workers and the Mangaheri, near Mamboia,
          in East Central Africa. *Proceedings of the Royal Geographic Society* 5:581–
          592.

1886   *Grammar of the Kagúru Language*. London: Society for Promoting Christian Knowledge.

Leach, E. R.
1961   *Rethinking Anthropology*. London: Athlone.
1962   Beasts and Triangles. *New Society* 1:21–23.
1972   *Humanity and Animality*. London: South Place Ethical Society.

Levine, Donald N.
1971   Introduction. In *Georg Simmel on Individuality and Social Forms*, edited by Donald N. Levine, pp.ix–lxv. Chicago: University of Chicago Press.

Lévi-Strauss, Claude
1958   The Structural Study of Myth. In *Myth*, edited by Thomas Sebeok, pp.50–66. Bloomington: Indiana University Press.
1963   *La Pensée sauvage*. Paris: Plon.

Ley, W.
1968   *The Dawn of Zoology*. Englewood Cliffs, N.J.: Prentice-Hall.

Lindblom, G.
1920   *The Akamba*. Upsala: Appelbergs.

Lloyd, G. E. R.
1966   *Polarity and Analogy*. Cambridge: Cambridge University Press.

Maagano ya Kale
    (Old Testament in Swahili). London: British and Foreign Bible Society.

Maberly, C. T. A.
1960   *Animals of East Africa*. Capetown: Trimmins.

Mackay, Louis
1965   Aristotle and Feidelson on Metaphor: towards a Reconciliation of Ancient and Modern. *Arion* 4:272–285.

McVicar, T.
1935   Sibs, Privileged Familiarity and Cross-Cousin Marriage among the Waluguru. *Primitive Man* 8:57–67.
1941   Wanguru Religion. *Primitive Man* 14:13–30.
1945   Death Rites among the Waluguru and Wanguru. *Primitive Man* 18:26–35.

Mauss, Marcel
1979a   Body Techniques (Les techniques du corps, 1936). In *Sociology and Psychology*, translated by Ben Brewster, pp.95–123. London: Routledge and Kegan Paul.
1979b   A Category of the Human Mind: the Notion of Person, the Notion of 'Self' (Une catégorie de l'esprit humain: la notion de personne, celle de 'moi,' 1938. In *Sociology and Psychology*, translated by Ben Brewster, pp.263–281. London: Routledge and Kegan Paul.

Mauss, Marcel (with the collaboration of Henri Beuchat)
1979   *Seasonal Variations of the Eskimo (Essay sur les variations saisonnières des sociétés Eskimos: études de morphologie sociale*, 1904–5), edited by James Fox. London: Routledge and Kegan Paul.

Mawinza, J.
1968   Reverence for Ancestors in Tanzania with Reference to the Luguru and Other Bantu Tribes. *Cahiers de religions africaines* 4:239–248.

Melbin, Murray
1978   Night as Frontier. *American Sociological Review* 43:3–22.

Meyer, Hans
  1909   *Das Deutsche Kolonialreich* I. Leipzig and Vienna: Bibliographische Institut.
Middleton, John
  1954   Some Social Aspects of Lugbara Myth. *Africa* 24:189–199.
  1960   *Lugbara Religion*. London: Oxford University Press.
  1961   The Comparative Study of Food Habits, *Tavistock Institute Document* 647. London.
Mills, C. Wright
  1961   *The Sociological Imagination* (1959). New York: Grove Press.
Moreau, R. E.
  1941   Suicide by 'Breaking the Cooking Pot.' *Tanganyika Notes and Records* 12:49–50.

Needham, Rodney
  1960   The Left Hand of the Mugwe *Africa* 30:28–33.
  1978   *Primordial Characters*, Charlottesville: University Press of Virginia.
  1980   *Reconnaissances*. Toronto: University of Toronto Press.

Onions, Richard B.
  1951   *The Origins of European Thought*. Cambridge: Cambridge University Press.
Osgood, Charles
  1952   The Nature and Measurement of Meaning. *Psychological Bulletin* 49:197–237.
Osgood, Charles and G. Suci, P. Tannenbaum
  1957   *The Measurement of Meaning*. Urbana: University of Illinois Press.
Oyono, Ferdinand
  1966   *Houseboy (Une vie de boy*, 1960). London: Heinemann.

Partridge, Eric
  1961   *Origins*. 3rd Edition. London: Routledge and Kegan Paul.
Puhvel, Martin
  1976   The Mystery of Cross-Roads. *Folklore* 87:167–177.

Rees, D.
  1902a   *History of the Church Missionary Society in German East Africa*, Manuscript. London: Church Missionary Society Archives.
  1902b   Superstition in Usagara. *Church Missionary Gleaner* 29:52–53.
Richards, Audrey
  1950   Some Types of Family Structure amongst the Central Bantu. In *African Systems of Kinship and Marriage*, edited by A. R. Radcliffe-Brown and D. Forde, pp.207–251. London: Oxford University Press.
  1956   *Chisungu, a Girl's Initiation Ceremony among the Bemba of Northern Rhodesia*. London: Faber.
Richards, I. A.
  n.d.   *Principles of Literary Criticism* (1925). New York: Harvest Books.
Ricoeur, Paul
  1979   The Metaphysical Process as Cognition, Imagination and Feeling. In *On*

Metaphor, edited by Sheldon Sacks, pp.141–157. Chicago: University of Chicago Press.

Rigby, Peter
1968   *Cattle and Kinship among the Gogo*. Ithaca, N.Y.: Cornell University Press.

Sapir, Edward
1963   Symbolism (1934). In *Selected Writings of Edward Sapir*, edited by David G. Mandelbaum, pp. 564–568. Berkeley: University of California Press.

Sartre, Jean-Paul
n.d.   *The Psycholgy of Imagination (L'imaginaire; psychologie-phénomenol-ogigue de l'imagination*, 1940). Seacaucus: Citadel Press.

Scheler, Max
1954   *The Nature of Sympathy (Zur Phänomenologie der Sympathiegefühle und von Liebe und Hass*, 1913). London: Routledge and Kegan Paul.

1972   *Ressentiment (Ueber Ressentiment un moralisches Werturteil*, 1912), edited by Lewis A. Coser. New York: Shocken Books.

Schutz, Alfred
1967   *The Phenomenology of the Social World*. Evanston: Northwestern University Press.

Shortridge, G. C.
1934   *Mammals of South West Africa* I. London: Heinemann.

Simmel, Georg
1968   *The Conflict of Modern Culture and Other Essays*. New York: Teachers College Press.

1971   *Georg Simmel on Individuality and Social Forms*, edited by Donald N. Levine. Chicago: University of Chicago Press.

Spender, Stephen
n.d.   The Making of a Poem (1946). In *The Creative Process*, edited by Brewster Ghiselin, pp.112–125. New York: Mentor.

Spinnage, C. A.
1962   *Animals of East Africa*. London: Collins.

Spriggs, E. R.
1910   The Day of Small Things, *Awake!* 20:32–33.

Stanford, W. Bedell
1972   *Greek Metaphor* (1936). New York: Johnson Reprint.

Stapleton, W. H.
1905   The terms for 'Right Hand' and 'Left Hand' in the Bantu Language. *Journal of the African Society* 16:431–433.

Stefaniszyn, Bronislaw
1964   *Social and Ritual Life of the Ambo of Northern Rhodesia*. London: Oxford University Press.

Stuhlmann, F.
1894   *Mit Emin Pascha ins Herz von Afrika*. Berlin: Reimer.

Tanganyika
1947   *The Laws of Tanganyika*. Watmought, London: Tanganyika Government Printer.

Tempels, Placide
  1959   *Bantu Philosophy (Le Philosophie bantoue*, 1945). Paris: Présence
           Africaine.
Turner, Victor W.
  1953   *Lunda Rites and Ceremonies*. Occasional Papers of the Rhodes-Livingston
           Museum No. 10. Lusaka.
  1959   *Schism and Continuity*. Manchester: Manchester University Press.
  1962a   Three Symbols of *Passage* in Ndembu Circumcision Ritual. In *Essays in
           the Ritual of Social Relations*, edited by Max Gluckman, pp.124–173.
           Manchester: Manchester University Press.
  1962b   Ritual Symbolism, Morality and Social Structure among the Ndembu.
           Rhodes-Livingston Journal 30:1–10.
  1967   *The Forest of Symbols*. Ithaca, N.Y.: Cornell University Press.
  1968   *The Drums of Affliction, a Study of Religious Processes among the Ndembu
           of Zambia*. Oxford: Clarendon Press.
  1969   *The Ritual Process*. Chicago: Aldine.

Warnock, Mary
  1976   *Imagination*. Berkeley: University of California Press.
Watt, Rachel
  n.d.   *In the Heart of Savagedom*. 3rd edition. London: Pickering and Inglis.
Weiner, Annette
  1976   *Women of Value, Men of Renown*. Austin: University of Texas Press.
  1977   Trobriand Descent: Female/Male Domains. *Ethos* 5:54–70.
Werner, Alice
  1904   Notes on the Terms Used for 'Right Hand' and 'Left Hand' in the Bantu
           Languages. *Journal of the African Society* 13:112–116.
  1933   *Myths and Legends of the Bantu*. London: Harrap.
White, C. M. N.
  1961   *Elements in Luvale Beliefs and Rituals*. The Rhodes-Livingstone Papers
           No. 32. Lusaka.
Wieschhoff, H.
  1938   Concepts of Right and Left in African Cultures. *Journal of the American
           Oriental Society* 58:202–217.
Winch, Peter
  1964   Understanding a Primitive Society. *American Philosophical Quarterly*
           1:307–324; reprinted in *Rationality*, edited by Bryan Wilson, pp.78–111.
           New York: Harper Torchbooks.
Wittgenstein, Ludwig
  1963   *Philosophical Investigations*. Oxford: Blackwell.
  1964   *The Blue and Brown Books*, Oxford: Blackwell.
  1969   *On Certainty*. New York: J. & H. Harper.
  1971   Remarks on Frazer's *Golden Bough* (1931, 1936). *The Human World* 3:18–
           41.
Wood, A. N.
  1908   An Idol Pulled Down. *Awake!* 13:121–122.

Zipes, Jack
  1983   *Fairy Tales and the Art of Subversion*. London: Heinemann.

Index

Affines, 16, 20, 25n.4
  in folktales, 162–173, 176
  and joking relations, 128–134
  See also Brideservice; Bridewealth; Cross-
  cousins; Incest; Joking relations; Kinship;
  Marriage; Residence
Analogy, 5, 7, 206
  See also Metaphor; Metonymy
Ancestors
  and control by elders, 17, 114, 192–193
  and folktales, 106–111
  genealogies, 86, 120n.4
  location of rituals of propitiation, 41, 122
  and matrilineages, 105, 111–115, 120n.9
  and names, 94–97, 115
  prayers to the dead, 114–115
  propitiation of, 45, 89, 111–119, 120n.9,
  122–124
  and rituals of death and pollution, 120n.9,
  121–137
  See also Dead; Matrilineality; Names
Animals
  deviant animals, 99–100
  in folktales, 169–173
  relation to the dead, 106–108, 116, 125
  related to witches, 141
  symbolic comparisons and contrasts with
  humans, 29, 35–36, 38, 40, 41–42, 47n.7,
  60, 63–64, 186
  See also Birds; Bush; Hare; Hyena; Livestock
Aristotle, 7
Autonomy, 12, 15–17, 196, 211–212
  See also Individual; Resentment

Bachelard, Gaston, 6, 37
Bakhtin, M. M., 161, 164
Baraguru, 15, 68–69, 71, 79, 81, 147
  See also Ethnicity; Foreigners;
  Maasai; Raiding
Barrenness
  of women, 22–23
  See also Households; Witchcraft; Women
Birds
  in folktales of the dead, 110, 111, 118

symbolism of, 39, 90, 98–99, 104n.15, 115
  See also Divination; Omens, Witchcraft
Birth
  abnormal, 99–102, 112
  birth rituals related to initiation, death, and
  marriage, 80, 126, 134–135, 180
  and naming, 96, 115
  rituals of, 57–58, 118, 120n.12
  symbolism of, 32, 34–35, 64, 86, 115, 117
Blood, 33–35, 37–38, 47n.5, 116
  See also Bloodwealth; Body; Bone; Fertility;
  Fire; Heat; Kinship; Matrilineality; Men-
  struation
Bloodwealth, 44
Body (human)
  orientation, 77
  symbolism of, 30–37, 63–64
  See also Blood; Bone; Circumcision; Fertil-
  ity; Grooming; Hair; Heat; Incest, Kinship,
  Matrilineality; Menstruation; Nakedness;
  Paternal kin groups; Ritual; Sexuality; Stone
Bondei, 137n.10
Bone, 33–34
  See also Blood; Body; Paternal kin groups
Brideservice, 17, 129, 133
  See also Affines; Bridewealth; Residence
Bridewealth, 16–17, 25n.2, 43–44, 117, 129,
  133, 164–165, 175–177
  disputes leading to witchcraft, 149–150, 175
  See also Affines; Brideservice; Residence
Burke, Kenneth, 4, 5, 6, 7, 9, 30
Burkert, Walter, 5, 7
Bush
  concepts of, 14, 29, 34, 41–42, 57, 80–81,
  85, 122, 139, 169, 172
  and the dead, 122
  wild animals overstepping the bush, 100
  See also Animals; Creation; History; Initia-
  tion; Space; Witchcraft

Caves
  and sexual symbolism, 74, 79–81, 107, 116,
  173
Circumcision, 36, 38–39, 41, 47n.9, 66n.3,
  74, 80–81

Dry season; Environment; Food

Fantasy
  and folktales, 161, 180, 204
  as subversion, 7–9
  and witchcraft, 158
  See also Imagination; Resentment; Symbols

Fertility (human), 19–20, 33–35, 40
  and witches, 142
  See also Ancestors; Birth; Blood; Body; Infidelity; Kinship; Marriage; Menstruation; Sexuality

Fire (and the hearth)
  Symbolism of, 37–39, 54–55, 57–59, 73, 80, 88–89, 123, 125, 208
  See also Blood; Food; Funerals; Heat; House

Firth, Raymond, 4

Folktales, 5, 8, 10n.5, 32, 41–42, 85–86, 90, 106–111, 160–199

Food (alimentation)
  and aggressive alimentary ritual, 128, 136n. 7, 182nn. 7, 14, 15
  and cannibalism and witchcraft, 140, 180, 193
  ceremonial distribution of, 63
  and ethnicity, 69, 70–71
  and etiquette, 62–63, 193
  and the house, 53–56
  and matrilineality, 188–197
  oral expression of affection (licking), 44, 63
  and sexuality, 193, 211
  and sexual separation of alimentation, 55, 62
  sharing of, in folktales, 162–169, 188–197
  symbolism of, 29–30, 37–40, 55–56, 58, 80, 88–89, 135
  and witches and gluttony, 141–142, 174, 179, 193
  See also Crops; Drinking; Etiquette; Famine; Fire; Sexuality

Foreigners
  Kaguru views of, 29, 67–71
  negative sexual views of, 47n.8
  and personal names, 93
  and witches, 146–147
  See also Ethnicity

Fry, Northrop, 7, 8, 161

Funerals
  ceremonies at, 43–44, 60, 90, 93, 95, 131
  graves and burial, 47n.4, 76, 83n.11, 113, 122, 124–126, 141, 182n.8
  mourning, 52, 57–59, 74
  See also Ancestors; Dead, death; Ritual

Gender
  and age, 61

  and attributes of men and women, 29–35, 208–210
  and division of labor, 18
  etiquette and grooming, 64
  and names reflecting sexual subordination, 94
  relations between men and women, 18–19, 22–24, 61–62
  symbolism of, 31–41, 207–210
  and use of space and time, 91
  See also Barrenness; Circumcision; Dichotomy; Households; Initiation; Mothers; Ritual; Sexuality; Spouses; Women

God, 47n.2, 89, 113, 120n.8, 122–123, 127, 138–139

Gogo, 15, 48n.16, 68, 70, 72, 77, 94

Grandmothers (old women), 63, 48n.11, 101, 139, 193

Grandparents
  as marital partners, 129–133
  and names, 96, 115
  See also Ancestors; Elders; Joking relations; Names

Grooming, 63–64
  and witches, 143
  See also Body; Hair; Initiation; Witchcraft

Hair
  symbolism of, 35–36, 63–64, 117, 126
  See also Body; Initiation; Grooming

Hallpike, C. R., 10n.5, 103n.2, 181n.3

Handedness (right and left sides), 31–33, 42–45, 46n.2, 47nn.3, 4
  See also Body; Dichotomy; Ritual; Sexuality

Hare, 48n.14, 187–188, 198–199n.2, 199n.3
  in folktales, 187–192
  See also Hyena

Heat
  and ritual, 38, 123–124
  symbolism of, 37–39, 47n.5
  See also Fire; Food; Gender; Sexuality

Heavenly bodies, 87–88
  See also Time

Hehe, 15, 68, 76, 77, 79, 81, 128

History
  Kaguru notions of, 67
  and legends 71–82

Hocart, A. M., 207

House
  construction of, 52, 65–66n.2
  form of, 50–51
  inside and outside, 91
  and latrines, 55–56
  sexual aspects of thatching, 47n.6, 52, 126
  symbolism of, 30, 39–40, 49–50, 53–60, 137n.11